Miracle on the Eastern Shore

Miracle on the Eastern Shore

*The 1937 Salisbury Indians
and Baseball's Greatest Comeback*

David A. Ranzan

McFarland & Company, Inc., Publishers
Jefferson, North Carolina

ALSO OF INTEREST
―――――――――――

Hero of Fort Schuyler: Selected Revolutionary War Correspondence of Brigadier General Peter Gansevoort, Jr. by Peter Gansevoort, Jr. Edited by David A. Ranzan and Matthew J. Hollis (McFarland, 2014)

Surviving Andersonville: One Prisoner's Recollections of the Civil War's Most Notorious Camp by Ed Glennan. Edited by David A. Ranzan (McFarland, 2013)

ISBN (print) 978-1-4766-9184-8
ISBN (ebook) 978-1-4766-5004-3

LIBRARY OF CONGRESS AND BRITISH LIBRARY
CATALOGUING DATA ARE AVAILABLE

Library of Congress Control Number 2023037095

© 2023 David A. Ranzan. All rights reserved

No part of this book may be reproduced or transmitted in any form or by any means, electronic or mechanical, including photocopying or recording, or by any information storage and retrieval system, without permission in writing from the publisher.

On the cover: 1937 Salisbury Indians—(top row) Jorge Comellas, Juan Montero, Frank Trechock and Frank Deutsch; (middle row) team treasurer John Milton, Fred Thomas, manager Jake Flowers, John Bassler, Leon Revolinsky, Joe Garliss, Joe Kohlman and business manager Melvin Murphy; (bottom row) batboy Maurice Fields, Bill Luzansky, Jose Salazar, Mike Guerra, Charles Quimby, Jerry Lynn and Edgar Leip (courtesy Judy Bowen and Jane Musser)

Printed in the United States of America

*McFarland & Company, Inc., Publishers
Box 611, Jefferson, North Carolina 28640
www.mcfarlandpub.com*

Table of Contents

Acknowledgments	vi
Abbreviations	vii
Preface	1
One—A New Era of Delmarva Baseball	5
Two—First 26 Games (May 19–June 18)	19
Three—The Brady Infraction	51
Four—The Climb (June 19–July 31)	58
Five—Domination on the Diamond (August 1–31)	93
Six—The Final Stretch (September 1–6)	126
Seven—Playoff Series	137
Eight—Exhibition Games	149
Nine—Indians in the Major Leagues	154
Player Biographical Sketches	157
Chapter Notes	213
Bibliography	245
Index	249

Acknowledgments

I would like to extend my appreciation to Dick Wheatley of the Federalsburg Historical Society, Donnie Davidson of the Dorchester County Historical Society and Peggy Morey and Kayla Weber of the Talbot Historical Society for their help while selecting several images of the other teams of the Eastern Shore Baseball League. One of the best repositories for Delmarva's rich history is at Salisbury University. The Edward H. Nabb Research Center for Delmarva History and Culture contains an extraordinary photographic collection of all things on the Eastern Shore. Ian Post, its local history archivist, was very helpful with my requests.

A special thanks go to Charlie and Deborah Silcott of the Eastern Shore Baseball Hall of Fame Museum for opening the museum early to allow me to scan several items from their wonderful displays.

I am humbled McFarland published this manuscript. I am indebted to McFarland's president Rhonda Herman, senior editor Gary Mitchem, editorial assistant Sophia Lyons, marketing coordinator Kristal Hamby, managing editor Susan Kilby, and their colleagues who assisted with the preparation of this book for publication.

And finally, I would like to express my heartfelt gratitude to the relatives of the 1937 Salisbury Indians ballplayers who shared their photographs, materials and especially their recollections of stories told to them about the good ol' days with me: Bonnie and Mark Briese, Kevin Ellis, Terry, Casey and Tom Elliott, Carole Krout, Buddy Kruk, Patricia Larson, Mary Jane Martinez, Jane Musser and Judith Bowen, Gary Pucci, George Shafnacker, Aubrey Shelton and Eric Steinfadt.

Abbreviations

Alabama-Florida League (ALFL)
American Association (AA)
Appalachian League (APPY)
Arizona-Texas League (AZTX)
Bi-State League (BIST)
Blue Ridge League (BLRI)
California League (CALL)
Canadian-American League (CAML)
Carolina League (CARL)
Central League (CENL)
Coastal Plains League (CPL)
Colonial League (COLL)
Cotton States League (CSTL)
Cuban League (CUBL)
Eastern League (EL)
Eastern Shore League (ESHL)
Evangeline League (EVL)
Florida East Coast League (FECL)
Florida International League (FINL)
Florida State League (FLOR)
Georgia-Florida League (GFL)
Georgia State League (GASL)
Illinois-Iowa-Indiana League (IIIL)
International League (IL)
Interstate League (ISLG)
Kentucky-Illinois-Tennessee League (KITTY)

Mexican League (MEX)
Middle Atlantic League (MATL)
Mountain State League (MTNS)
Nebraska State League (NSL)
New York-Pennsylvania League (NYPL)
North Atlantic League (NATL)
North Carolina State League (NCSL)
Ohio State League (OSL)
Pacific Coast League (PCL)
Pennsylvania-Ontario-New York League (PONY)
Pennsylvania State Association (PASA)
Piedmont League (PIED)
Pioneer League (PION)
Provincial League (PROV)
Quebec Provincial League (QUPL)
South Atlantic League (SALL)
Southeastern League (SEAL)
Southern Association (SOUA)
Tar Heel League (THL)
Tri-State League (TRIS)
Virginia League (VIRL)
West Texas-New Mexico League (WTNM)
Western Association (WA)
Western International League (WINT)

Preface

There were plenty of historically significant moments in 1937, and one does not have to look far to find them. In the literary world, J.R.R. Tolkien's *The Hobbit* and John Steinbeck's *Of Mice and Men* were published. Margaret Mitchell won a Pulitzer Prize for her epic novel *Gone with the Wind*. On the big screen, the first full-length animated feature film, *Snow White and the Seven Dwarfs*, premiered at the Carthay Circle Theatre in Los Angeles in December. San Francisco Bay's Golden Gate Bridge and the Lincoln Tunnel in New York City opened. President Franklin D. Roosevelt, after defeating Kansas governor Alf Landon, held his second inauguration on January 20. Around the globe, several events transformed the political arena. In the United Kingdom, the coronation of King George VI was held, Joseph Stalin purged the Soviet government, and the Second Sino-Japanese War began. And there were tragedies: The German airship the *Hindenburg* exploded in flames while attempting to land on the airfield at Lakehurst, New Jersey; aviation pioneer Amelia Earhart disappeared over the central Pacific Ocean near Howland Island while attempting to circumnavigate the globe; and the worst school disaster in American history, the New London School explosion, claimed more than 295 lives.

In sports history, too, the year brought noteworthy events. In football, Cleveland was granted an NFL franchise, which would become the Rams, and the Boston Redskins moved to Washington, D.C., and went on to defeat the Chicago Bears in the NFL Championship Game. War Admiral won the Triple Crown. Joe Louis, the Brown Bomber, knocked out Cinderella Man James J. Braddock in the eighth round in front of 60,000 spectators at Comiskey Park to claim the heavyweight boxing title. In baseball, 1937 saw Cy Young, Tris Speaker and Nap Lajoie inducted into the Hall of Fame. On May 30, New York Giants pitcher Carl Hubbell won his 24th consecutive victory over two seasons. And

Preface

the New York Yankees won their sixth championship, and second of what would be four in a row, beating the New York Giants four games to one in the 34th World Series.

It takes a longer, closer look at history to find what might be the most remarkable sports story of the year, however. On September 18, 1937, the inaugural season of the reconstituted Eastern Shore Baseball League came to an end. At 4:20 in the afternoon, the final out was registered and the Salisbury Indians defeated the Centreville Colts for the league championship. This completed one of the most amazing comebacks in professional sports.

After starting the season with a win-loss record of 21–5, the Salisbury Indians were informed by the league president, J. Thomas Kibler, that the ball club had violated league rules by having more than four players on its roster with previous professional baseball experience. Their penalty, the forfeiture of their 21 victories, sent the team plummeting to the cellar of the standings. Behind extraordinary pitching keyed by the unmatchable duo of Jorge Comellas and Joe Kohlman and relentless team hitting led by Jerry Lynn, Frank Trechock and Fermin Guerra, the Indians went on to win 59 of their final 70 games to secure first place, the league pennant and its playoffs championship.

Throughout the summer months, and at first well outside the headlines, the unbelievable story of this Class D minor league farm team unfolded. By the end of the season, news of the Indians' accomplishment had reached a level of celebrity, appearing in newspapers across the nation. Decades later, there is still wonderment at the comeback and the club itself, which in 2001 was named by the Minor League Baseball Association as one of the greatest minor league teams of all time.

But what makes a team great—and what, specifically, made *this* team great? Was it the Indians' utter dominance of their opponents? Or was it their remarkable resilience in the face of an unexpected obstacle? After all, in addition to suffering a severe penalty—going, overnight, from 21–5 to 0–26—the team overcame a season of dead arms, charley horses, sprained hands, broken ankles, spiked feet and players jumping contracts to storm back and take the league title. It hardly seemed possible, as Bill James points out: "Not only were their wins in the bank converted to losses, but also losses by the opposition had been converted into wins," adding to the distance between Salisbury and the league's other teams. They responded by going 59–11, good for an eye-popping .843 winning percentage, over the remainder of the season.[1]

Preface

This book tells the story of their extraordinary comeback, still the greatest in the history of the game.

A Note on the Research

Newspapers were the key primary source material for this book. Sifting through pages and pages of them, most from the Chesapeake Bay region, I attempted to locate all the box scores for games played by the Salisbury Indians in 1937. Although many newspapers have been digitized and are accessible online, several remain available only through in-person visits to historical societies and archives.

It is hoped that those readers previously familiar with the abridged storyline, along with those who have never heard of the Salisbury Indians, will find the complete story of this remarkable but now largely forgotten team all the more compelling for the added depth and detail.

ONE

A New Era of Delmarva Baseball

Revival of the Eastern Shore Baseball League

The first establishment of the Eastern Shore Baseball League existed from 1922 to mid–1928. Operated on the Delmarva Peninsula, the league featured teams from Maryland, Delaware and Virginia but unfortunately closed after a collapse in farm prices that preceded the Great Depression. On July 10, 1928, the directors of the Eastern Shore League passed a motion by a four-to-two vote to disband the league on account of poor attendance. Under the leadership of Walter B. Miller of Salisbury (1922), M. Brevoort Thawley of Crisfield (1923) and J. Harry Rew of Parksley (1924–1928), the league could not sustain the necessary financial backing to be viable.[1]

The Great Depression pushed all the minor leagues across the country into financial instability. Judge William Gibbons Bramham,[2] the president of the National Association of Professional Baseball Leagues, pointed to three factors that led to the woes of the minor leagues. First, it was the "lack of funds on the part of patrons. ... The necessities of life have first call upon the purse."[3] The second cause was what he described as a "Ponzied operation."[4] After World War I, leagues raised salaries and underwent park expansion with great fervor. However, admission prices remained unchanged and low. Unlike other businesses, the minor leagues did not "adjust and balance their budgets" before the Great Depression hit and had to take huge losses during the 1931 and 1932 seasons.[5] The third factor, in Bramham's opinion, was the selfishness of the leagues that naively thought that large sums of money would continue to come in while the nation suffered.

Miracle on the Eastern Shore

William G. Bramham (1874–1947), the third president of the National Association of Professional Baseball Leagues, sitting at his office desk in Durham, North Carolina, in the 1930s. He successfully served in this capacity from 1933 through 1946, expanding the number of minor leagues from 14 to 52 (author's collection).

In 1933, the Minor Baseball League Association began a five-year plan to rehabilitate its program to support Major League Baseball. The plan contained several components to establish healthy minor league operations: a compact circuit, local ownership and established rivalries. From 1933 to 1936, association membership expanded from 14 leagues across the nation to 25 leagues.

In 1934, Dan Pasquella,[6] a Crisfield businessman and player-manager from the old-time loop, conceived the idea of reestablishing the Eastern Shore League. Pasquella reached out to Joe F. Carr,[7] a nationally known organizer who was the promotional director of the Minor Leagues of Professional Baseball. Carr expressed interest in the endeavor and by March 1935, Carr sent out a letter to the officials of the old clubs urging them to organize. Not until January 1937 did Carr

ONE—A New Era of Delmarva Baseball

come around and make the appropriate arrangements for a meeting to discuss this revival.

On January 14, 1937, representatives of towns and major clubs gathered for a meeting at the Salisbury Chamber of Commerce building to discuss the possibility of starting the league. The outlines for the league, as sketched out by Carr, who was presiding over the meeting, called for a Class D loop to serve as a farm system for Class AA teams and the major league. A dozen ball clubs would form the new league. Attending the meeting were representatives from the Maryland towns of Easton, Salisbury, Cambridge, Federalsburg, Centreville, Princess Anne and Crisfield, and Dover, Delaware, and Cape Charles, Virginia. Carr was able to rack up interest from Class AA teams; major league teams that included the Washington Senators, the New York Giants and the Philadelphia Phillies; the Class AA Baltimore Orioles; and the Class A Trenton Senators. In total, between 50 and 75 representatives for the various interested towns and a small group of agents for major and minor league organizations attended the meeting. Spokesmen for the towns included Ralph Clas (Cambridge); Mayor Alfred Truitt (Salisbury); Dr. Kenneth Knotts (Federalsburg); H.C. Butler and Hanson Horsey (Centreville); Hoyt Bloodsworth (Princess Anne); J.C.W. Tawes, J. Millard Tawes and Dan Pasquella (Crisfield); Frank "Home Run" Baker (Easton); and H.M. Walters, A.P. Schoolfield and E.W. Ross (Pocomoke City).[8]

All of the delegates present, although differing on questions of local financing, agreed on one point—the Eastern Shore was "baseball conscious."[9] The chief obstacle to a permanent formation was the inability of some delegates to speak officially for the towns they represented. Salisbury, Centreville, Crisfield and Dover were quoted as "ready to sign."[10] Pocomoke City could sign provided that outside financial aid could be obtained from some major or minor league club. Easton, described as the "most baseball-conscious" town on the Shore, lacked official confirmation, as did Cambridge and Federalsburg.[11] The town of Princess Anne was left out of the possibilities of joining pending further study of the prospects there.

John Ogden, general manager and vice president of the Baltimore Orioles, announced that the International League team would sponsor a club in Dover if the town built a new ballpark. If this deal fell through, Baltimore would back another club in the circuit. "Poke" Whalen, who managed Salisbury's last two years in the old loop, announced that Joe

Miracle on the Eastern Shore

Cambria, owner of the Trenton Senators of the New York-Pennsylvania League, would sponsor a club in Salisbury.

Carr explained the National Association, under which the league would operate, imposed a salary limit of $1,000 a month—with a minimum of $700. No club would be permitted to exceed this limit. The loop would have a minimum of six clubs with each club playing between 100 and 120 games a season during the summer months. A town should figure on a budget of $7,500 a season for expenses. Ogden and Patsy O'Rourke, representing the Philadelphia Phillies, suggested a working budget of about $6,000.

One of the "celebrities" who attended the meeting was Trappe, Maryland, native Frank "Home Run" Baker, a four-time home run champion and three-time league champion with the Philadelphia Athletics. After his major league career, he settled down as a farmer and businessman in his hometown. Although this was an exciting venture and he shared his support for it, he expressed his hesitation by forewarning attendees that to have a successful league, financial stability for all participants was absolutely necessary. Financial instability was the downfall of the old loop. Several clubs back then established their salary limits too high and the gate receipts could not maintain that amount and eventually the club owners had to walk away. He believed that the communities on the Eastern Shore would pay to watch baseball again and that there was "plenty of home talent" to fill the clubs.[12]

During the meeting, upon the suggestion of Baltimore Orioles general manager John Ogden, Tom Kibler,[13] veteran director of athletics at Washington College in Chestertown, Maryland, was unanimously elected to serve as temporary president of the new circuit, tentatively composed of Salisbury, Centreville, Crisfield, Dover, Pocomoke City, Cambridge, Easton and Federalsburg.

A second meeting was arranged to be held in the town of Cambridge on January 24. On the agenda would be the permanent organization of the league and the execution of franchise applications. However, Kibler was informed by Carr that the official formation meeting at Cambridge Hotel had to be postponed to January 31, owing to the fact that Carr had some important information to place before club representatives but it could not reach them by January 24.

On January 31, the Eastern Shore Baseball League, a Class D professional circuit, was formed with six clubs—five from Maryland and

ONE—*A New Era of Delmarva Baseball*

In 1937, while serving as the athletic director at Washington College, J. Thomas Kibler (1886–1971) was elected president of the Eastern Shore Baseball League. He became infamous when he decided to hand down the severe penalty to forfeit the Salisbury Indians' first 21 victories (courtesy Washington College Archives).

one from Delaware. Representatives of Cambridge, Easton, Salisbury, Federalsburg, Centreville and Dover submitted formal applications for franchises. Representatives of Pocomoke City and Crisfield indicated they intended to join to increase the league to an eight-club circuit but needed a little more time to drum up interest. They were given to the next scheduled meeting in Easton on February 14 to make any final arrangements for affiliating with an upper-level franchise. Michael J. McGonegal applied on behalf of Wilmington, Delaware, for inclusion in the league but those at the meeting agreed that the city was too large for Class D ball and tabled the application. The most populous town in the proposed league, Salisbury, was approximately 12,000. The city of Wilmington had close to 110,000 residents.

At the meeting, Whalen and Kibler proposed a preliminary plan of a 99-game schedule with doubleheaders slated for Memorial Day, July Fourth and Labor Day with the season opening on May 19 and closing on Labor Day. There would be six days of play each week with Monday designated as an off day in the circuit. Sunday ball would be played in each town.

Easton and Dover announced that they had plans to play night baseball as well. Others favored the option of night baseball but informed the group that they lacked the budget at that moment to construct the lighting apparatus. The circuit implemented the Shaughnessy system,[14] which was being used in the International League, to determine the playoffs for the league championship. At the end of the regular season, the first four clubs in the standings would meet in three-game series to decide the title.

The league voted for a 14-player limit for each club's roster and the $1,000-a-month salary limit. The players would consist of 10 raw recruits with no professional experience or "rookies," two one-year men and two class men. In case a club had a player-manager on the roster, $75 a month of his salary would be charged off against the monthly salary limit. Kibler was elected president for a one-year term and designated acting treasurer. He and Poke Whalen would draw up a set of schedules. In addition, the league voted that no player trades would transpire after August 1 in each season and a club could waive a player away but could use only a "rookie" as his replacement. Two sets of uniforms were voted on for players and the use of the double-umpire system was confirmed. The league also agreed that the home club would keep all the revenue from the gate receipts. This would incentivize each club to do their own hustle to maximize home-game attendance since it would be their primary revenue stream for the season. The minimum admission prices were set at 40 cents for seats in the grandstands and 25 cents for seats in the bleachers.

At the February 14 meeting, the directors voted for a 100-game schedule that would start on May 19 and end on Labor Day, September 6. Kibler was elected to serve as secretary and treasurer in addition to being president of the loop. He would receive a salary of $1,000 if the

ONE—A New Era of Delmarva Baseball

league was made up of six clubs and $1,200 if there were eight clubs. This included a $300 office budget. The directors' ultimate decision made Kibler, as one reporter wrote, "the executive and judiciary department with more cabinet portfolios and prerogatives than Mussolini. As the schedule committee, he was to arrange the hundred-game playing program. He was to decide what brand of baseball the clubs would use, his authority to hire and fire umpires and arrange the amount of their salary was absolute. His was the power to enforce all regulations and impose fines."[15]

The directors withheld action on Pocomoke City's formal application for admission pending a decision by the baseball interests at Crisfield on whether it would join the circuit. The admission of only one club would throw the league schedule out of balance. To expedite Crisfield's decision, Pasquella called a meeting of baseball patrons and businessmen residing in Crisfield.

On February 26, J.C.W. Tawes presided over a meeting in Crisfield to see if the town could foster enough support to enter the newly formed Eastern Shore League. After a heated discussion, it was decided that the town would formally apply for a franchise the next day. This action allowed Pocomoke City to enter the league and make it an eight-club league. For the Pocomoke City franchise, a board of directors was established with Arthur H. Ehlers, a Baltimore bowling alley proprietor, as its president and principal owner.

A setback occurred involving Crisfield's involvement in the league when on March 11, Robert M. Clarke, former major league umpire and holder of the Crisfield franchise, told Kibler he was relinquishing the franchise as he had been unable to agree with the local municipality on terms for the use of the Crisfield grandstand. Luckily, three days later, several men came to the rescue and Clarke formally informed Kibler that an agreement had been reached and he would hold the franchise. Pasquella was appointed player-manager of the Crisfield club.

To help secure the financial stability needed for a successful season, each club had to deposit $800 into the league treasury, which would hold the funds in escrow for that club's obligations, including players' salaries. An initial payment of $200 was required when they submitted their application. Another $100 deposit was due on May 10 and after the season opened, the fund payment of $50 would be deposited for the first 10 weeks.

Miracle on the Eastern Shore

The league directors met for one more meeting on May 9. Kibler announced he had selected and signed under contract eight umpires: James Boyer and James J. O'Connor of Baltimore; Albert Clark of Wilmington; Thomas Crane of Franklinville, Pennsylvania; James Gilbert of Lambertville, New Jersey; John Toach of Trenton, New Jersey; Henry Carrington of Waterbury, Connecticut; and George L. Ekaitis of Chestertown.[16] In an attempt to evaluate the applicants, Kibler invited several of them to Washington College to audition their skills by officiating college baseball games. The double umpire system would be used with one umpire behind the plate and the other positioned in the field. For recordkeeping duties, President Kibler offered Salisbury native Charles J. Truitt[17] the position of league statistician.

At the meeting, the Eastern Shore Baseball League finalized the official composition with seven of the eight ball clubs affiliated with major league teams.

They were:

Cambridge Cardinals—St. Louis Cardinals
Centreville Colts—Boston Red Sox
Crisfield Crabbers—New York Giants
Dover Orioles—Baltimore Orioles (IL)
Easton Browns—St. Louis Browns
Federalsburg Athletics—Philadelphia Athletics
Pocomoke City Red Sox—Brooklyn Dodgers
Salisbury Indians—Washington Senators

Mr. Cambria's Salisbury Indians

Owned by Baltimore sportsman Joseph Carl Cambria,[18] the Salisbury Indians began working on the managerial composition of the club. Born in Messina, Italy, in 1890, Cambria followed his father and immigrated in 1893 with his two brothers to Boston, Massachusetts. Cambria played amateur and semiprofessional ball in Massachusetts, Rhode Island and Canada. After military service during World War I, Cambria relocated with his wife, Charlotte, to Baltimore to purchase the Bugle Coast and Apron Co., a laundry business on North Chester Street. In 1928, Cambria purchased a semiprofessional baseball club and entered the world of baseball ownership. For several years, Cambria continued to sponsor several professional teams in the Baltimore area.

ONE—A New Era of Delmarva Baseball

"Papa Joe" Cambria (1890–1962), the scout extraordinaire for the Washington Senators, pioneered the recruitment of Latin American players, especially from Cuba. In the 1930s and 1940s, he owned several minor league clubs, including the Trenton Senators and the Salisbury Indians (courtesy Eastern Shore Baseball Hall of Fame Museum).

In 1933, Cambria purchased the Albany Senators of the International League and began a close working relationship with Clark Griffith, owner of the Washington Senators. Cambria was one of the most prolific scouts in Major League history, signing hundreds of men to professional contracts for Griffith and the Washington Senators for 26 years. Cuba was the focus of Cambria's major contribution to baseball history. He signed well over 400 young Cuban ballplayers to professional contracts from 1934 until his death in 1962. Cambria made his headquarters in Havana, taking a room at the American Club. A scout would typically offer a young Cuban player $75 a month and put him on a plane for Key West. There the players would catch a bus to their final destinations.

When Cambria heard of the reincarnation of the Eastern Shore Baseball League, he rushed to purchase the franchise option for the Salisbury ball club. He would own the franchise until 1940. Cambria's first move was to find the right person to pilot the club. He approached recently retired Major League Baseball player and Eastern Shore League alumnus D'Arcy Raymond "Jake" Flowers.[19] A 34-year-old native son of Cambridge, Maryland, Flowers played 10 seasons of professional baseball from 1923 to 1934 for the St. Louis Cardinals, Brooklyn Dodgers and Cincinnati Reds. Before the majors, Flowers attended Washington College and was a flashy infielder for the Cambridge Canners in the old league in 1922. By May 6, Flowers signed on.

To round out the team's administrative staff, Melvin E. Murphy, a 34-year-old former salesman of a meat packing business, was hired as business manager; John Milton as secretary; Ernest T. Foskey, trainer, groundskeeper and bus driver; and Elijah Disharoon, in charge of the center field scoreboard.[20] To serve as the ball club's general manager, John Joseph "Poke" Whalen was chosen. Maurice Fields, a local teen, was selected as the team's batboy.[21]

Cambria approached the local municipality and negotiated an agreement for the use of Gordy Park for the club's home games. Built in 1922 on the corner of Oak and Pine streets, the park, named after former Salisbury White Clouds catcher Samuel E. Gordy, was touted as the second-finest ballpark in Maryland, after Oriole Park in Baltimore. In early April 1937, a lease was signed and renovation of the grandstands and bleachers at Gordy Park was underway. Procurement of equipment for illuminating the park for night games was also placed. Cambria sent Len Shires,[22] a former Texas League player and coach for the Albany Senators, to oversee the ballpark's restoration. On May 4, the local newspaper reported that the old wooden stands had been torn down and offered as firewood to anyone who could haul them away.

Next on the list for Cambria: build a strong roster. Before the official formation of the league, Whalen began scouting and by February 5, the local newspaper reported that he had signed three pitchers and a first baseman (Baltimore semipro right-hand pitchers Frank S. Spring

ONE—A New Era of Delmarva Baseball

A view of the grandstands and bleachers of Gordy Park, the ballpark used by the Salisbury Indians, situated on the corners of Oak and Pine streets in Salisbury, Maryland. It was originally built in 1922, and Indians owner Joe Cambria renovated the park to expand seating from 3,500 to 5,000. Today, the Salvation Army football field occupies the site (courtesy Mary Jane [Revolinsky] Martinez).

and John "Woodey" Bates, right-hander James A. Ralph of Laurel, Delaware, and local semipro outfielder Charles Quimby), all classified as rookies.[23] By May 5, Whalen reported that 30 players were signed to report to Salisbury for tryouts. Most of the prospects were sent to the training camp with the Cambria-owned Class AA Trenton Senators of the New York-Pennsylvania League and would not assemble at Salisbury until about four days before the opening of the league, scheduled for May 19. The recruits received both preliminary training and actual experience with the Trenton club with some even getting a turn in the regular lineup. Most of the Salisbury recruits composed an augmented Trenton club, having barely failed to make the regular lineup for lack of experience.

The players signed were:

> Catchers—Fermin Guerra, Claude Larned, William Lyman and Clifton Keyser[24]
> Pitchers—Along with Frank Spring, "Woodey" Bates and James Ralph, Leslie Butcher, Russell Gurth, Herbert F. Pierson, John Bassler, Leon Revolinsky, Alexander Trippe and an unnamed lefthander from Trenton[25]

Miracle on the Eastern Shore

First Basemen—Robert Brady, Arthur Steinfadt and Francisco Hernandez of Havana, Cuba[26]

Infielders—Frank Trechock, Tony Miller, Paul Jarrett, Sam Kravitz, Armando Paytuvi, Carman Soltis, Edgar Leip (who played 10 games with the Trenton club) and Thaddeus Cash[27]

Outfielders—along with Charles Quimby, Walter Andrews, Sam Britton, William Luzansky and Frank James[28]

By May 12, four prospects had not shown up, infielder Tony Miller, pitcher "Woodey" Bates and an unnamed left-hander from Trenton. Catcher Claude Larned had to stay with the Trenton club because of an injury to one of the Senators' receivers.

Some players did not accept Salisbury's proposal to try out for the team. One such person was Walter John "Babe" DeFreitas, a Lakewood (New Jersey) high school baseball star, who declined the offer. He received a scholarship from Long Island University and decided to attend the institution after graduation.[29]

By the next day, all the prospects had reported to Salisbury, which afforded Flowers a full week to evaluate them. At first, the plan had been to keep most of the candidates with the Trenton club so they could work out with the regular players in New Jersey and gain some upper-level experience through practice and scrimmages. However, it was decided that sending them down to Salisbury would enable the players to become better acquainted with each other and Flowers could look them over in a preseason workout. The early arrivals numbered about 25, to be augmented later by pitching candidates from Trenton.

Flowers was still wavering on the option of a player's role for the squad. Several clubs in the loop had individuals exercising that option of a player-manager: Crisfield's Dan Pasquella, Federalsburg's George E. Short, Pocomoke City's Vic Keen and Cambridge's Fred Lucas.[30] The Cambria organization was concerned primarily in developing players for sale to major league clubs and they came to a consensus that it would be best that Flowers be the "mastermind from the bench" in order for the players on the squad to receive the greatest playing time.[31] Their developmental plan echoed that of other Class D leagues whose priorities were to initiate the building process of young players as they moved up through the leagues so they could be sold to major league clubs.

Management arranged two exhibition games to further evaluate

ONE—A New Era of Delmarva Baseball

the recruits. They lost to the Trenton regulars by the score of 11 to 7. Also, two days before the start of the season, the Indians played a five-inning exhibition game with the Salisbury State Teachers College baseball team that turned into a slugfest. While Gordy Park was being renovated, Dr. Jefferson Davis Blackwell, president of Salisbury State College, offered the college's athletic field, dressing rooms and showers for use of the players. On May 17, the team bus was delivered.

The season's prices for admission into Gordy Park were set as follows: seats in the grandstand at 55 cents, seats in the bleachers were 35 cents, ladies paid 25 cents and children under the age of 14 paid 15 cents. An advertisement appeared in the local newspapers announcing box seats and season ticket prices: season tickets for general admission to the grandstand were $22.50, boxes (season for four seats) were $100, boxes (season for six seats) were $125 and box seats for one game were 75 cents.

Finally, the day had arrived. From Dan Pasquella's passion to revive the league a few years ago to the formal establishment of the eight-team circuit, Wednesday, May 19, was a day that all baseball fans on the Eastern Shore had hoped for. After a 10-year hiatus, organized baseball had returned. In preparation for the day, businesses around the town of Salisbury arranged to be closed during the game to allow workers to attend. For the Salisbury Indians, Jake Flowers completed his evaluation and selected his team, which was composed of "rookies" from the coal region of Pennsylvania, the eastern European neighborhoods in middle New Jersey

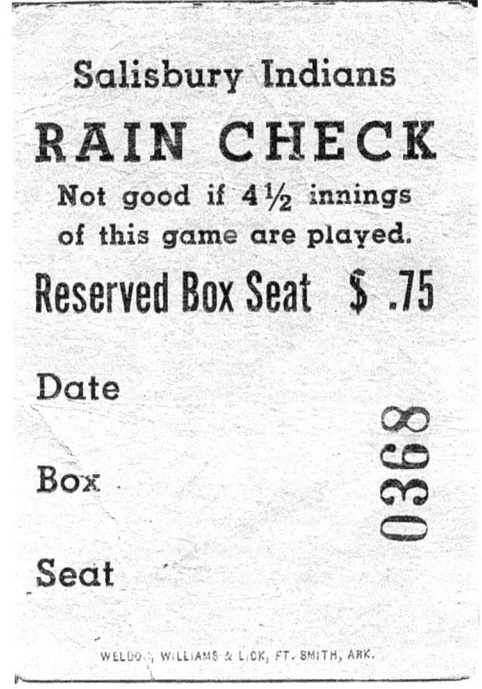

Ticket stub for a Salisbury Indians game at Gordy Park in 1937 (courtesy Eastern Shore Baseball Hall of Fame Museum).

A Salisbury Baseball Club, Inc., courtesy card for entrance to Gordy Park given to the wife of "Doc" Cash, signed by owner Joe C. Cambria and general manager J.P. Whalen, 1937 (courtesy Kevin Ellis).

and from the states of Wisconsin, Virginia, Tennessee, Ohio and Connecticut along with Philadelphia natives, Cuban nationals and one local boy from Centreville, Maryland. What Joe Cambria, Poke Whalen and Jake Flowers had assembled, many believed, before the season began, to be the best franchise in the league.

Two

First 26 Games (May 19–June 18)

Salisbury 7, Cambridge 5   (1–0)   May 19

	1	2	3	4	5	6	7	8	9	R	H	E
Cambridge	0	1	0	1	0	0	0	2	1	5	8	5
Salisbury	6	0	0	0	0	0	0	1	X	7	4	3

Comellas (winner), Kohlman (save), Brown (loser) Trechock (2)—RBI; Trechock—HR

On Wednesday, May 19, 1937, the new baseball season of the revived Eastern Shore League finally arrived. The Salisbury Indians started the season hosting the Cambridge Cardinals, their traditional rival of the old loop as well as manager Flowers's former minor league team, known as the Canners during his tenure. To help celebrate the event, approximately 2,000 fans, recalling memories of the bygone days of the first incarnation of the league, excitedly descended upon the hub of Wicomico County and took their seats in Gordy Park's unfinished grandstand and bleachers. Located on the corner of Pine and Oak streets, the ball field had dimensions of 310 feet to the left field foul pole, 450 feet to center field and 300 feet to the right field foul pole.

Preceding the game, a parade led by the 53-piece Laurel High School marching band formed at one o'clock in the afternoon at the corner of Main and Baptist streets. The line of march grandly proceeded west on Main Street to Market Street, Market Street to Camden Avenue, Camden Avenue to South Division Street, South Division Street to Locust Street and Locust Street to the ballpark. The parade entered the park and marched to deep center field. The visiting and home teams stood at attention while the American flag was hoisted to the top of the pole. The crowd then stood as the band played the national anthem.

Miracle on the Eastern Shore

Ceremoniously, Salisbury mayor Alfred T. Truitt threw the first ball to the acting catcher, former mayor E. Sheldon Jones.[1] Indians owner Joe Cambria powered the pitch through the infield while 83-year-old Lewis W. Gunby, the sole surviving veteran of the Salisbury White Clouds, the town's first baseball team, stood behind Mayor Jones as the honorary umpire.

The Salisbury fans eagerly waited to see the starting lineup Flowers had assembled. Ed Leip (3B) led off, followed by Doc Cash (2B) and Bill Luzansky (LF). Fermin "Mike" Guerra (C) batted cleanup. Charles Quimby (RF) was in the five hole, Walt Andrews (CF) batted sixth, Bob Brady (1B) batted seventh and Frank Trechock (SS) batted eighth. Flowers sent to the mound Jorge "George" Comellas, the 20-year-old Cuban right-hander.

At 3:32 in the afternoon, umpire Henry Carrington brushed off home plate and bellowed, "Play ball!" while his officiating partner, Thomas Crane, took his position along the baseline.

Comellas faced four batters in the first inning with no incident. During the bottom half of the inning, the Indians faced southpaw Larry Brown,[2] a Salisbury (Maryland) youth. Notably nervous in his league debut, Brown issued walks to the first three batters. The cleanup hitter, Guerra, the Indians' Cuban catcher, laced a shot near third base. Cards third baseman Charles Mast[3] gathered up the grounder and overthrew second base. Center fielder Frank Jackson retrieved the ball in center field and wildly threw the ball to the catcher, Chip Marshall.[4] When the play was completed, four runs were chalked up on the scoreboard for the Indians and Mast and Jackson were each officially charged with an error. Unaware to those watching the play, a miscommunication occurred between the Indians' manager and their catcher. Flowers, noticing Brown's unusual wildness, instructed Guerra to "take the first ball,"[5] which in baseball lexicon means to not swing at the first pitch. Unfortunately, or fortunately because of the outcome of the play, Guerra understood little English and took the four English words at their face value, swung and connected Brown's offering. When he first came to Salisbury, Flowers asked Guerra his first name. After having "Fermin" spelled and pronounced several times, Flowers asked Guerra if he would mind being called "Mike" as it would be easier to remember and pronounce. The nickname stuck all through his baseball career. After Brady drew a walk with two outs, Trechock belted a long shot over center field onto the roof of the factory to end the scoring.

Two—First 26 Games (May 19–June 18)

In the top of the second inning, Cardinals player-manager Fred Lucas hit a homer to put the visitors on the scoreboard. In the fourth inning, second baseman Ed Hayden[6] earned a walk, Marshall singled and Hayden scored on Brown's clean hit to right field, making the score 6 to 2. In the eighth inning, Cambridge scored two runs when Jackson doubled down the third baseline and Lucas brought Jackson in with his second home run of the game.

In the bottom of the eighth, Salisbury answered when Cash scored on shortstop Dan Murtaugh's[7] throwing error after fielding Guerra's grounder.

In the top of the ninth inning, Comellas began to tire and had trouble locating the strike zone. Quickly the bases were loaded and with one out, Flowers sent in southpaw John Bassler, who struck out Jackson. The next batter, Lucas, who had already hit two home runs, stepped to the plate. Flowers made another call to the bullpen and signaled for Joe Kohlman, who walked Lucas. Before that, Sam Ronchetti,[8] who had pinch-hit for Brown, scored on a failed attempt by Kohlman to pick him off as Ronchetti wandered down the third baseline. With the bases still loaded, Kohlman refocused and threw three balls past Hayden to end the game.

Cardinals pitcher Brown had a credible performance, holding the Indians to four base hits and striking out five. His only downfall was issuing 10 walks. For the Indians, Comellas had a below-average outing, issuing six walks, striking out five and scattering eight hits in 8⅓ innings.

News from around the league had the Dover Orioles losing to the Pocomoke City Red Sox by the score of 5 to 3. Delaware governor Richard C. McMullen threw out the first ball at the game. The Federalsburg Athletics lost their home opener by the score of 9 to 4 against the Easton Browns. Maryland governor Harry W. Nice tossed out their first ball. The Centreville Colts were victorious against the Crisfield Crabbers in their home opener by a 13-7 score. Maryland Attorney General Herbert R. O'Conor tossed out the first ball.

Cambridge 5, Salisbury 4   (1–1)   May 20

Salisbury	1	0	0	1	1	0	1	0	0	4	10	2
Cambridge	0	0	3	1	1	0	0	0	X	5	4	1

Kohlman (loser), Semple (winner)
Cash, Steinfadt—2B; Trechock, Guerra—HR; Luzansky, Guerra, Cash, Trechock—RBI

Miracle on the Eastern Shore

Day two had the Indians travel to the town of Cambridge in Dorchester County, Maryland, to play the Cardinals in front of approximately 1,500 Cambridge fans. The Cambridge Recreation Company Inc., which owned the franchise, agreed to a five-year lease for 25 acres within the old fairgrounds along South Race Street extended. The owners erected new stands at the ballpark, whose dimensions measured 306 feet to left field, 362 feet to center and 298 feet to right.

Just like the season opener at Salisbury, Cambridge had its own opening day celebration with a parade preceding the game. The two ball clubs marched through the main business section of town accompanied by the Rescue Fire Company. For the flag-raising ceremony, the players were joined by former governor Emerson C. Harrington, his son, Emerson C. Harrington, Jr., Cambridge mayor Charles Brohawn, C.H. Seward, Granville Hooper, Joseph Fowler and the Reverend T. Applegarth. Mayor Brohawn tossed out the first ball, with Governor Harrington at bat. Harrington swung and missed while Granville Hooper caught it.

Flowers sent Joe Kohlman to the mound and Fred Lucas, the Cardinals' skipper, countered with Thomas Semple.[9] Kohlman had a solid performance, striking out nine Cardinals and giving up four hits (although three were doubles). Salisbury scored in the first inning when Luzansky's deep flyout to center brought in Leip.

In the bottom of the third, Cambridge scored three runs. Cardinals catcher Marshall walked, followed by a double by Semple. After an out by shortstop Murtaugh, first baseman Bob Iwanicki[10] hit another double, and then scored on center fielder Jackson's base hit. In the fourth, Guerra collected his first home run of the season to cut the score to three to two. The Cardinals added another run in the bottom of the fourth. In the next inning, the Cardinals scored the winning run when Iwanicki scored after opening the inning with a double. In the seventh inning, Kohlman, after reaching first on an error, scored on Cash's single.

Along with Trechock and Guerra hitting home runs, Cash went three for five with a double. The Indians collected 10 hits from Semple but he scattered them effectively, leaving nine runners stranded. They could never overtake the Cardinals. Fred Lucas would later recall that if a Salisbury player had not overrun second base, the Indians would have won the contest.

Two—First 26 Games (May 19–June 18)

Salisbury 4, Crisfield 2   (2–1)   May 21

Crisfield	0	0	2	0	0	0	0	0	0	2	6	1
Salisbury	1	1	0	0	1	0	0	1	X	4	9	6

Bassler (winner), Anderson (loser)
Luzansky—2B; Luzansky, Cash, Trechock—SB; Luzansky (2), Leip, Quimby—RBI

Salisbury hosted the Crisfield Crabbers for the first night game on the Eastern Shore. To christen the moment, State Comptroller William S. Gordy, Jr., was chosen to toss out the first ball. After roughing up the Spalding horsehide and warming up his right arm, he launched the ball from his grandstand box and weakly fell short of his mark, the glove of Salisbury catcher Guerra.

Salisbury was the first of four ball clubs in the league that planned to play night games. Cambridge, Dover and Pocomoke City had yet to install their klieg arc lights. With a start time of 8:15 in the evening, approximately 4,000 fans, nearly twice the number than opening day, mobbed the grandstands, bleachers and along the foul lines to view the American pastime under the floodlights. The Indians' Midwestern southpaw, John Bassler, held the Crabbers to a scoreless first inning. The Indians scored once during their part of the inning and again in the second. Manager Dan Pasquella replaced starter Tony O'Buzz[11] with Anderson, a 17-year-old right-hander, when Salisbury occupied two bases with no outs in the second inning. Anderson quieted the Indians' bats until the fifth inning, when they tallied another run. In the eighth, they added one more. Bassler held the Crabbers to six hits. Crisfield's tallies came in the third inning when its two runs came about without a hit (a walk, an error and a wild pitch).

Indians owner Joe Cambria came to the game, checking up on his investment, and announced his plan to enlarge the park to accommodate 5,000 fans. At that time, the park could hold 3,500, with 2,500 in the grandstands and 500 on each side of the bleachers. Fifteen hundred seats would be added to the bleachers, forming a half-moon around the outfield.

Salisbury 7, Crisfield 5   (3–1)   May 22

Salisbury	0	0	1	0	0	2	0	4	7	7	2
Crisfield	0	0	3	2	0	0	0	0	5	7	0

Comellas (winner), Kohlman (save), Levan (loser)
Guerra—3B; Trechock—HR

Miracle on the Eastern Shore

The Indians defeated the Crisfield Crabbers 7 to 5 in the bay town of Crisfield with a four-run rally in the ninth inning. In the final frame, Anthony Levan,[12] the Crisfield pitcher, became unsteady with three walks and a triple by Guerra that was followed by a single, leading to four runs and the victory for Salisbury. For the Indians, a new pitching prospect was making his debut on the mound. From the northern Virginia suburb of Washington, D.C., 20-year-old Vernon Shelton[13] had been pitching for the semipro Quantico Indians since 1935. During the game, he struggled a bit, allowing seven hits and five runs. In the fifth, Comellas relieved Shelton and kept the Crabbers hitless for the next 4⅔ innings to earn the win. Kohlman pitched a perfect ninth. Before the game, Dan Pasquella stepped down as the Crabbers' skipper. Bob Clarke, the general franchise holder and a former manager, player and umpire, took over the managerial duties. Clarke reported that no dissatisfaction occurred between him and Pasquella but the Crisfield team had not been performing well and both felt possibly someone else could do better. For the benefit of the club, Pasquella offered his resignation.

Situated on the McGrath property in the Jacksonville section of town, Clarke Park was one of the largest fields in the league, measuring 275 feet from home plate to the right field foul pole, 282 feet to the left field foul pole and 422 feet to deep center field. The carpentry work was done by Ryland Ward, Ollie Harrison and Fletcher Harrison.[14] The preparation of the field was under the direction of Harold Cullen, and throughout the season, Hezekiah Brittingham[15] served as the groundskeeper. The scoreboard, donated by two well-known businessmen of Crisfield, Lewis and Thomas Saltz, was erected along the right field foul line against the fence. It measured 17 feet high and 20 feet wide and was considered the largest on the shore. A 30-foot flagpole, donated by Freeston Sterling,[16] was installed in deep center field. Advertising signs were painted on the fence by Wallace Dize and Preston Thomas.[17] A concession stand, operated by Dana Thomas and Warren "Hoss" Sterling,[18] sold soft drinks, peanuts and other fan favorites. For home games, the Crabbers donned cream-colored uniforms with black-and-white stockings and black caps. Their away uniforms were gray with black lettering.

The town of Crisfield was regarded by Eastern Shore veterans as the best baseball town in the loop. The watermen, who made up the majority of the 15,000 residents in and around Crisfield, were "dyed-in-the-wool

Two—First 26 Games (May 19–June 18)

fans" and could balance their work tasks of oystering, clamming and crabbing with an enjoyable quantity of baseball.[19]

Salisbury 7, Federalsburg 6   (4–1)   May 23

Salisbury	1	0	5	0	1	0	0	0	0	7	8	1
Federalsburg	0	0	0	3	0	2	1	0	0	6	9	2

Kowal (winner), Ratterree (loser)
Steinfadt, Quimby, Cash, Lynn (2), Guerra—RBI; Guerra—2B; Steinfadt, Lynn—HR

The Salisbury Indians' next outing was an away game against the Federalsburg Athletics. On the mound, 26-year-old Middletown, Connecticut, native Frank Kowal[20] won his pitching debut by the score of 7 to 6. Kowal was a seven-year veteran of the Middlesex County (Connecticut) baseball leagues. In the fifth inning, he was relieved by Comellas, who held Federalsburg to two hits. Throughout the game, the Indians made their eight hits count against five Federalsburg pitchers (William Ratterree, Tom Waldron, Maynard Schoen, Kendall Moran and James Toland).[21]

The Salisbury Indians attacked first in the initial frame, when 22-year-old Cuyahoga County Ohioan Art Steinfadt, who was taking his turn at first base, launched a moon shot over the fence. The third inning was a big one for Salisbury, in which four hits, a hit batsman and a fielder's choice added five runs. Kowal walked and scored on Lynn's two-run homer. Luzansky followed with a base hit and Steinfadt was hit by a pitch. Guerra then crushed a three-run home run. In the fifth stanza, three hits by Guerra (a double), Cash and Quimby and a fielder's choice by Trechock added another run.

Behind 6 to 0, the A's finally got on the scoreboard with three runs in the fourth inning. Left fielder Robert Stant[22] singled and scored on center fielder Zip LeGates's base hit. Stant and right fielder Charles Miller,[23] who earned a base on balls, scored on third baseman Charles Morris's double. In the sixth inning, the A's added two more runs on three straight walks and a two-run single by Morris. The A's added one more run when right fielder Dink Boyce[24] worked a walk and scored on Miller's double.

The Federalsburg ownership purchased the site for its new park and decided to place the playing field in the northwest section. With the assistance of Congressman T. Alan Goldsborough, the construction of the ballpark received presidential approval as a Works Progress Administration project. The ballpark measured 323 feet to left field, 346 feet to center and 335 feet to right. The town of Federalsburg was the smallest in the circuit with a population of around 1,200 but was known as the center of the best baseball region on the Delmarva Peninsula.

A view of the grandstands and some of the bleachers down the third base line during a game at the Federalsburg ballpark prior to 1947 (courtesy Federalsburg Historical Society).

An action shot showing a batter at home plate during a game at the Federalsburg ballpark prior to 1947 (courtesy Federalsburg Historical Society).

Two—First 26 Games (May 19–June 18)

Salisbury 9, Dover 3   (5–1)   May 25

Dover	0	0	0	0	0	0	2	0	1	3	7	4
Salisbury	3	0	5	0	0	1	0	0	X	9	14	2

Kohlman (winner), Riley (loser)
Trechock, Reznichak (3), Steinfadt, Cash (3), Kohlman—RBI;
  Lynn, Reznichak, Cash—2B; Trechock—3B; Guerra—SB

Some 3,000 fans sitting in the recently expanded grandstands at Gordy Park witnessed the Salisbury Indians display some newly founded batting power by slugging 14 resounding blows, which led to a 9-3 win over the Dover Orioles in the afternoon game of a doubleheader. Indian hurler Kohlman was in total control with his full arsenal of fastballs, curves, drops, changes of pace and occasional screwballs. In the first inning, he gave up a single to Orioles shortstop Michael Mosher.[25] After that, the Orioles batters did not reach third base until the sixth inning, when the game was safely in hand by a score of 9 to 0. Kohlman struck out 12.

The Salisbury bats drove Riley, the bespectacled starting Orioles pitcher, off the mound in the third inning with no outs. The Indians scored three runs in the first inning on doubles by Lynn and Trechock, singles by Guerra and Reznichak and an error on Steinfadt's hit. After smashing six hits off Riley, the Indians continued the onslaught against his relief, Stephen Finta,[26] for another eight hits.

Trechock connected with a triple, a double and a single in four trips to the plate and scored three runs. Lynn went three for four with a double. Cash batted in three runs, and newcomer Joe Reznichak hit a double and a single with three runs batted in. A football star from Bucknell University, Reznichak attained national recognition by leading the Bison over the University of Miami in the first Orange Bowl. He debuted in left field and was designated the backup catcher for the Indians.

Salisbury 10, Dover 6   (6–1)   May 26

Salisbury	3	0	1	3	0	2	0	0	1	10	8	3
Dover	3	3	0	0	0	0	0	0	0	6	10	4

Comellas (winner), Wittig (loser)
Guerra (4), Steinfadt, Comellas—RBI; Guerra (2)—HR;
  Guerra (2), Quimby (4)—SB

The Salisbury ball club traveled to the Blue Hen State for the first night game at Orioles Park. Located just east of the Legislative Building,

Miracle on the Eastern Shore

the ballpark was only a five-minute walk from the business section of the city. Measuring 318 feet from home plate to left field, 340 feet to center field and 318 feet to right field, it was illuminated by 180,000 watts of total candlepower from clusters of eight and 12 lights installed on 10 tall poles.

The Dover fans who attended the game witnessed the Indians quickly put three runs on the scoreboard in the first inning. Salisbury sent out Midwest portsider John Bassler, who struggled early with his control, walking three Orioles and fanning one. This, with two hits, enabled the Dover hitters to tally six runs in the first two innings.

In the first inning, shortstop Joe Archer[27] started it off with a walk. After right fielder Mosher struck out, second baseman Ed Roetz[28] brought Archer in with a base hit. Center fielder Charles Stotz walked and first baseman Paul Swoboda was awarded first base after Bassler hit him with a pitch.[29] Roetz and Stotz scored on third baseman Edwin Vandegrift's fielder's choice.[30]

In the next inning, Bassler issued a walk to Lyle Elliott and a single to catcher Hal Stock.[31] Indians first baseman Steinfadt mishandled Dover pitcher Wittig's[32] slow roller. Flowers saw enough and called upon Comellas to relieve Bassler and, after allowing two hits that brought in the three runs, Comellas plugged the leak. Comellas allowed an average of one hit per inning for the last eight frames, along with striking out 11 Orioles.

The Indians also scored three runs in the first inning, on Guerra's three-run homer. In the third inning, Guerra connected with his second home run, this time a solo blast. The Indians took the lead in the fourth with a three-spot on hits by Quimby and Steinfadt, a walk to Leip, a sacrifice bunt by Comellas, a fielder's choice hit by Lynn and an error on Luzansky's base hit. In the sixth inning, they added two more runs. Lynn started the inning earning a free pass. After Luzansky laid down a sacrifice hit, Steinsfadt hit a single that allowed Lynn to cross home plate. Guerra worked a walk and came in to score on an error by Vandegrift on Trechock's hit. The Indians' last run came on a walk to Quimby, who then scored on Comellas's single.

Guerra had a remarkable game in his short minor league career. He made five trips to the plate and registered one walk, one hit by pitch, two home runs and a single. Guerra drove in four runs and he crossed the plate three times. The Indians played "heads-up" baseball offensively and took advantage of timely hitting by collecting eight hits that led the

Two—First 26 Games (May 19–June 18)

Indians to score 10 runs. Guerra completed his night by stealing two bases. Fleet-footed left fielder Charley Quimby stole four bases.

Federalsburg 6, Salisbury 5   (7 innings)   (6–2)   May 27

Salisbury	0	1	0	0	0	4	0	5	9	5
Federalsburg	1	0	0	3	1	0	1	6	9	6

Bassler (loser), Schoen (winner)
Trechock, Reznichak (2), Leip, Bassler—RBI, Steinfadt, Guerra—2B; Trechock—HR; Reznichak—SB

Salisbury, sporting a 6–1 record, traveled to the town of Federalsburg and left there with their second loss of the season even though they had a chance to at least tie the game. With runners on the corners in the eighth inning, umpire George Ekaitis called the game on account of darkness. There had been complaints from other clubs in the league about the late start time for the games at Federalsburg. The fact was that the Athletics management decided to start their home games at 5:15 p.m. to allow workers from the local factories to attend. However, because the ballpark was not equipped with floodlights, it affected the length of the games.

Even though the game was shortened, both teams garnered nine hits each. Steinfadt and Guerra collected extra-base hits and Trechock hit his fourth home run. Flowers sent Leon Revolinsky to the mound for his debut outing. Coming into the game, it was reported that Revolinsky had a "world of stuff on the ball." The hefty right-hander's performance was slightly wild in the beginning, walking four batters in the first inning. He settled down and played solidly until he pulled muscles in his back. He continued to pitch after consultation with Flowers, who believed Revolinsky could work through the muscle pull. Unfortunately, in the fourth inning, the injury worsened, making it too painful for him to continue, so Flowers called for Bassler to relieve him at the start of the fifth. During the fourth inning, Revolinsky gave up three runs on four hits, which allowed the A's to build a 5–1 lead.

In the sixth inning, the Indians jumped on Nick Butcher and Maynard Schoen for five hits and four runs to tie the game. After Steinfadt flied out to center, Guerra doubled. Reznichak launched a two-run moon shot. Schoen came in to relieve Butcher and was greeted by Trechock, Cash and Leip with consecutive singles, the latter scoring Trechock. Bassler hit into a fielder's choice that allowed Cash to score the tying run. Lynn grounded out to second to end the inning.

Miracle on the Eastern Shore

In the seventh, A's right fielder Les Christopher's[33] long sacrifice fly scored center fielder LeGates and gave the A's a 6-5 lead and the eventual margin of victory. In the top of the eighth, after a walk to Leip and a base hit by Brady, who pitch-hit for Bassler, the Indians had runners on the corners in the eighth inning when the game was called.

Federalsburg 6, Salisbury 5   (6–3)   May 28

	1	2	3	4	5	6	7	8	9	R	H	E
Federalsburg	0	2	3	0	0	0	0	0	1	6	11	2
Salisbury	0	0	0	0	3	0	2	0	0	5	9	6

Bassler (loser), Toland (winner)
Bassler (2), Lynn—RBI; Trechock—2B; Leip—SB

The Indians suffered their second straight loss, the third of the season. After having a game stolen from them, the Indians had one of those "off-days" that "befalls" every team during a long season.[34] The Indians were officially charged with six errors. Most of them occurred at the most costly time. Salisbury also executed poorly on the basepaths, being caught on four steal attempts. Frank Kowal, starting for Salisbury, was bombarded from the start, with the A's collecting nine hits and scoring five runs before Kowal retired in the fifth inning. He left with the bases loaded and one out. Bassler, working in relief for two consecutive games, took over the pitching duties and struck out the next two batters with eight pitches. After that, the Federalsburg ball club got just two hits off Bassler.

For the A's, Dale Hudson,[35] erstwhile Pittsville (Maryland) semipro hurler, kept the Indian bats at bay, allowing one hit—a single by Kowal—in the first four innings. During the next three innings, the Indians gathered six hits, led by Bassler and Guerra, to even the game at five each. The game settled down to a pitching duel between Bassler and James Toland until the ninth, when an error, a well-executed bunt down the first baseline and another error gave the A's a run and the victory. Salisbury did threaten in the bottom half of the inning but fell short.

On the same day Salisbury lost to Federalsburg, the Salisbury Ministerial Association sent a resolution to the Maryland state attorney of Wicomico County, Rex A. Taylor, calling for him "to exercise his office" regarding the Salisbury baseball club playing games on Sundays. They believed that the ball club had violated state law and therefore requested Taylor to investigate the matter.[36] In 1924, Maryland passed a blue law that included a section that prohibits any person from performing any

Two—First 26 Games (May 19–June 18)

work or bodily labor on Sundays. The association's call to Taylor was quite peculiar, for semiprofessional games on the peninsula had been played on Sundays since 1934.

Salisbury 9, Crisfield 2   (7–3)   May 29

Crisfield	0	0	0	0	0	0	0	1	1	2	7	4
Salisbury	0	3	1	4	0	1	0	0	X	9	7	2

Kohlman (winner), Gatier (loser)
Brady, Lynn, Kohlman, Guerra—RBI; Trechock—HR; Lynn, Luzansky, Guerra, Trechock, Quimby—SB

On May 29, Salisbury returned to the winner's circle with a 9-2 victory over the Crisfield Crabbers. Aided by the opposing pitchers' wildness, the Indians collected seven hits. Crisfield hurlers Steve Gatier, James Titcomb and Tony O'Buzz walked a total of 11 batters.[37] Indian hurler Kohlman pitched a stellar game, scattering seven hits.

On the same day, the papers reported that the Trenton Senators signed University of Maryland standout catcher Fred Thomas.[38]

Salisbury 6, Federalsburg 1   (8–3)   May 30

Federalsburg	0	0	0	0	0	0	0	1		1	7	0
Salisbury	5	0	0	0	0	0	0	1	X	6	7	4

Comellas (winner), Ratterree (loser)
Guerra, Leip (2), Comellas—RBI; Guerra—2B; Brady—SB

Salisbury got their revenge on the Federalsburg Athletics, who held a 2–1 advantage against the Indians during the young season. Before the game, Clark Griffith, principal owner of the major league Washington Senators, threw out the first pitch. In usual Indian fashion, they struck first, putting up a five-spot in the first inning behind three hits and three walks. After that, it became a pitchers' duel between Comellas and Nick Butcher,[39] William Ratterree's relief. Comellas pitched so effectively that only two runners got past second base.

Salisbury 7, Easton 2   (9–3)   May 31

Salisbury	0	0	1	0	0	1	5	0	0	7	9	1
Easton	0	0	0	1	1	0	0	0	0	2	12	3

Pucci (winner), Zarowsky (loser)
Leip—RBI; Guerra, Quimby, Reznichak, Luzansky—2B; Luzansky—3B

Miracle on the Eastern Shore

Decoration Day brought another hurler to the Eastern Shore. Perth Amboy native Moe Pucci[40] traveled to Easton after pitching a game in his hometown. Performing on one hour of sleep, he scattered 11 hits through seven innings for a 7-2 Salisbury victory in the first game of a unique doubleheader. Pucci tired in the seventh and, with one out, requested to be relieved. Comellas came in and pitched 1⅔ scoreless innings.

In the first inning, Luzansky was stranded at third after hitting a triple. In the third inning, Salisbury got on the scoreboard when Leip reached safely on shortstop Zimmerman's error, advanced to second on Pucci's single and moved to third when Lynn hit into a 6–4–3 double play. He scored on a single by Brady.

In the fourth inning, Easton tied it up when Browns catcher Clyde Lessig doubled and scored on first baseman Richard Poydock's single to left.[41] The next inning, Easton took the lead when second baseman Bert Pultz earned a free pass, advanced to third on a throwing error by Leip

The 1937 Easton Browns finished second behind the Salisbury Indians with a record of 56–41. Back row, from left: president Ernest C. Landgraf, George "Doc" Jacobs (manager), William Zarowsky, Leroy Mikus, Frank Lee, Albert Kubski, George Diehl, James "Mickey" Vernon and Harry Kuntashian; front row, from left: Frank Radler, Fred Webber, Michael Stiles, Edward Zimmerman, Louis Weimer, Kenneth Eck and Edgar Beidleman (H. Robins Hollyday Collection, Talbot County Historical Society).

Two—First 26 Games (May 19–June 18)

on a hit by Michael Stiles and scored on left fielder Robert Etts's base hit.[42]

Salisbury knotted up the score when Brady, after working a walk, scored on Guerra's double. The score was tied twice until the seventh inning, when Salisbury broke the game wide open, scoring five runs on three doubles, a single and two sacrifice bunts that resulted in all runners being safe. Quimby started it off with a two-base hit, followed by two consecutive sacrifice bunts by Leip and Pucci. Lynn singled and, after Brady grounded out to second, Luzansky connected with a hot shot for a two-base hit. Guerra walked and Reznichak doubled. Trechock and Quimby finished the inning with a groundout to short and a flyout to left field. Quimby, Leip, Pucci, Lynn and Luzansky scored during the inning.

Federal Park was built with the dimensions of 300 feet to left, 375 feet to center and 310 feet to right. After the Brooklyn Dodgers decided

An aerial view of Federal Park, the ballpark for the Easton Browns, in 1937 (H. Robins Hollyday Collection, Talbot Historical Society).

Miracle on the Eastern Shore

not to sponsor the Easton franchise, the St. Louis Browns stepped in and assigned Ernest Landgraf,[43] a scout in the St. Louis organization, to serve as president of the Easton Browns. Landgraf negotiated a two-year lease for use of the ballpark. He also arranged for A.L. Nichols to repair the stands, improved the grounds and hired Ivon T. Morton to manufacture the fence signs.[44] The Easton ballplayers' uniforms were a set of whites for home games and grays for away games.

Salisbury 4, Easton 3   (10–3)   May 31

Easton	2	0	0	0	0	0	0	0	1	3	5	2
Salisbury	0	0	0	0	1	0	3	0	X	4	8	0

Revolinsky (winner), Comellas (save), Kuntashian (loser)
Luzansky (2), Brady, Reznichak—RBI; Luzansky—2B

The Salisbury ball club packed into the team bus and traveled home to host the Browns for the nightcap. In front of approximately 3,000 spectators within Gordy Park, the Indians and the Browns put on an exciting game that led to a 4-3 victory for the Indians. Leon Revolinsky, recovered from a spastic back, began the game a little wild but calmed down in the second inning, limiting the opponent to one hit. He struck out 12 hitters and walked 10. Throughout the game, he would allow one or two batters to reach base, only to shut the door to end the inning. In the ninth inning, with one down, Comellas relieved him, making it the second time that day he entered the game in a relief role. The game ended on a miscall by the umpire at first base. With the score 4 to 3, Easton was robbed out of at least tying the game when, with a baserunner on third, their batter was called out at first base even though it was clear to the fans that Brady dropped the ball. Easton manager George "Doc" Jacobs[45] sprinted to umpire Clark to protest, seized Clark by the coat lapels and shook him vigorously as he verbally argued his point. After all that, Easton management decided not to protest the game but Jacobs was fined $10 for his offense.

As the month of May ended, the Salisbury Indians stood on top of the standings with a 10–3 record. Easton was one game behind at 9–4. Federalsburg was next with an 8–4 record, followed by Centreville 6–6, Dover 5–6, Cambridge 4–8, Pocomoke City 4–9 and Crisfield 3–9.

Two—First 26 Games (May 19–June 18)

Salisbury 17, Centreville 4 (11–3)   June 2

Centreville	0	3	1	0	0	0	0	0	0	4	5	1
Salisbury	6	3	2	3	0	0	3	0	X	17	15	2

Kohlman (winner), Gross (loser)
Lynn, Brady, Guerra, Reznichak (4), Trechock, Quimby (4), Leip, Kohlman—RBI; Leip—2B; Lynn, Quimby—3B; Reznichak—HR; Leip (2)—SB

Several hundred baseball fans witnessed a hitting rampage at the fog-enshrined Gordy Park. When the game was over, the scoreboard displayed Salisbury Indians 17, Centreville Colts 4. The local newspaper noted that the Colts had a "much heralded heavy artillery" coming into the game.[46] The Centreville ball club led the league in team batting average (.277), doubles (11), home runs (13) and RBI (48). On the mound for the Indians, Kohlman allowed one hit after the third inning and threw a five-hit, 10-strikeout evening. The Colts opened up the game with the first three men retired in order. In the second, Colts first baseman Norman Wurst and second baseman Ted Tomczyk singled with two outs and scored on catcher Pete Weimer's long fly that had enough distance to clear the left field fence.[47] In the third, Kohlman hit shortstop Ed Feinberg with a pitch and Feinberg

Son of Philadelphia Phillies executive Patsy O'Rourke, Joe O'Rourke (1904–1990) managed the Centreville Colts for two seasons (1937–1938) (courtesy Donnie Davidson).

Miracle on the Eastern Shore

scored when Trechock mishandled left fielder Alex Pitko's[48] hot shot and overthrew first base.

On the Indians' side, Lynn tripled to start the bottom half of the first inning. He scored on Brady's single. Luzansky struck out and Brady moved to second on Lloyd Gross's[49] wild pitch. Guerra walked and Reznichak singled, scoring Brady while Guerra stopped at third. Both Guerra and Reznichak scored on Quimby's triple, which led to Gross exiting the game. His relief, John Boylan,[50] threw a wild pitch that allowed Quimby to score. Leip and Kohlman struck out to end the inning. When the dust settled, the Indians placed a six-spot on the scoreboard.

In the second inning, Brady singled and Luzansky reached first base on a fielder's choice. Reznichak drove the ball far over the left field fence for a two-run home run, his first of the season. With two outs in the third inning, Leip singled, stole second and third bases and scored on Lynn's single. Brady was hit by a pitch and advanced to second when Luzansky walked. Lynn scored on the infield grounder hit by

Centreville Colts slugger Alex "Spunk" Pitko (1914–2011) led the league with 20 home runs. He had a two-year career in the major leagues, playing for the Philadelphia Phillies (1938) and Washington Senators (1939) (courtesy Donnie Davidson).

Two—First 26 Games (May 19–June 18)

Guerra. All were safe when the Colts failed to throw Luzansky out at second base.

In the fourth inning, Trechock and Quimby walked. Trechock scored on Leip's two-bagger. In the seventh, Luzansky walked and Reznichak singled. Quimby hit a single that brought both runners in. Leip walked and Quimby scored on Kohlman's flyout to the outfield.

By the end of the day across the league, all ball clubs reduced their roster to 14 players. The Salisbury Indians' permanent roster for the season consisted of:

Robert Brady, 1B	Joseph Reznichak, RF
Jerry Lynn, 2B	Fred Thomas, OF/C
Frank Trechock, SS	Joseph Kohlman, P
Edgar Leip, 3B	George Comellas, P
Fermin Guerra, C	John Bassler, P
Charles Quimby, LF/IF	Leon Revolinsky, P
William Luzansky, CF	Frank Kowal, P

Salisbury 8, Centreville 7   (12–3)   June 3

Salisbury	0	2	0	1	1	2	0	0	2	8	12	2
Centreville	2	0	1	1	1	0	0	2	0	7	9	1

Kowal (winner), Gross (loser)
Lynn (2), Brady, Luzansky (2), Guerra (2)—RBI; Leip, Lynn (2)—2B; Guerra—HR

On June 3, the Centreville Colts hosted the Salisbury Indians and the ball clubs put on an exciting game that kept the fans on the edge of their seats throughout the night. The game began with the Indians failing to score in the initial stanza when Lynn doubled to center and Brady walked. Unfortunately, both players were left stranded. In the bottom of the inning, Centreville jumped to an early lead when Colts second baseman Ed Feinberg hit a two-run homer, scoring third baseman Gordon Troy.[51]

Salisbury tied it up in the top half of the second inning. Trechock singled and was out on Quimby's fielder's choice. Quimby advanced to second on Leip's single. Leip was out at second when Bassler weakly tapped back to the pitcher, Theodore Mezours.[52] Quimby and Bassler scored on Lynn's second double of the game. In the bottom of the third, Bassler lost the strike zone. With one out, he walked the next three batters (Feinberg, Pitko and Wurst). Colts center fielder Toddy Carroll[53] then hit a long fly to center field that allowed Feinberg to score. Both the Colts and the Indians scored in the fourth with the Colts protecting a 4–3 lead.

In the fifth inning, Brady suffered a charley horse and had to leave the game. Quimby moved from left field to first base. Kohlman came into the game to play left field. Salisbury took a one-run lead in the sixth that sent Mezours to the showers. Gross entered the game in relief. In the eighth inning, Salisbury lost the lead when Centreville scored twice off Kowal, who had replaced Bassler. In the top of the ninth, Luzansky singled and Guerra lifted a moon shot over the right field fence to plate the deciding runs. Comellas entered the game in the bottom of the ninth and, after he struck out Colts left fielder Pitko, first baseman Wurst hit a booming triple. Center fielder Carroll struck out and Comellas walked right fielder John Davis.[54] With the tying run on third and the winning run on first, Weimer hit a sharp liner right into Trechock's glove to retire the side.

Easton 6, Salisbury 5   (10 innings)   (12–4)   June 4

Salisbury	1	1	0	0	0	0	1	2	0	5	13	0
Easton	0	0	0	1	1	3	0	0	1	6	9	2

Bassler (loser), Kuntashian (winner)
Lynn, Leip (2)—RBI; Quimby (2); Lynn—2B; Lynn—HR

On June 4, before the Easton-Salisbury game started, Joe Cambria, owner of the Salisbury Indians, submitted a statement declaring that all Sunday home games would be moved to Monday night. His action was in response to the Salisbury Ministerial Association's resolution to State Attorney Taylor asking for an investigation. It was not his desire to violate the state "blue laws," which prohibited playing baseball on Sunday. His decision on the matter focused on "the players to be popular and good citizens."[55]

Jerry Lynn led off the game by belting Harry Kuntashian's[56] second offering over the fence, his second home run of the season. In the second inning, Reznichak reached first base with a single and scored on Quimby's double. Salisbury kept a two-run advantage until the fourth inning, when the Browns' right fielder, Ed Beidleman,[57] hit a home run over the right field fence. In the fifth, the Browns tied the score on a base on balls issued to catcher Lessig, a sacrifice laid down by Kuntashian and shortstop Ed Zimmerman's[58] single to center. In the sixth, the Browns scored three runs when center fielder Stiles singled, first

Two—First 26 Games (May 19–June 18)

baseman Mickey Vernon and left fielder Charles Metro walked and Lessig tripled to left field to clear the bases.[59] Kowal was sent in to relieve Revolinsky and struck out Kuntashian to end the inning. Kowal pitched a scoreless seventh inning. In the eighth, Salisbury refused to give up. Guerra drew a walk. Trechock singled and Leip drove Guerra in with an infield hit. The ninth started with Lynn collecting his third hit of the day and stealing third on Fred Thomas's base on balls. A 23-year-old recruit from Washington, D.C., Thomas was assigned to left field. Quimby, normally the Indians' starting left fielder, operated first base while Brady was still nursing a charley horse. Lynn scored when Kuntashian threw a wild pitch. Thomas scored the tying run when Lessig lost his cool reacting to Kuntashian's wildness and threw the ball to the ground in front of him in disgust. The ball bounced away toward first base. Thomas, seeing his opportunity, sprinted around the bases and scampered home.

In the bottom half of the ninth, Kuntashian singled off Bassler,

A casual group photograph with several members of the 1937 Salisbury Indians at Gordy Park. Standing, from left: Bill Luzansky, Jake Flowers, Fred Thomas and Leon Revolinsky; kneeling, from left: Frank Trechock and Mike Guerra (courtesy Mary Jane [Revolinsky] Martinez).

Miracle on the Eastern Shore

who took the mound in the eighth inning. After Zimmerman flied out to center, second baseman Pultz sacrificed Kuntashian over to second. Center fielder Stiles was intentionally walked and Beidleman hit a fielder's choice to short. Salisbury threatened in the 10th with runners on second and third but could not bring them home.

Easton, in the bottom half, started with third baseman Kenneth Eck[60] flying out to second. Vernon's hot shot ricocheted off a stone in the infield and allowed him to occupy second base. Metro hit a two-base hit, which allowed Vernon to score the winning run.

A hard-fought battle fell short with the Indians receiving their fourth defeat of the season. Aside from the fielding miscues, the Salisbury Indians collected 13 hits and executed three double plays.

Salisbury 15, Pocomoke 2 (13–4) June 5

Pocomoke	x	x	x	x	x	(2)	0	0	0	2
Salisbury	x	x	x	x	x	(4)	11	0	X	15

[Box score not found]
Comellas (winner), Savitsky (loser)

In the next game, the Indians played a close-knit game with the Pocomoke City Red Sox for the first six innings. In the seventh inning, Bill Savitsky,[61] the Pocomoke pitcher, suddenly got bombarded with base hits from the Indians' bats. Vic Keen, Red Sox player-manager, replaced him and the Indians continued the onslaught. After it was all finished, the Indians scored 11 runs. During the inning, Guerra drove a shot just inside the left field foul post with two men on base. Keen and Pocomoke catcher Stephen Sefick[62] disputed the home run but the umpire ruled it fair. For the game, the Indians collected 10 hits and George Comellas won his fifth victory of the season.

The next game, scheduled with the Centreville Colts on June 6, was rained out. This would be the first of many weather-effected cancellations throughout the season.

Salisbury 2, Cambridge 1 (14–4) June 8

Cambridge	0	0	1	0	0	0	0	0	0	1	4	1
Salisbury	0	0	0	1	0	0	0	0	1	2	9	1

Kohlman (winner), Koons (loser)
Quimby, Lynn—RBI; Quimby—2B; Lynn, Trechock, Luzansky, Brady—SB

Two—First 26 Games (May 19–June 18)

On June 8, Kohlman took the mound against Cambridge and pitched a four-hit outing. He yielded three hits in the first two innings. In the third, the Cardinals scored their lone tally without a hit. Cardinal catcher Marshall walked and was sacrificed to second by pitcher Michael Koons.[63] Right fielder James Ettner[64] hit a grounder that was misplayed, allowing Marshall to score. After that inning, Kohlman allowed only one hit, which came in the seventh inning, a double by second baseman Murtaugh. He struck out 12 Cardinal batters, walked one and faced only 30 batters. As the game progressed, Kohlman grew stronger. In the top of the ninth, he struck out third baseman Silvio Giovanelli, shortstop William Gagain and first baseman Iwanicki.[65] Salisbury gathered nine hits in the tight game, during which they had opportunities but could not execute.

In the bottom of the fourth with two outs, Trechock singled and scored on Quimby's double. In the seventh, the Indians started with both Lynn and Brady hitting singles but the rally failed. Brady had returned to the lineup after nursing a charley horse. At the bottom of the ninth, Leip started the rally by drawing a walk. Kohlman laid down a sacrifice bunt to move him over to second. Lynn brought him in with his fourth single in five at-bats.

The game had great defensive plays from both teams. In the fifth with the bases loaded and two outs, Reznichak launched a shot into center field. Cardinals center fielder Jackson ran to the factory wall and snow-coned the catch. Defensively, for the Salisbury Indians, Leip made a running catch near the left field fence on Koons's foul ball in the fifth. The Indians also played "heads-up" baseball by being aggressive on the basepaths with Lynn, Trechock, Luzansky and Brady each stealing a base.

Kohlman's season record so far: in 45 innings, he gave up 15 runs on 28 hits, striking out 55 batsmen.

Salisbury 2, Cambridge 1 (10 innings) (15–4) June 9

Salisbury	0	0	0	0	0	1	0	0	0	1	2	8	0
Cambridge	0	0	0	0	0	0	1	0	0	0	1	6	2

Bassler (winner), Kovis (loser)
Reznichak—RBI; Thomas—2B; Thomas—SB

Just like what happened the night before, the game was an old-fashioned pitchers' duel, this time between Bassler and Ed Kovis,[66] the Cardinals hurler who was making his pitching debut. Kovis gave

Miracle on the Eastern Shore

up eight hits while Bassler held the Cardinals to six hits and fanned 12 batters. Unlike the previous night, this game went to extra innings and Salisbury won the game in the 10th. During that inning, Luzansky, standing on first, sprinted for second when Kovis delivered the ball to home plate with Thomas in the batter's box. Marshall, the Cardinals' catcher, tried to gun down Luzansky but overthrew the bag. Center fielder Jackson retrieved the ball as it rolled into the outfield and, in a moment of excitement seeing Luzansky heading toward third, threw offline to third baseman Giovanelli. Luzansky touched third base and continued down the basepath to score the winning run.

The Indians got on the board first when Thomas led off the fifth inning with a double and came in to score on Reznichak's single. In the seventh, Cambridge tied the game when, after hitting a double, left fielder Bernard Healy scored on shortstop Bill Myska's single.[67]

In the lineup, Thomas took his turn as the catcher, giving Guerra a day off. Reznichak occupied left field and Kohlman was in right field again. Thomas, offensively hitting in the three hole, had a double and a single and stole a base.

Salisbury 5, Dover 2   (16–4)   June 11

Salisbury	0	0	0	0	1	1	0	0	3	5	10	0
Dover	0	0	0	1	0	0	1	0	0	2	2	2

Revolinsky (winner), Finta (loser)
Lynn, Quimby (3)—RBI; Luzansky, Leip, Lynn, Quimby—2B; Reznichak, Leip, Luzansky—SB

On June 11, Salisbury extended its league lead by three full games. The fans attending the Indians-Orioles game in Delaware's state capital were kept on the edge of their seats for a couple of hours. The game, which was postponed by rain the night before, started as a pitchers' duel with both teams unable to tally a score through the first three innings. In the fourth, Dover broke through when Orioles manager Ed Roetz, playing second base, and center fielder Stotz earned a base on balls off Salisbury's starting pitcher, Leon Revolinsky. Left fielder Charles Coleman[68] sacrificed the runners over and Roetz scored when third baseman Edwin Vandegrift lifted a high fly to left center field.

The Indians answered in the top of the next inning. Leip was issued a free pass, stole second and came around on Lynn's single. Salisbury took a lead in the sixth inning, beginning with Luzansky's base hit. He

Two—First 26 Games (May 19–June 18)

was thrown out at second on a grounder by Thomas. The next two batters, Reznichak and Trechock, walked to load the bases. Thomas then scored on Quimby's infield grounder.

The Orioles tied the score in the seventh on a peculiar play. Revolinsky walked Vandegrift and first baseman Paul Swoboda. Finta, who batted left-handed, hit a hot shot to the opposite field that rolled toward the corner of the fence. All three runners raced around the basepaths as Quimby hustled for the ball. Encircling the area four times, Quimby frantically searched for the ball before motioning that he could not find it. Other players, along with umpires Toach and Clark, quickly jogged to the spot where the ball was last seen. Umpire Clark even scaled the fence to take a look on the other side. The umpires consulted and decided that it was a case of a lost ball. They awarded Finta a ground-rule double, scoring Vandegrift, and returned Swoboda to third base. The supposition was that the dirt under the fence was probably washed away by the previous storm and the ball slipped underneath.

A baseball was a precious commodity. Maurice Fields, the batboy, described his duties during a game. If a foul ball was hit into the stands, Fields had to retrieve it. If fans caught it, he would have to go to them and ask for the ball back. If the ball went outside the ballpark, two or three kids were there patrolling the grounds. For every ball retrieved, the kids would get 25 cents.

In the ninth, Lynn started off the inning with a double. He moved to third on Brady's bunt. Luzansky then executed the perfect squeeze play, dropping a bunt down the third baseline, allowing Lynn to score. Reznichak and Trechock both drew walks to load the bases. With Quimby at the plate with the count at 1–0, Howard Killen,[69] a Felton, Delaware, native, came in to relieve Finta. Killen had recently shut down the Centreville Colts' bats by striking out 19 batters and allowing only two hits in his debut. Quimby smashed Killen's first offering off the fence in deep right center for the game-winning two-base hit, scoring Luzansky and Reznichak. After Leip walked, Revolinsky flied out to short to end the inning.

For the game, Quimby batted in three runs. Salisbury was again active on the basepaths with Reznichak, Leip and Luzansky stealing a base. The game also exhibited spectacular defensive moments. Orioles center fielder Stotz's difficult catch in deep center prevented two possible runs and Quimby made a running catch near the left field foul line.

Miracle on the Eastern Shore

Salisbury 3, Pocomoke 2   (17–4)   June 12

Salisbury	0	3	0	0	0	0	0	0	0	3	7	2
Pocomoke	2	0	0	0	0	0	0	0	0	2	6	3

Comellas (winner), Messick (loser)
Trechock (2), Comellas—RBI; Leip—2B; Trechock—HR; Leip—SB

During the afternoon of June 12 at Sportsman's Park, Salisbury and Pocomoke City played a close game that involved a pitchers' duel between Comellas, the Indians' ace, and the Red Sox's pitching duo of Bill Savitsky and Frank Messick.[70] Pocomoke got on the board early in the first inning when they took advantage of Comellas's unsteadiness and pushed two tallies across home plate. Second baseman Wexler started the inning drawing a base on balls and shortstop Irv Hall[71] singled. Schluter flied out to first and right fielder Nelson Jester followed with a base hit.[72] Center fielder Maurice Dugan reached first on an error and Denenberg lined a base hit.[73] Wexler and Hall scored during the inning. After that, Comellas shut down the Red Sox's offense by limiting

Group photograph of the 1937 Pocomoke City Red Sox, who finished sixth with a 42–55 record. A few individuals identified are (back row) Irv Hall (second from left) and Henry Schluter (third from left), and (front row) Vic Keen (manager) (second from left) (courtesy Eastern Shore Baseball Hall of Fame Museum).

Two—First 26 Games (May 19–June 18)

them to six hits and striking out 10 batters in nine innings. In the top of the second, Trechock crushed a two-run homer off Savitsky. Comellas followed that up by driving in the winning run. Messick came in to replace Savitsky in the inning and quieted the Indians' bats for the rest of the game. Both sides placed goose eggs for the remainder of the game.

The dimensions of Sportsman's Park were 300 feet to left, 325 feet to center and 300 feet to right. Parts of the stands and field were renovated by a detachment of the Civilian Conservation Corps. An oddity of the park was the light pole, padded with old mattresses for players' safety, located in the middle of left field that sometimes obstructed the flow of action.

Salisbury 7, Centreville 6 (18–4) June 13

Salisbury	2	0	0	3	1	0	0	1	0	7	12	1
Centreville	1	0	0	0	0	0	0	2	3	6	6	4

Kohlman (winner), Ogden (loser)
Reznichak, Trechock, Kohlman (2), Lynn (2)—RBI;
Reznichak (2), Guerra—2B; Lynn—HR

Next, the Indians traveled to Queen Anne County Park. The park, owned by the Queen Anne County Sports Activities Association, was situated on the old Meredith lot off Belvedere Avenue, measuring 360 feet to left field, 425 feet to center field and 262 feet to right field. The infield was designed as a "skin diamond" or void of grass.[74] Kohlman, who was next to toe the rubber, notched 11 strikeouts and limited the Centreville Colts to six hits. For the first seven innings, the Colts collected only two hits, and with the game comfortably in hand, Kohlman took his foot off the gas. This allowed the Colts to put together a great rally during the last two innings that eventually fell short. Kohlman's counterpart, Tom Ogden,[75] was chased off the mound in the fourth inning when he gave up seven hits. Usually defensively solid, Centreville left fielder Pitko committed three errors during the game.

In the first inning, Lynn earned a walk and scored on Reznichak's double. Trechock then singled in Reznichak. In the bottom of the inning, Pitko tied the game with a solo home run. In the fourth inning, Salisbury chalked up three more runs. Guerra, Quimby and Leip hit consecutive singles and Guerra and Quimby scored on an error by left fielder Pitko on Kohlman's hit. Lynn's flyout to center field allowed Leip to cross home plate. In the next inning, Kohlman grounded out, bringing in Guerra, who previously doubled. Salisbury scored one more run in the eighth on Lynn's solo homer.

Centreville began their rally in the bottom of the eighth when center fielder Carroll singled and catcher Mysel walked and third baseman Troy doubled them in. During the inning, Kohlman registered the three outs with strikeouts to right fielder Rist, pitcher Mezours and shortstop Miller. In the final stanza, Pitko walked, followed by strikeouts of second baseman Feinberg and first baseman Boylan. Kohlman walked the next batter, Rist, then allowed consecutive singles to center fielder Carroll and catcher Mysel. Dick Petock,[76] pinch-hitting for Mezours, popped out to Guerra at home plate to end the game.

The next day, June 14, Salisbury hosted the South Philadelphia ball club in an exhibition game and won 1 to 0.

Pocomoke 5, Salisbury 4 (18–5) June 15

Salisbury   0 1 0 0 0 2 0 0 1   4   8   0
Pocomoke   1 0 0 0 0 0 4 0 X   5 11   1

Bassler (loser), Harris (winner)
Guerra (3), Quimby—RBI; Guerra (2)—HR; Leip—SB

If you live by the sword, you die by the sword, proverbially speaking. Four out of the past six games, the Salisbury ball club won by one run. So it was certain that they would lose by one run eventually. Pocomoke City's star hurler, Hank Harris,[77] scattered the Indians' eight hits. The Indians did get a big game from Guerra. After spending a few days on the bench, he returned to collect his seventh and eighth home runs of the season and a single in four at-bats. He knocked in three of the Indians' runs. Quimby contributed two hits in four trips to the plate.

For Indians southpaw Bassler, the 11 hits that he allowed were the most in the early season. The hometown ball club struck first in the initial frame when shortstop Irv Hall scored on right fielder Jester's base hit. After that, Bassler settled down and kept them at bay until the seventh inning, when the Red Sox staged a four-run rally that notched the win. After striking out center fielder Dugan and left fielder Denenberg, Bassler issued two consecutive singles to first baseman Daddino and catcher Sefick and a base on balls to pitcher Harris. Second baseman Wexler delivered a two-run hit and Hall followed up with a base hit. Third baseman Schluter ended the inning with a fielder's choice. Salisbury fought hard, tying the game in the second inning when Trechock

Two—First 26 Games (May 19–June 18)

scored on a double play that Quimby hit into. They took the lead on Guerra's two-run blast in the sixth. After relinquishing the lead in the seventh, Salisbury tried to conjure up another comeback win but sent only one run across the plate, Guerra's second homer of the game, and the rally ended there. The Indians still continued to showcase their defensive prowess by executing three more double plays, all started by Trechock.

Salisbury 10, Pocomoke 4   (19–5)   June 16

Pocomoke	1	0	0	0	0	0	1	2	0	4	8	4
Salisbury	4	0	5	0	1	0	0	0	X	10	14	3

Revolinsky (winner), Messick (loser)
Luzansky (2), Trechock (4), Quimby (2), Leip, Lynn—RBI;
Luzansky, Trechock—HR; Leip, Reznichak—SB

The Indians returned to Gordy Park and avenged their one-run loss against the Pocomoke City Red Sox with a 10-4 victory. Revolinsky toed the mound and was a contradiction throughout the game. He fanned 11 batters but handed out eight free passes. Pocomoke City took advantage of Revolinsky's lack of control and scored first. In the initial frame, Red Sox second baseman Wexler struck out. Shortstop Irv Hall walked and right fielder Jester singled. Hall advanced to third on a wild pitch. Center fielder Dugan walked to load the bases and left fielder Denenberg walked to force in a run.

Salisbury answered with a four-spot in the bottom half of the first. Lynn flied out and Brady reached first base on Wexler's error. Luzansky then launched a shot over the right center field fence. Reznichak singled and Trechock crushed the ball over the factory building in center field. Next up, Guerra drove a long drive into the corner between left and center fields that would have been an easy homer but Denenberg soared high in the air and speared it with the tips of his glove. Quimby singled and Dugan made a shoestring catch of Leip's blooper to short center to end the inning.

Revolinsky scattered eight hits and put it in cruise control when his teammates gave him a nine-run lead. In the third inning, the Indians put up a five-spot. It started when Luzansky singled. Reznichak walked and Luzansky scored on Trechock's single.

For the game, Trechock went three for five and drove in four runs. Luzansky went three for five and Reznichak walked twice and had three singles in five trips to the plate.

Miracle on the Eastern Shore

Salisbury 10, Crisfield 5   (20–5)   June 17

Crisfield	0	0	1	0	0	3	0	1	0	5	6	1
Salisbury	0	0	0	3	3	0	1	3	X	10	14	2

Comellas (winner), Barnes (loser)
Trechock (3), Guerra, Leip, Quimby (2)—RBI; Lynn, Trechock, Guerra—2B; Trechock—HR; Trechock, Luzansky—SB

On June 17, the ominous rain clouds were the main story when the Crabbers came to the hub of Wicomico County. Rain delayed the start of the game and interrupted the action twice. Some 800 fans braved the weather to witness the Indians continue their winning ways. Comellas earned his seventh straight victory while delivering a not-so-stellar performance on the mound obviously affected by the weather conditions. He held the Crabbers to six hits and struck out 12 batters. Crisfield got on the scoreboard first, which involved a hit, an error and what the newspaper described as "other contributing factors" in the third inning. In the fourth, Salisbury made their move. Thomas was issued a free pass and Reznichak singled. Thomas scored on Trechock's double. Reznichak scored on Guerra's double, then Leip's grounder scored Trechock. In the next inning, they tallied three more runs. Lynn singled and went corner to corner on Luzansky's single. Lynn scored on Semple's wild pitch. During the play, Luzansky was thrown out at second. Thomas and Trechock singled and Guerra walked. Quimby connected with a two-run single.

In the sixth inning, Crisfield fought back, adding three in the stanza with second baseman Mickey Urban, first baseman Tex Gilmartin and third baseman Hal Marnie singling along with a walk and an error.[78]

In the seventh, Trechock collected his third hit in the eighth and ended up at third base when Crisfield catcher Crawford tried to throw him out at second. Trechock scored on a wild pitch by Semple.

The Salisbury Indians tallied three more times. Lynn started with a running mishap. He hit a smash down the third baseline and would have had a double if not for the fact that he did not touch first base and was called out. Luzansky singled and stole second base. Crawford let a ball get past him, which allowed Luzansky to score. Reznichak then walked and Trechock lifted his fourth hit of the evening over the left field fence. The Crisfield pitchers, Sherwood Barnes[79] and Semple, could not quell the hot-hitting Indians, who ended up with 14 hits.

Two—First 26 Games (May 19–June 18)

Salisbury 13, Crisfield 1   (21–5)   June 18

Salisbury	3	4	1	5	0	0	0	0	0	13	11	2
Crisfield	1	0	0	0	0	0	0	0	0	1	4	4

Kohlman (winner), Cahall (loser)
Luzansky, Thomas, Reznichak (3), Trechock (4), Guerra, Quimby, Kohlman—RBI; Luzansky—2B; Trechock, Reznichak, Guerra, Quimby—HR; Leip—SB

On June 18, the Salisbury Indians exhibited a balanced attack of hitting and pitching against the hometown ball club from Somerset County. Joe Kohlman inked his sixth consecutive win after losing his first game. He retired 10 Crisfield Crabbers by strikeout, gave up four singles and walked only two. The Salisbury batters started strong in the first inning by notching three tallies. Lynn started off grounding out to Crabbers shortstop Joseph Reha.[80] Luzansky smashed a two-base hit and Thomas walked. After Reznichak lifted a weak flyout to second baseman Urban, Trechock hammered a three-run homer. Guerra struck out to end the inning.

In the next frame, they added four more runs that chased Joseph Cahall[81] off the mound. Quimby and Leip connected on consecutive base hits. Kohlman flied out to left field, which allowed Quimby to tag up and scamper home. Lynn got plunked, Luzansky singled and Thomas got hit by a pitch as well. Reha fumbled Reznichak's hot shot, which allowed Lynn and Luzansky to score. Trechock blasted an RBI single.

Stanley Solinski entered the game but could not cool off their bats.[82] The Indians chalked up one run in the third and five more in the fourth, which included three solo home runs, one each by Reznichak, Guerra and Quimby. Quimby's home run happened in an unusual manner. He rocketed a long drive to deep center field. Center fielder Spike Webb[83] retreated back to the fence and reached out to snag the ball. Unfortunately, or fortunately for Quimby, the ball deflected off the tip of Webb's glove and landed on the other side of the fence. After that Solinski walked the next three batters, Leip, Kohlman and Lynn. Buzz Mahrer[84] came in to relieve Solinski and walked the next two batters, Luzansky and Thomas, allowing two more runs to score.

For the Crabbers, the only run came in the first inning when Webb scored on second baseman Urban's flyout to center field.

After the game, the Indians held a lead of 4½ games with a winning

Miracle on the Eastern Shore

percentage of .808. Little did the team or its fans know what devious plan the baseball gods had devised for the Salisbury ball club for the rest of the reason. By the next day, the Indians would be pushed off the proverbial pedestal to the bottom of the standings with a winning percentage of .039.

Three

The Brady Infraction

One month into the "inaugural" season, the 21–5 Salisbury Indians' run to the pennant hit a snag. An unnamed official from one of the clubs in the circuit requested a rating of the Salisbury players, which gave rise to a reported protest. The complaint lodged against Salisbury inquired if the Indians had violated a league rule regarding the eligibility of its players. According to league rules, each club in the Eastern Shore League was permitted 10 rookies, two non-class men and two class men. Non-class men were defined as players with one year of professional league experience. Class men were defined as players with multiple years of experience. At the start of the season, Salisbury listed Fermin Guerra, Jorge Comellas, Jerome Lynn and Joe Kohlman as having one or more previous years of experience. Comellas and Guerra played for the York White Roses/Trenton Senators. Lynn played for several clubs in the New York-Penn League and Kohlman played for the Beckley Miners and the Baltimore Orioles.

On June 17, league president Tom Kibler requested that the Salisbury club send its roster to him for review. The violation revolved around the status of Indians first baseman Robert Brady. Under National Association rules, a player under contract for 30 days or more was considered to have had at least one year's experience. It was understood that Brady, a resident of Hanover, Pennsylvania, had signed a contract with a professional club, the NYPL's Harrisburg Senators, but was prevented from reporting or playing due to illness. Flowers argued he had a written and signed statement from each of the club's players citing their past baseball experience. Flowers defended Brady by stating that the first baseman was not under contract for 30 days prior to signing with the Salisbury Indians and therefore would still be classed as a "rookie."

From 1934 to 1936, Brady, a product of Hanover's lot baseball diamonds, received yearly invitations to try out for the Senators' first base position. On May 22, 1934, the *York Gazette and Daily* newspaper reported Brady received a telegram from Bobbie Fuchs,[1] president of the Harrisburg Senators, asking him to report to the Hotel Governor the next day. Unfortunately, after trying out, Brady was nosed out by older and more experienced players. A year later, the *Hanover Evening Sun* reported he was trying out again for the Harrisburg club and on April 18, 1936, the local newspaper reported that after playing a short stint with the Taneytown club in the Frederick League in early spring, Brady signed a contract with the Hanover club of the semipro York-Adams County League.

Although acknowledging that Brady did not play a game for the Harrisburg Senators, was released before the season opened and was not compensated one cent from the club, Kibler said his release was not registered. The league president believed the Salisbury club's error in signing Brady was made in "good faith" but added "the records of the National Association show that he is a one-year man. It is necessary, therefore, for [Kibler] to order all games ... forfeited."[2] Even though Salisbury was innocent of any conscious deception to break league rules, "each club is responsible for determining the status of its players."[3] Indians owner Cambria commented, "Kibler has always impressed me as being level-headed but in this case, he seems to have forgotten the word common sense in the English language."[4]

In the early days of the 1937 schedule, Brady and Arthur Steinfadt were candidates for the infield position at first base for the Indians. Flowers eventually decided upon Brady and Steinfadt was released. Brady appeared in 15 games, and three of those were among the five the Indians had lost. Later Brady strained a leg muscle and Quimby replaced him at first base for several games. Guerra held down the initial sack for the July 19 game against the Crisfield Crabbers, pending a decision regarding Brady's status.

Following a conference with Flowers, President Kibler issued an executive order on June 20 that sent the Salisbury ball club plummeting from the top of the league to the subcellar. The order instructed the Indians to forfeit to the other seven teams all the games won before June 19.

After receiving the notification, the club reached out to Judge Bramham, president of the Minor League Baseball Association, for his thoughts on the matter, and by June 21, he notified them that he believed that he would not intervene as this was an intraleague issue

Three—The Brady Infraction

and therefore hoped that some good judgment would be used. Flowers then wired Kenesaw Mountain Landis,[5] high commissioner of organized baseball, the next day to set up a meeting regarding the case and indicated that he was prepared to travel to Chicago upon receipt of notice if the meeting was granted. "In all my seventeen years in professional baseball I never thought of doing a crooked or questioned thing and I intend to see this thing through until the club is cleared," promised Flowers.[6]

Salisbury also appealed to the directors of the Eastern Shore League. Confronted with requests from the ball clubs of Dover, Pocomoke, Easton and Federalsburg, Kibler called a special meeting of Eastern Shore League directors for June 25. The agenda for the meeting: to afford the officials from the Salisbury Indians an opportunity to present their case. Under certain circumstances, the league's board of directors may override rulings and decisions of the league president by a vote of the board.

"Before the league opened," Cambria accusatorily said, "the Salisbury club submitted a list of players to the league president. As is his duty, President Kibler okayed the list—and that OK satisfied Salisbury that its men were all right. Under league rules, Kibler must examine the roster of all clubs; he had as much knowledge about Brady as Salisbury did. The decision to throw out 21 games has floored the team—but it'll never quit. I've instructed the manager and the team to carry on the fight on and off the ball field."[7]

Roger Pippen,[8] sports editor of the *Baltimore News-Post*, asserted in his column on June 23 that Kibler's action in forfeiting the games was unnecessarily drastic. His opinion continued: "If it is true that the officials of the Salisbury Club were not aware they were violating the rules in playing infielder Brady, I think President Kibler of the ESL was far too drastic in his handling of the case.... In view of the telegram the Salisbury officials received from the president of the NY-Penn League, explaining that Brady had not participated in a single game, Kibler could have been more lenient without establishing a bad precedent."[9]

Even Brady's local newspaper came to his defense. Al Clark, the *Harrisburg Telegraph* sportswriter, spoke of Brady as an 18-year-old first base candidate four years ago and his recollection about Brady never appearing in the Senators' lineup except in practice games of the intraclub variety. Clark recalled, "Brady never signed a contract with Harrisburg." "He was too young to sign without this mother's consent so far as

Miracle on the Eastern Shore

I know and when he asked me for my opinion of signing a contract with Les Mann,[10] I told him not to sign anything." "Brady was the lad Johnny Evers[11] wanted signed and retained as a regular," Clark recalled. "Mann, however, couldn't see eye-to-eye with Evers and advised Brady to wait a year or two before signing any contracts."[12]

On June 25, the directors gathered from all the clubs in the league except Cambridge. Cambria displayed the telegram from Perry B. Farrell,[13] the NYPL president since 1930, confirming the fact that Brady had never played professional ball before coming to Salisbury.

The telegram read: "Our records show Robert Brady signed a contract with Harrisburg club on June 15, [1934] and the contract had on it a notation 'For future services.' The official records do not show that Brady ever played with Harrisburg or any other club in this league. It is my personal opinion this transaction was a cover-up on the part of the Harrisburg club officials. It is my further opinion this contract should never have been recorded."[14] Thus the contract was illegal because he was a minor—18 years old—and that it did not contain his parents' signatures.

After hearing the evidence, the directors of the Eastern Shore Baseball League voted unanimously to uphold Kibler's decision of imposing a penalty on the Salisbury club for having more experienced men than the rules allowed. The committee said that Brady's only recourse would be to have his record with the National Association of Professional Baseball Leagues changed.

The directors also imposed a $100 fine on the Salisbury club for having eight men on the suspended list, when the league rules allowed only four.[15] The $100 fine was far less than the $500 penalty the rules provided but Kibler felt the larger sum would be too stiff since Salisbury apparently was not guilty of intent. The players on the suspended list were placed there for failure to report and should have been referred to the National Association as ineligible players.

Kibler allowed the Indians to keep their win over Dover on June 19 in consideration of Brady's release. The order gave the Easton Browns first place by two full games. Kibler said he acted in accordance with a ruling from Judge Bramham. Flowers announced the club "would appeal to higher authorities for a common sense ruling."[16] Since the matter may hinge upon the validity or legality of the contract filed in 1934 by the Harrisburg club, which at that time was a farm team of the Boston Braves, an ultimate decision may rest with Commissioner Landis.

Three—The Brady Infraction

Following the executive order, Brady was released pending a decision from Landis.

Cambria filed a protest with Landis and emphasized he would personally carry it, if need be, to him. "We'll see this thing through to the finish, for we have just begun the fight," Cambria proclaimed. "Salisburians have been loyal to their club and I'll spend my last cent before I'll let them bow."[17] Additionally, Salisbury held out hope that, even if they were unable to recover their 21 victories, they might be able to recover the seven victories in which Brady did not play.

On August 3, Bob Brady, accompanied by Salisbury's business manager, M.E. Murphy, traveled to Chicago to appear before Landis about the possibility to have the contract that Brady signed with the Harrisburg Senators voided. Brady gave Murphy letters from the officials of the now-defunct Harrisburg club stating he was under contract illegally. Brady claimed that the contract, signed in 1934, was illegal since it was not signed by his parents and he was only 18 years of age at the time. He contended the contract was a cover-up by club officials by marking it suspended after he had been released verbally.

In August, Clark Griffith, the owner of the Washington Senators, stepped into the fray and expressed his opinion about the Brady incident. "I don't think the Salisbury Indians need the return of the 21 games they were robbed of on a technicality," he opined to the *Daily Times* on August 9.[18] "Joe Cambria has the greatest little ballclub I've ever seen anywhere. The way they're going now they'll make the biggest comeback in baseball history," he prophesized. "It will be one for the 'believe it or not books.'" Griffith claimed that there was "no sensible hearing" given to allow the ball club a chance for an argument to be presented.[19]

The action taken by league president Kibler in declaring the games forfeited was, in Griffith's opinion, "hasty and ill-advised." The hearing before the league board of directors "was a farce" and he was quite annoyed that Judge Bramham had flatly refused to intervene.[20]

Commissioner Landis had expressed "keen interest" in the case to Griffith. However, the legislative powers that the minor leagues possessed denied him to act in a case of this sort. To reverse Kibler's ruling, Griffith believed that an appeal for a hearing before the Executive Committee of the National Association of Minor League Baseball was necessary. This appeal was already being executed by M.E. Murphy but no answer had been received.[21]

Clark Griffith (1869–1955) owned the Washington Senators from 1920 until his death. The Salisbury Indians were affiliated with the Senators. Nicknamed "The Old Fox," he was known as an advocate for Latin American players, particularly those from Cuba (Library of Congress, Prints & Photographs Division, photograph by Harris & Ewing [LC-H22-D-8921]).

  Letters from Commissioner Landis to Griffith outlined the proper procedure for the Brady case. According to the letters, Brady must first go before the Executive Committee of minor league baseball. If they offered him no relief, Landis could then consider the case.

  While the fans roared, screamed and pleaded to the world "we wuz robbed!," Kibler stuck to his guns and the decision remained. Clark Griffith phoned him angrily. "You're tearing up the league." "Well, Mr. Griffith, if we can't play by the rules of the game, let's tear up the

THREE—The Brady Infraction

league!"[22] Kibler emphatically exclaimed. No further comment was made.

Griffith insisted that Brady was eligible. He spat vicious verbal blasts at Kibler, threatening a lawsuit for damage incurred to his team. "The Old Fox" (Griffith) lost his patience with telephone calls. He motored down to Chestertown, Maryland, to have it out with Kibler face-to-face. He came away the loser. Kibler stuck by his decision, which was backed up a few days later by Bramham.

Bob Brady returned to his hometown of Hanover, Pennsylvania. In early August, he reported to the Zanesville Bees (MATL) to be an outfielder when the Bees negotiated for him. Unfortunately, when he reported it became clear that he had no experience in the outfield. He was released because the club had no use for a first baseman. In 1938, he played for the Taneytown ball club and the Reistertown ball club.

Four

The Climb
(June 19–July 31)

Salisbury 10, Dover 0   (1–26) (22–5)   June 19

Salisbury	3	0	1	0	2	0	0	3	1	10	14	0
Dover	0	0	0	0	0	0	0	0	0	0	4	3

Bassler (winner), Taylor (loser)
Luzansky (2), Thomas (3), Trechock, Guerra (2), Leip—RBI; Luzansky, Thomas, Guerra—2B; Luzansky—HR; Leip, Trechock—SB

The Salisbury Indians trounced the Dover Orioles 10 to 0 while waiting to hear the verdict over the alleged Brady violation. Bassler pitched a four-hitter with only two Dover players reaching second base. He struck out eight and walked only one. Going against his moniker of "Hard Luck Lefty," he registered the Indians' first shutout of the season. Salisbury's batters shelled Dover pitcher Thomas Taylor[1] for 14 hits.

Cambridge 8, Salisbury 4   (1–27) (22–6)   June 21

Cambridge	0	0	4	0	0	2	0	2	0	8	10	3
Salisbury	0	0	0	1	1	1	0	1	0	4	10	5

Revolinsky (loser), Kovis (winner)
Trechock, Luzansky (2)—RBI; Revolinsky—2B

Several hours after hearing the announcement from the league president that had them forfeit their first 21 victories, the Salisbury Indians hosted the Cambridge Cardinals. Postponed the night before, the game was, as a writer put it, "an exhibition of good and bad baseball, pugilistic prowess and that often-indulged-in American pastime 'rassberry.'"[2] "Gordy Park was a hot spot that night," recalled Jim Boyer, who officiated the game along with Jim O'Connor.[3]

Four—The Climb (June 19–July 31)

The Cardinals won the game 8 to 4, not because they played better baseball but more to do with circumstances that bounced their way. Salisbury pitcher Revolinsky kept the Cardinals to just one hit until the third inning. During that inning, the Cardinals put two men on with two singles when Giovanelli, the Cardinals' third baseman, launched a shot that hit the top of the fence and bounced over, scoring three runs. The Cardinals added another run to take a 4–0 lead. The Indians scored a run in the fourth and fifth innings. In the sixth inning, the home plate umpire, O'Connor, missed a call. With one out and the bases loaded, Cardinals catcher Marshall flied out to short left field. Center fielder Jackson, who was on third base, tagged up and dashed toward home plate. Quimby, having caught the flyout, fired a perfect strike to Thomas, the Indians' catcher, who tagged Jackson before his foot touched the plate but O'Connor called him safe. Jackson's slide ended almost a full yard from the plate. "In fact, the runner has not yet touched the plate," a sportswriter joked.[4] The fans shouted their displeasure about the call. Flowers left the dugout to protest. He hardly got out a dozen words when O'Connor gestured for Flowers to return to the dugout. Flowers then protested vehemently and left the field. O'Connor's decision stood and the Cardinals added another score in the inning, making it 6 to 2. Jackson's play would have been the third out.

In the seventh inning, the umpire crew appeared to have made their second "grave" mistake, this time involving a play at first base, and the fans in the stands began to grumble again. In the eighth, they quieted down a bit until Cambridge came to bat. From the Cambridge dugout, someone shouted an insulting epithet at Thomas, the Indians' backstop. The former University of Maryland baseball star turned, threw off his mask and started walking toward the visitors' dugout, demanding "Who said that?"[5] Gagain, who had replaced Jackson in center field, and second baseman Murtaugh left the dugout bench to meet him. A fight ensued where the city police, ballplayers and about two hundred fans swarmed the field to try to separate three players. This led to an all-out brawl with players swinging at one another and rival fans going at one another. Daniel Murtaugh recalled how Flowers, the Indians manager, saved his baseball career during the fight. He had more bark than bite, in retrospect. He never swung his fist at any person as he was a little guy, standing 5'9" tall, and understood he had no business fighting the big bruisers. During the melee, Murtaugh was punched twice with the second one dropping him to the ground. While sitting there, rubbing

Miracle on the Eastern Shore

his jaw, Murtaugh saw Flowers rushing toward him. Fearing that he was going to be hit again, he started to crawl away. Instead, Flowers knocked a spectator out with a one-two punch. The man was standing over Murtaugh, holding an empty quart-sized soft drink bottle. It could have splintered his skull. After all was settled, Thomas, Murtaugh and Gagain were ejected from the game.

While the field was being cleared, Revolinsky began warming up. One of his pitches got away and struck Quimby on the ankle, which forced him out of the game. Flowers moved Guerra from first base to behind the plate to replace Thomas. Bassler came in to cover first base and Kohlman replaced Quimby in left field. To make matters more complicated, one section of the lighting system shorted out and cast shadows along the third base side of the field. In addition, drizzling rain began to pick up intensity near the end of the game.

While leaving the ballpark, several fans, disgusted by the officials' misjudgments during the game, angrily approached O'Connor. Fearing for the worse, the umpire swung his mask about to defend himself and escaped without harm.

The league standings before June 21:

Salisbury 21–5
Federalsburg 16–9
Easton 15–10
Dover 12–12

Centreville 11–13
Cambridge 9–15
Crisfield 8–17
Pocomoke 8–19

The league standings after June 21:

Easton 20–8
Federalsburg 18–10
Dover 16–11
Crisfield 15–12

Centreville 14–13
Cambridge 13–13
Pocomoke 13–16
Salisbury 1–27

Salisbury 4, Easton 3   (2–27) (23–6)   June 22   (11 innings)

Salisbury	1	0	0	0	0	0	0	2	0	0	1	4	13	4
Easton	0	1	1	0	0	0	0	1	0	0	0	3	7	4

Kohlman (winner), Radler (loser)
Reznichak, Quimby, Trechock—RBI; Luzansky—2B

On June 22, it took 11 innings for the Indians to defeat the Easton Browns 4 to 3. On the hill, Comellas held the Browns to four hits for the

Four—*The Climb (June 19–July 31)*

first seven innings. He struck out eight and walked none. In the eighth, leading 3 to 2, Comellas passed the ball to Revolinsky, who found himself in a serious jam when he loaded the bases with a double from shortstop Weimer, a sacrifice laid down by center fielder Stiles and walks issued to right fielder Beidleman and left fielder Crompton. Flowers called on Kohlman in relief. The first man to face him, first baseman Vernon, hit a long fly to center to score a run. After that, he silenced the Easton bats to one hit and one walk for the next 2⅔ innings.

The Indians tallied one run in the first inning when Luzansky scored on Reznichak's single. The Browns knotted up the score in the second inning when Reznichak dropped third baseman Eck's long fly that would have been the third out. A single by second baseman Pultz scored Eck. In the third inning, Easton scored a run on a single by Weimer and two errors. In the eighth, consecutive singles by Trechock, Guerra and Quimby and a long fly ball to left field from Lynn scored two runs for the Indians. In the 11th inning, Salisbury scored the winning run when an error occurred at second base that allowed Thomas, who was stealing second, to be safe. It was followed up with two singles from Reznichak and Trechock. In Easton's half of the inning, Vernon hit a single. The next man, Eck, grounded out to first and the game ended on a failed attempt at a hit and run from Pultz, which resulted in a double play. The Indians collected 13 hits off the Browns' star pitcher, Frank Radler.[6] Trechock went three for six, extending his hitting streak to 16 games. Luzansky contributed with a double and a single and Reznichak, Quimby and Leip each hit a pair of singles.

News from around the league reported that Federalsburg held their first night game, hosting the Cambridge Cardinals. There were also plans to modify Federalsburg's grounds by increasing the distance from home plate to the fence by 21 feet.

Easton 5, Salisbury 1   (2–28) (23–7)   June 23

Easton	0	0	2	0	0	0	0	2	1	5	6	2
Salisbury	0	0	0	0	0	0	0	0	1	1	6	4

Bassler (loser), Kuntashian (winner)
Guerra—SB

With several mistakes that cost them the game, Salisbury lost to the Easton Browns 5 to 1. The game was mostly a pitchers' duel between Bassler and Kuntashian, each handing out six hits apiece. Bassler

Miracle on the Eastern Shore

allowed only two hits until the sixth inning. In the third inning with one out, Bassler issued a free pass to Kuntashian. Kuntashian was out at second on Easton shortstop Weimer's grounder. The play should have resulted in a double play. However, the ball heading to first base was overthrown. The ball was retrieved and a rundown ensued. After all was done, Weimer was safe at second when the ball got away from Guerra, who was covering first. Weimer scored on center fielder Stiles's two-base wallop. Stiles scored on right fielder Beidleman's single. In the eighth and ninth innings, the Indians had rallies that fell short when they loaded the bases in each inning. Trechock hit for the 17th game in a row and Bassler's two singles led the Salisbury offense. Dealing with a short bench owing to injuries, Kohlman played left field and Quimby manned second base. Newspapers reported that Mike Depko,[7] a new recruit from Plymouth Township, Pennsylvania, was sent to Salisbury after signing a contract with the Trenton Senators. Depko pitched for the Wilkes-Barre Barons in 1936.

Salisbury 7, Federalsburg 1   (3–28) (24–7)   June 24

Salisbury	0	4	0	1	0	1	0	1	0	7	6	1
Federalsburg	0	0	0	0	0	0	0	0	1	1	4	6

Kohlman (winner), Hudson (loser)
Luzansky (2), Quimby, Lynn (2), Leip—RBI; Leip—HR; Leip—SB

At the Federalsburg Athletics' home field, Salisbury rebounded and defeated the Caroline County ball club 7 to 1 behind Kohlman's superb pitching. Kohlman limited the A's batters to four hits and struck out six. In 76 innings, Kohlman had struck out 85 batters. Hudson, the A's counterpart to Kohlman, held the Indians to six hits but his teammates committed six errors behind him.

In the second inning, Salisbury tallied four runs on a single, two errors and three walks. Reznichak started it off with a single and advanced to second on Trechock's groundout to third. Guerra walked and Quimby reached safely on right fielder Dink Boyce's fielding error. Leip walked and after Kohlman flied out to first baseman Al McNally,[8] Lynn worked another base on balls. Luzansky reached on an error by second baseman Millman. In the fourth inning, Leip clubbed a solo shot over the fence. In the sixth, with two outs, Kohlman was safe on A's shortstop Charles Morris's error. He scored when A's left fielder

Four—The Climb (June 19–July 31)

Robert Stant mishandled Lynn's fly ball. In the eighth inning, Leip was issued a free base and scored on Lynn's base hit. For the A's lone score, Manczak,[9] after earning a walk, scored on Stant's base hit.

Salisbury 4, Federalsburg 1 (4–28) (25–7) June 25

Federalsburg	0	1	0	0	0	0	0	0	1	4	2
Salisbury	0	0	0	3	0	0	1	0	X	4	10	2

Comellas (winner), Ecker (loser)
Quimby, Thomas, Leip—RBI; Quimby, Luzansky—2B; Thomas, Luzansky—3B; Lynn, Trechock—SB

For his eighth straight victory of the season, Comellas held the Athletics batters to four hits, struck out nine and issued three walks. The A's lone tally in the 4-1 defeat came in the second inning when A's right fielder Boyce reached first base on Lynn's error and advanced to third when Comellas, in the attempt to pick him off, threw the ball into the ground. Short, the A's catcher, then brought Boyce in on a sharp single.

In the fourth, the Indians got on the scoreboard and took the lead after Trechock was safe at first when A's third baseman John Manczak committed an error. He scored on Quimby's double. Thomas laced a triple to deep right field that brought in Quimby. Thomas scored on Leip's fielder's choice. In the eighth, Luzansky tripled and scored when Turney Ecker[10] balked.

During the past five games, the Indians had been dealing with physical and emotional setbacks. The roster had been cut to 13 players with the release of Bob Brady. Leip had been coping with a charley horse, Lynn with a sprained thumb and Quimby with a bruised spiked foot. Thomas, the only utility man on the bench, had been behind the plate. For this game, Bassler played right field as Reznichak's replacement. It was reported that Reznichak suffered a sprained ankle during the last game. Leip and Trechock swapped positions (3B and SS) and performed admirably.

Salisbury 8, Dover 7 (5–28) (26–7) June 26
[Box score not found]
Revolinsky (winner), Wittig (loser)

The Salisbury Indians displayed their fighting spirit against the Dover Orioles with a come-from-behind ninth-inning rally for an 8-7

Miracle on the Eastern Shore

victory. Revolinsky did not have his best stuff that night, allowing 14 hits to the Orioles batsmen. He was a man left on an island as he had nobody to relieve him. The Indians' bullpen was empty. Kowal was incapacitated with a sore arm and Bassler injured his finger. Comellas and Kohlman were spent; they already took their turns in the two previous games.

Before the last inning, Salisbury had four hits and three runs on the scoreboard. Even with their lineup being patched together, the Indian bats came alive in the ninth inning. They started the rally with two singles and two walks that brought in one run. The next batter, Trechock lifted John Wittig's offering over the fence for a three-run home run. Lynn singled in the fifth and game-winning run.

Salisbury 6, Cambridge 0   (6–28) (27–7   June 27

Salisbury	0	0	0	1	2	0	0	2	1	6	9	0
Cambridge	0	0	0	0	0	0	0	0	0	0	6	5

Kohlman (winner), Raffensberger (loser)
Luzansky, Leip, Comellas, Trechock—RBI; Quimby,
   Luzansky, Lynn—2B

On June 27, Kohlman took the mound and, as a newspaper reporter stated, "was master of the situation at all stages of the game," throwing a 6–0 shutout against the hometown Cardinals.[11] He scattered the Cardinals' six singles around and fanned nine, bringing his strikeout total to 94 through 10 games. Bernard Healy, the Cardinals' left fielder, recorded a golden sombrero by striking out four times. Cardinals third baseman Giovanelli broke up the no-hitter in the fourth inning. Flowers continued to be creative when putting together the lineup card. Comellas played right field and batted eighth. He contributed by batting in a run.

The Indians got on the scoreboard in the fourth inning. After Guerra's groundout to third, Trechock singled and came around to score when Cambridge shortstop Bill Myska mishandled Thomas's strong grounder. In the fifth, the Indians scored two runs when Lynn reached on a fielding error from Myska. Luzansky doubled in Lynn. Guerra struck out and Luzansky scored when Myska committed another error, this time on Trechock's liner to short. The Indians added two more runs in the eighth on an error from Myska's replacement, Gagain, which allowed Trechock to reach first base safely. After Quimby's strikeout,

Four—The Climb (June 19–July 31)

Thomas singled. Trechock scored on Leip's flyout to center field and Trechock scored on Comellas's base hit. The Indians ended their scoring spree in the ninth when Lynn hit a two-bagger and scored on Trechock's single.

After forfeiting the 21 victories, the Indians were nine games behind the seventh-place Cardinals and 15½ games from the league-leading Easton Browns. The Cambridge Cardinals had been running into some issues with overall attendance at their ballpark. A strike at the Phillips Packing Company, which started on June 22, affected the residents' finances, which hindered them from going to the hometown games. The strike ended on June 30 but the effects lingered throughout the region.

Salisbury 11, Centreville 5   (7–28) (28–7)   June 29

Centreville	0	0	0	0	3	0	0	2	0	5	8	1
Salisbury	0	2	1	0	4	0	1	3	X	11	12	3

Comellas (winner), Ogden (loser)
Trechock, Thomas, Luzansky (2), Guerra (2)—RBI; Quimby, Reznichak—2B; Trechock, Guerra, Quimby—HR

Since June 19, the Indians had won seven of nine games. On June 29, at Gordy Park, they walloped the Centreville Colts 11 to 5. George Comellas gave the crowd a pitching spectacle by striking out 21 Colts. In the second inning, the Indians began the scoring when Trechock crushed Ogden's pitch over center field near the right corner of the factory. After working a walk, Guerra scored on Quimby's double. In the third inning, Comellas was hit by a pitch. Lynn, Reznichak and Trechock singled with the latter batting Comellas in.

In the fifth, the Colts tied the game. Third baseman Troy singled, then Lynn fumbled Colts shortstop Harold Miller's[12] grounder near second base, allowing all runners to be safe. Troy scored on catcher Ike Mysel's[13] soft single. Ogden singled to right field. Miller sprinted home as Reznichak fielded the ball and threw it to the relay man, Lynn, who in turn threw the ball badly to Thomas. The ball rolled into the Centreville dugout and Miller and Mysel scored. All three runs were unearned.

In the bottom half, Comellas and Lynn hit back-to-back singles. Comellas was thrown out at third on Luzansky's fielder's choice. Lynn and Luzansky scored when Trechock was safe on an error. Guerra then connected on a two-run homer. Centreville manager Joe O'Rourke saw enough and sent in Lee to relieve Ogden.

In the seventh, Lynn singled and scored on Reznichak's double. Centreville put up two runs in the eighth inning. Guerra committed an error allowing Colts first baseman Wurst to be safe at first base. Troy doubled and Miller and Mysel singled. In the bottom half of the inning, Quimby launched a shot over the fence that was delivered by Lee's replacement, Buck Smyth.[14] Smyth issued a walk to Thomas, who advanced to second on Leip's single. Comellas walked to load the bases. Thomas scored on Lynn's fielder's choice and Luzansky's sacrifice fly allowed Leip to score.

In the ninth inning, Comellas struck out right fielder Ray Rist[15] and left fielder Pitko for his 20th and 21st strikeouts to establish the league record.

On the same day (June 30), the directors of the league met and decided to grant Kibler authority to approach the president of the Bi-State League to discuss the possibility of setting up a postseason series between the winners of the Bi-State and the Eastern Shore Leagues.

Salisbury 5, Cambridge 0   (8–28) (29–7)   July 1

Cambridge	0	0	0	0	0	0	0	0	0	0	3	1
Salisbury	0	1	0	0	0	0	4	0	X	5	5	1

Kohlman (winner), Stanfield (loser)
Leip, Kohlman, Lynn, Reznichak (2)—RBI

In the next game following Comellas's magnificent 21-strikeouts pitching performance, Joe Kohlman wrenched it up a little with a three-hit shutout while dealing out 18 strikeouts. The Indians got on the scoreboard in the second inning without a hit. Trechock worked a walk and advanced to second base when a Cambridge infielder committed an error that allowed Quimby to be safe at first base. Thomas walked to load the bases and Trechock scored on Leip's sacrifice fly. The game remained 1–0 until the seventh inning, when Quimby started the rally with a single. Salisbury's new recruit, Buck Elliott, Jr.,[16] 18-year-old son of former Baltimore Orioles and Bucknell University standout Buck Elliott, Sr., placed down a perfect bunt and both runners were safe. Thomas then repeated the same play and again all runners were safe. Leip lifted an infield fly for the first out. Cambridge pitcher Stanley

Four—The Climb (June 19–July 31)

Stanfield,[17] so shaken with how the inning was going, walked Kohlman and Lynn, scoring Quimby and Elliott. Luzansky struck out, then Reznichak drove in Thomas and Kohlman with a single. Overall, Stanfield did pitch a pretty solid game, holding the Indians to five hits, but struggled with his control.

Cambridge 8, Salisbury 2   (8–29) (29–8)   July 2

Salisbury	0	1	0	0	0	0	0	0	1	2	2	5
Cambridge	0	0	0	1	0	4	3	0	X	8	8	3

Bassler (loser), Raffensberger (winner)
Elliott, Leip—RBI; Guerra—2B

Finally, a pitcher solved and quelled the hot-hitting Salisbury Indians. Cambridge hurler Ken Raffensberger[18] held the Indians to two hits. Only Trechock and Guerra made contact with a pitched ball, the former a single and the latter a double. Six blows were intended to be hits but were not due to sensational glove work by the Cardinal fielders. The Indians did get on the board first when Guerra doubled in the second inning. He advanced on an error by second baseman Murtaugh on Quimby's grounder. Guerra then scored on Elliott's flyout to deep center. In the ninth, Raffensberger developed wildness and the Indians scored one run without a hit. Trechock popped out at home plate. Guerra and Quimby earned walks and Elliott was safe on a throwing error by shortstop Reds Hoffner[19] on his fielder's choice. Guerra scored on Leip's flyout to left field. Revolinsky struck out to end the game.

Bassler was unlucky again as shaky support behind him cost him a victory. "Bad throwing, muffed grounders and misjudgments were costly," noted one reporter.[20] Lynn, in particular, was ineffective at second base with two errors. In the fourth inning, Cambridge tied the score when left fielder Healy was safe at first on an error by Trechock, who was playing third base. Second baseman Murtaugh drove Healy home with a base hit. In the sixth inning, the Cardinals exploded for four runs to break up a 1–1 tie behind two doubles, two singles and a walk. This included Cambridge catcher Marshall's two-bagger with the bases loaded. Third baseman Giovanelli brought in Murtaugh with a single. In the next inning, the Cardinals ended the rout with a three-spot on the board. Hoffner started the inning off with a single and advanced to second on a well-placed sacrifice bunt executed by Healy down the third baseline. First baseman Iwanicki followed it up with a walk and center

Miracle on the Eastern Shore

fielder Jackson hit into a fielder's choice that allowed Hoffner to score. Murtaugh hit a two-run double that brought in Iwanicki and Jackson.

Concerning the Indians' roster, *The Daily Home News* reported that pitcher Joseph Shafnacker[21] of South Amboy was spending several days in Maryland to try out with the Salisbury Indians. This was in response to Kowal's recent injury to his arm.

Salisbury 12, Federalsburg 5 (9–29) (30–8) July 3
[Box score not found]
Comellas (winner)

On July 3, the Salisbury Indians, behind Comellas's pitching, manhandled the Federalsburg Athletics 12 to 5. Two days later, an official report came out that the Salisbury Indians had released several players from their contracts: Thad Cash, Arthur Steinfadt, Casimir Macklin, Walter Andrews, Frank James, Philip Sherr and Clifton Keyser.[22]

By July 6, Salisbury had six postponed games due to the weather, two each with the baseball clubs of Centreville, Dover and Easton.

Salisbury 5, Dover 4 (10–29) (31–8)
July 7 afternoon game (7 innings)

Dover	3	1	0	0	0	0	0	4	6	0
Salisbury	0	2	0	2	1	0	X	5	11	3

Comellas (winner), Toland (loser)
Thomas, Leip, Luzansky (2), Trechock—RBI;
 Trechock—2B; Luzansky, Trechock—HR;
 Thomas—SB

On July 7, Salisbury hosted a doubleheader at Gordy Park. In the opener, 22-year-old Sayreville, New Jersey, native Joseph Shafnacker was sent out to the mound and the Dover Orioles took advantage of him by scoring three runs in the first inning on two hits and a walk. With just two outs in the first inning, Revolinsky was sent in to relieve Shafnacker. In the second inning, the Orioles added another run on a hit, a sacrifice and a wild pitch. The Indians scored two runs on three hits in the bottom of the second and tied the game in the fourth when Lynn singled and "Little Bill" Luzansky sent a booming drive between the center field warehouse roof and the scoreboard. Trechock added his own warehouse roof homer in the fifth to put the Indians in front for good. Comellas, who relieved Revolinsky in the third, notched his 11th

Four—The Climb (June 19–July 31)

win as he held the Orioles to two hits in five innings while striking out six batters.

Salisbury 2, Dover 1   (11–29) (32–8)   July 7 night game (11 innings)

												R	H	E
Dover	0	0	0	1	0	0	0	0	0	0	0	1	7	1
Salisbury	0	0	0	0	0	1	0	0	0	0	1	2	11	1

Kohlman (winner), Wittig (loser)
Trechock, Bassler—RBI; Trechock—2B; Quimby—SB

In the nightcap, Joe Kohlman and John Wittig went head to head in an 11-inning pitchers' duel with Kohlman coming out the winner. The game remained scoreless for the first three innings. This included three strikeouts thrown by Kohlman. In the fourth, Orioles center fielder Marnie dunked in a Texas Leaguer and advanced to second on Guerra's error on third baseman Joe Archer's single. Marnie crossed the plate on Orioles shortstop Vandegrift's single. In the top part of the sixth inning, Kohlman executed what one sportswriter penned as "one of the prettiest fielding plays by a pitcher" at Gordy Park this season.[23] An Oriole batter hit a grounder down the first baseline. Kohlman sprinted over and snatched the ball under the runner's foot. With a backhand underhand toss, he flipped the ball to Quimby, who received it in time for the putout.

During the bottom half of the inning, Salisbury was able to even the score with two hits and two sacrifices. This included Luzansky hustling to second base and sliding hard, taking Vandegrift's foot off the bag. Reznichak bunted him over to third and scored on Trechock's double.

The game remained tied until the Indians' half of the 11th inning. Quimby started it off with a single and advanced to third on Leip's single. He scored on a perfect squeeze play by Bassler, pinch-hitting for Kohlman, who had been overcome by heat at the end of the Orioles' half of the inning and could not bat when his turn came up.

Salisbury 14, Dover 5   (12–29) (33–8)   July 8

									R	H	E
Salisbury	1	2	2	3	0	1	1	4	0	14	18	3
Dover	3	0	0	0	1	0	0	1	0	5	8	4

Revolinsky (winner), Killen (loser)
Lynn (4), Bergen, Quimby (2), Reznichak, Trechock (2),
   Thomas—RBI; Lynn, Leip, Bergen—2B; Lynn, Quimby,
   Trechock—HR; Thomas (2), Luzansky—SB

Miracle on the Eastern Shore

On July 8, the Salisbury Indians pounded out a one-sided slugfest over the hometown Dover Orioles by a 14-5 score. For the second time, Jerry Lynn started the game with a lead-off home run, lifting Killen's first pitch over the left field fence. The Orioles answered with three runs of their own off of Indians starter Shafnacker, who did not get out of the first inning. With two men on, Cardinals shortstop Vandegrift tripled to right field, allowing third baseman Archer and second baseman Roetz to score. Right fielder Reznichak, in a hurry to return the ball back to the infield, threw off target, which allowed Vandegrift to score. After left fielder Ed Weatherlow[24] doubled, Shafnacker was relieved by Revolinsky with one out in the inning. In the second inning, the Indians evened the score when Leip and Lynn hit singles and new recruit James Bergen[25] crushed a hot smash to center field, scoring Leip and Lynn. The next inning had Thomas hitting a single, followed by Quimby homering. Salisbury put the game on ice when, in the fourth inning, Reznichak brought in Luzansky with a single and Trechock went yard for the 14th time, scoring Reznichak. In the sixth inning, the Indians scored one run on Reznichak's base hit that allowed Lynn to score. In the seventh inning, Thomas scored on an error on Quimby's grounder to shortstop. The Indians finished their onslaught with four runs in the eighth on Thomas's single and an error committed by Marnie on Lynn's deep fly to center field.

The Orioles played to the last out, scoring two more times. In the sixth inning, Weatherlow hit a solo home run, and Revolinsky walked in a run in the eighth. Offensively, the Indian bats woke up with 18 hits. Thomas went two for three, Lynn three for five with a double and a home run, Reznichak three for five and Trechock, Bergen and Leip each went two for four. Defensively, the game had several outstanding plays by Leip and Thomas of Salisbury and third baseman Archer of Dover. Revolinsky, in relief, pitched 8⅔ innings of five-hit ball. He struck out nine but walked eight.

Easton 3, Salisbury 1   (12–30) (33–9)   July 9

Easton	2	0	0	1	0	0	0	0	0	3	6	1
Salisbury	0	0	0	0	0	0	0	0	1	1	4	5

Bassler (loser), Kuntashian (winner)
Lynn—2B

In an attempt to increase attendance and to enhance the family entertainment value of the American summer pastime, the July 9 game

Four—The Climb (June 19–July 31)

against the Easton Browns was promoted as "Wheaties Night." All children under 15 years old could enter the ballpark for one cent if they presented the top of a Wheaties cereal carton.

Bassler lived up to his moniker "Hard Luck Lefty" when he faced the Browns. He performed quite well, limiting Easton to six hits while striking out 12. However, his teammates' bats quieted and could not support his performance. They also committed fielding mishaps, four of which directly enabled the Browns to score their three runs.

Starting in the first inning, Browns shortstop Zimmerman walked and advanced to second on second baseman Pultz's blooper. Center fielder Stiles sacrificed the two runners over to second and third. Next up was right fielder Beidleman, whose hot shot ate up Quimby at first base, allowing Zimmerman and Pultz to score while Reznichak retrieved the ball. Third baseman Eck and first baseman Vernon ended the rally with strikeouts.

In the second, Salisbury prevented Easton from scoring. Weimer, Easton's left fielder, doubled and advanced to third while catcher Lessig beat out a well-placed bunt. Zimmerman put down a bunt for a squeeze play but Bassler sprang off the mound and tossed the ball to Guerra, who tagged Weimer out at home plate. The third run was added in the fourth. Vernon walked and Weimer was safe at first on Leip's error. Lessig drove a ball to right field. Reznichak made a shoestring catch and doubled off Weimer at first. Vernon, in the meantime, hustled around the bases and scored.

The Indians tried to rally but just could not finish the deal. In the sixth inning, Lynn, standing on second base after his shot caromed off the factory wall in left field, became a victim of the "old hidden ball trick" when he drifted away from the bag and Zimmerman tagged him out. In the eighth, Thomas, who replaced Quimby at first base, executed a perfect drag bunt between the pitcher's mound and first base. After Leip struck out and Bassler flied out, Lynn walked but, unfortunately, Luzansky grounded out to end any chance of a rally.

The Indians' solo run occurred when Bergen singled and Reznichak walked. Lessig, the Easton catcher, attempted to catch Reznichak off first base but overthrew the ball past Vernon. Bergen took off from second base and hustled around the bases to score. The rally flamed out when Trechock flied out and Guerra and Thomas struck out. Kuntashian, Easton's star hurler, struck out nine Indian batsmen and yielded just one hit in each of the first four innings.

Miracle on the Eastern Shore

Salisbury 9, Cambridge 1   (13–30) (34–9)   July 10

Cambridge	0	0	0	0	0	0	0	1	0	1	5	3
Salisbury	5	1	1	0	2	0	0	0	X	9	11	2

Comellas (winner), Desrosier (loser)
Bergen (2), Guerra, Quimby (2), Leip (2), Comellas—RBI; Lynn—2B; Luzansky, Guerra—SB

Behind Comellas's five-hit pitching performance, the Indians shook off a bad outing the night before and collected 11 hits in the 9–1 victory over the Cardinals. The Indian bats chased Cambridge starting pitcher Norbert Desrosier[26] off the mound in the first inning and continued with his replacement, Michael Koons. During the game, there were two sensational fielding performances. The first one came from Luzansky, who made a leaping catch against the center field warehouse that robbed a Cardinal batter of a two-base hit. The second one was when Quimby, who was positioned at first base, raced back to the fence to catch a foul fly.

Salisbury 17, Dover 4   (14–30) (35–9)   July 11

Salisbury	0	4	0	1	1	5	3	3	0	17	22	2
Dover	1	0	0	0	0	2	1	0	0	4	9	0

Montero (winner), Wittig (loser)
Reznichak (2), Montero (3), Lynn (2), Leip (3), Luzansky (4), Trechock (2), Thomas—RBI; Montero, Lynn, Trechock, Leip—2B; Montero, Leip—3B; Reznichak, Luzansky (2)—HR; Bergen (2), Trechock—SB

The Salisbury Indians journeyed to the Blue Hen State capital and showcased a 22-hit exhibition that wilted three Orioles pitchers in a 17-4 blowout. Starting pitcher Wittig was sent to the showers in the second inning after allowing six hits. His replacement, James Toland, was driven off the mound after yielding 11 hits in 4⅔ innings, and Thomas Taylor finished the game by allowing five hits and six runs. The Indians started their scoring barrage in the second inning when the first man up, Reznichak, walloped the first pitch over the fence. They added three more runs in the inning. Guerra and Quimby singled and Montero[27] doubled them in. Lynn then doubled in Montero. In the fourth inning, Montero started the inning with a triple and scored on Lynn's groundout to shortstop. In the next inning, Guerra scored on Leip's triple. In the sixth inning, the Indians put up a five-spot. Lynn singled

Four—The Climb (June 19–July 31)

and Luzansky hit a two-run home run. After that, Bergen singled and scored on Trechock's double and Reznichak worked a walk. Trechock and Reznichak came around to score on a two-base hit by Leip. In the seventh, the Indians added three more runs on three singles by Lynn, Bergen and Trechock and a hit by pitch taken by Luzansky. The eighth inning had Luzansky smash a three-run homer, his second of the game. Luzansky, Salisbury's diminutive center fielder, had two hits, both home runs. Bergen had four hits and stole two bases. Guerra enjoyed a three-for-four game and Lynn, Trechock and Juan Montero, the new Indian pitcher from Cuba, each went three for five.

Dover began their scoring in the first inning when center fielder Marnie scored on shortstop Vandegrift's fielder's choice. In the sixth inning, catcher Richard Hutchison[28] belted a two-run base hit that allowed second baseman Roetz and left fielder Weatherlow to score. In the next inning, Marnie hit a solo home run to finish Dover's tallies.

Fans at Gordy Park also witnessed several outstanding defensive plays. Luzansky robbed an Oriole batter of a two-base hit with a leaping

In 1937, the Salisbury Indians' pitching staff racked up an impressive 2.07 ERA. Five of the Indians pitchers gathered for a group photograph: (from left) Jorge Comellas (22–1 1.31), Leon Revolinsky (13–2 3.27), Juan Montero (7–2 2.56), Joe Kohlman (25–1 1.19) and John Bassler (10–10 2.46) (courtesy Eastern Shore Baseball Hall of Fame Museum).

Miracle on the Eastern Shore

catch against the center field warehouse. Quimby, running like a deer, chased down a foul ball along the first baseline.

Montero, who was sent down from the Trenton Senators, made his pitching debut on the Eastern Shore and pitched a nine-hit game with six strikeouts and six walks. He never really had to bear down. Most of the Orioles' hits came in the late innings. Montero was the third Cuban signed by Joe Cambria to appear on the Salisbury roster.

Salisbury 9, Easton 1   (15–30) (36–9)   July 12

	1	2	3	4	5	6	7	8	9	R	H	E
Salisbury	0	0	2	0	2	0	0	0	5	9	11	2
Easton	1	0	0	0	0	0	0	0	0	1	5	5

Revolinsky (winner), Radler (loser)
Bergen, Trechock, Reznichak (2), Leip, Luzansky, Guerra—RBI; Reznichak (2)—2B; Luzansky (2), Bergen, Trechock—SB, Quimby

On July 12, a peculiar game was played in Salisbury. Originally scheduled in Easton two weeks earlier but postponed due to rain, it had Easton acting as the home team. The Browns scored their only run in the first inning. Shortstop Weimer walked and advanced to second on second baseman Pultz's sacrifice. Right fielder Beidleman then singled him in. On the mound for the Indians was the speed artist Revolinsky, who pitched a five-hit 9-1 victory, his sixth in seven starts. He also fanned seven batters and managed only three walks.

In the third inning, the Indians set some sort of record with three consecutive players stealing second base after garnering a hit. With two outs, Luzansky laid a bunt down the third baseline and beat the throw. On the next pitch, he stole second base. Bergen singled him in. Bergen, playing left field for the Indians, then stole second and scored on Trechock's single, who in turn stole second base. Reznichak grounded out to end the inning. In the fifth, Lynn walked and Luzansky singled. Reznichak ripped a double that brought in Lynn and Luzansky. In the ninth, errors committed by the Browns allowed the Indians to push over five more runs. Quimby walked and stole second base. He scored on Leip's single. Browns first baseman Vernon committed an error that led to Revolinsky being safe at first base. Next up was Lynn, whose grounder hit the base umpire and allowed him to reach safely. During the play, it looked like Leip had scored but the umpires ruled the ball dead and sent him back to third. With the bases loaded, Luzansky

Four—The Climb (June 19–July 31)

singled Leip and Revolinsky home. Bergen singled and Guerra hit into a fielder's choice that scored Luzansky.

The Browns, in the bottom of the ninth, tried to rally but with one out, the Indians executed a fast around-the-horn double play—Leip to Lynn to Quimby. The fans again witnessed solid defensive plays with Beidleman and Luzansky showcasing their excellent fielding prowess. The Indians also performed a fast double plays when Quimby, manning first base, picked up a hot smash and threw the ball to second, where Leip was covering and immediately returned the ball to Quimby for the infield's most difficult play.

Around the league, the *Morning Call* reported that Robert M. Clarke, sponsor and franchise holder of the Crisfield Crabbers, released catcher Dan Pasquella from the team. Pasquella was credited with reviving the Eastern Shore League as well as managing the team for the first four games of the season. It was unclear why he was released.

Salisbury 10, Pocomoke 5   (16–30) (37–9)   July 13

Salisbury	2	0	0	2	0	2	0	0	4	10	15	1
Pocomoke	2	2	0	0	0	0	0	0	1	5	9	1

Kohlman (winner), Harris (loser)
Lynn, Reznichak (2), Quimby (2), Kohlman, Trechock, Guerra (3)—RBI; Luzansky (2), Kohlman (2)—2B; Lynn, Quimby, Reznichak, Guerra—HR

The Indians' next game was against the Pocomoke City Red Sox in Worcester City. Along with his crafty pitching, Kohlman used his bat to win his 12th consecutive victory. During the 10-5 win, he went three for four with two doubles. Kohlman struck out nine but walked a season-high six batters.

Lynn started the game with his third lead-off home run of the season. Luzansky hit a double and Trechock drew a walk. Reznichak hit into a fielder's choice allowing Luzansky to score. In the bottom half of the initial frame, Pocomoke City evened up the score when Red Sox second baseman Emlyn Jones[29] walked. Third baseman Art Rosen[30] doubled and right fielder Jester hit a long fly to center. Tagging up, Jones scampered home. Rosen darted home when Luzansky threw wildly. In the second inning, the Worcester County team added two more runs on a single by first baseman Tom Daddino.[31] Left fielder John Halychik[32] followed that up with a home run. In the fourth inning, the Indians

Miracle on the Eastern Shore

mimicked the Red Sox when Reznichak hit a single and Quimby homered. After that, Kohlman blasted a two-bagger but was left stranded. In the sixth, Reznichak lifted a shot out of the park. Leip singled and scored on Kohlman's second double of the game. In the ninth, Luzansky doubled and scored on Trechock's single. Reznichak singled and Guerra hit a three-run home run. In the bottom half, Pocomoke added a run when Jones singled, Rosen worked a walk and Jester hit a single. For the game, nine Pocomoke runners were left stranded on the basepaths.

Salisbury 9, Pocomoke 4 (17–30) (38–9) July 14

Pocomoke	0	0	0	1	2	1	0	0	0	4	5	3
Salisbury	2	3	0	0	2	2	0	0	X	9	11	6

Comellas (winner), Messick (loser)
Luzansky (2), Trechock, Lynn, Bergen, Thomas, Reznichak, Comellas (2)—RBI; Reznichak, Comellas—2B; Luzansky, Bergen—3B

Comellas was not his normal self when the Pocomoke City team visited Gordy Park but he managed to sneak out his 13th consecutive victory. A "comedy of errors," one staff writer noted; Salisbury outhit and out-errored their opponent with 11 hits to five hits and six errors to three errors.[33] Comellas managed just four strikeouts while walking four batters. Both Comellas and Quimby committed two errors and Leip and Thomas had one apiece. On the Red Sox side, catcher Thomas Dousha committed two errors and pitcher Ray Humphreys made one.[34]

Salisbury started the scoring in the first inning when Lynn singled and Luzansky drove him in on a hard clout to right center. Luzansky sprinted home when center fielder Dugan made a beautiful stab and grab on Trechock's screamer to right center.

In the second inning, Quimby singled and Leip walked. Comellas placed down a bunt and was safe at first on Humphreys's error. With the bases loaded, Lynn hit into a fielder's choice that forced Comellas out at second while Quimby scored. Luzansky lifted a long flyout to center that allowed Leip to score. Bergen tripled, allowing Lynn to score. In the fourth inning, Leip injured himself and Guerra came in to replace him at third base. In the fifth, Reznichak doubled and Guerra walked. Comellas helped his cause when he doubled both of them in. In the sixth inning, the Indians tallied twice on singles by Luzansky and Bergen and walks to Trechock and Reznichak, the latter of which forced

Four—The Climb (June 19–July 31)

in Luzansky. The next batter up, Thomas, hit into a fielder's choice that allowed Bergen to score.

Pocomoke City got on the board in the fourth on singles hit by left fielder Halychik and right fielder Jester and three Indian errors, one by Leip and two by Quimby. In the next frame, they added two more runs on singles by catcher Dousha and relief pitcher Gray, a walk to second baseman Jones, a wild pitch and an error. In the sixth, Pocomoke shortstop Schluter scored on a three-base error by Comellas. Defensively, Dugan snagged two hits destined for extra bases from his center field perch.

Crisfield 7, Salisbury 5   July 15

Crisfield	0	2	2	0	0	0	0	3	0	7	9	3
Salisbury	0	1	1	0	1	0	0	0	2	5	10	5

[Protested Game—No Qualified Record]

On July 15, an advertisement appeared in the *Daily Times* welcoming the newest arrival to the Indians' bullpen: "Montero, the new Cuban pitcher, will toss them against the Crabbers tonight. Come out and see the boy who can't speak English but can do his talking with a baseball."[35] The 22-year-old Cuban was sent to Salisbury from the Trenton Senators, where he had a win/loss record of five to four. Unfortunately, Juan Montero and his relief, Leon Revolinsky, had a hard time finding the plate at crucial moments in a 7–5 defeat to the Crabbers.

In the first inning, Montero walked Crabbers center fielder Webb on four straight pitches. Webb took second on Montero's wild pitch. Second baseman Tony Hudson[36] walked on four straight pitches. Shortstop Joseph Reha bunted safely for a base hit. Right fielder Joseph Millar[37] grounded to Montero, who threw the ball to Thomas at home plate to force out Webb and Thomas pivoted and rifled the ball to first baseman Quimby to double off Millar. Montero retired the side when Crabbers first baseman Gilmartin popped out to him.

The Crabbers came back in the second inning and scored two runs. Left fielder Nathaniel Riggin drew a walk and advanced to third on catcher Roy Myers's single and Reznichak's error.[38] Riggin scored on Barnes's base hit bunt. Montero issued another walk, his fourth, to Webb to load the bases. Myers scored on a fielder's choice by Hudson. Millar grounded out to end the inning.

The Indians got on the scoreboard in the bottom half of the second inning with a moon shot onto the factory roof by Reznichak.

Miracle on the Eastern Shore

Crisfield chalked up two more runs in the third. Montero walked Gilmartin and Riggin. Marnie bunted safely and Gilmartin scored on Montero's error. Flowers had seen enough and sent in Revolinsky in relief, who struck out Myers. Riggin was forced out on Barnes's fielder's choice. Webb drew a walk and Hudson singled to right field, scoring Marnie. During the play, Barnes, while rounding third, missed the base and was called out, which ended the inning. The Crisfield Crabbers argued the call and the game was continued under protest.

In the bottom half of the third inning, Bergen and Trechock singled. Reznichak was intentionally walked. Bergen scored when Guerra grounded out. The next inning had the Crabbers halting an Indian rally with a quick double play, Reha to Hudson to Gilmartin. In the fifth inning, Bergen singled and stole second base. Myers, the Crisfield catcher, made a bad throw that allowed Bergen to come around and score.

In the eighth inning, the Crabbers scored three more runs. Revolinsky plunked Reha with a pitch, and he advanced to second on Millar's grounder. Gilmartin hit a single to bring Reha in. Riggin singled. A single by Marnie scored Riggin and Gilmartin.

In the ninth inning, Quimby singled but was forced out at second on Thomas's fielder's choice. Revolinsky drew a walk and Lynn singled Thomas in. Revolinsky stole third base. Dallas Rife[39] was sent in to relieve Barnes and struck out Bergen. Trechock drew a walk that forced in Revolinsky. With the bases loaded, Reznichak came up to bat. Rife fired an inside pitch that hit Reznichak's bat as he fell away and rolled harmlessly down the first baseline for an easy out, which unceremoniously ended the game.

Crisfield 3, Salisbury 1   (17–31) (38–10)   July 16

Salisbury	0	0	0	1	0	0	0	0	0	1	8	1
Crisfield	1	2	0	0	0	0	0	0	0	3	7	1

Bassler (loser), Rife (winner)
Quimby—RBI; Luzansky—2B; Quimby—SB

Before the July 16 game, Crisfield Crabbers president J.C.W. Tawes let loose a gang of "jimmy" crabs on the Crisfield ball field while the Indians took batting practice in an attempt to shake the Indians' confidence. The trick seemed to work as it unnerved the Indians enough to lead to a 3–1 loss to their Somerset County host.

It was Bassler's time on the mound and he pitched another winning

Four—The Climb (June 19–July 31)

contest, tossing a seven-hitter. Unfortunately, the Indians' bats were left silent by the Crisfield hurler, Rife, who scattered eight hits.

In the first inning, Lynn booted center fielder Webb's hot smash. Webb advanced to second base on second baseman Hudson's grounder and scored when shortstop Reha hit a single to center field. In the second inning, left fielder Riggin drove a ground-rule double that bounced over the left field barrier. He moved to third on third baseman Marnie's fielder's choice and scored on catcher Myers's single. Myers advanced to third base on Rife's ground-rule double in the same area as Riggin's shot. The Crabbers put on a squeeze play but Webb failed to bunt and Myers was tagged out at home plate. Webb brought in Rife with a base hit. In the fourth inning, the Indians scored their lone run on successive singles by Trechock, Guerra and Quimby.

After the third inning, the contest became an old-fashioned pitchers' duel. Rife stranded nine Indians on the basepath. Rife's teammates were spectacular behind him. The fielding of Webb and Reha was extremely tight. Crabber left fielder Riggin had a sensational one-handed catch when he sprinted 65 yards to the first baseline to rob Bassler of a certain double.

Salisbury 11, Centreville 3 (18–31) (39–10) July 17

Salisbury	2	1	2	5	1	0	0	0	0	11	12	4
Centreville	0	1	1	0	0	1	0	0	0	3	11	5

Kohlman (winner), List (loser)
Luzansky—2B; Reznichak—3B; Lynn—HR; Reznichak, Luzansky, Guerra—SB

In the afternoon game of a doubleheader with the Centreville Colts, the Indians exploded for 11 runs on 12 hits while Kohlman earned his 13th consecutive victory. He struck out seven and walked only one. The Indians' relentless hitting sent Centreville's bespectacled starting pitcher, Robert List,[40] to the showers in the fourth inning after the Indians collected seven hits, including a double by Luzansky. List's replacement, Smyth, kept the Indians in check, allowing just five hits.

In the initial stanza, Lynn and Luzansky started it off with consecutive singles. Guerra grounded out to shortstop Feinberg and Lynn scored on Trechock's flyout to left field. Reznichak and Quimby were issued walks. The latter pushed Luzansky across home plate. Thomas popped out to third baseman Miller to end the inning. In the next inning, Leip

Miracle on the Eastern Shore

walked and scored on Luzansky's base hit. The Indians scored two more runs in the third inning. Trechock and Reznichak singled and advanced on Quimby's groundout to shortstop. Trechock scored when he tagged up on Thomas's deep flyout to left field. A base hit by Leip brought home Reznichak. Kohlman struck out to end the third. The Indians racked up five tallies in the fourth inning. Lynn reached safely on an error by second baseman Troy. Luzansky hit into a botched fielder's choice with all runners being safe. Lynn scored on Guerra's single. Trechock walked and Reznichak smashed a triple that cleared the bases. Quimby drove in Reznichak with a base hit to finish the scoring for the inning. In the fifth, Lynn hit a home run to tally the 11th and final run for the Indians.

Centreville got on the board in the second inning when shortstop Feinberg led off with a double and scored on a single by right fielder Rist. In the next inning, left fielder Pitko blasted a moon shot over the right field fence. Their third run came in the sixth inning when third baseman Miller reached safely on a fielder's choice and scored on Smyth's single.

Centreville 4, Salisbury 2   (18–32) (39–11)   July 17

Salisbury	0	0	0	0	2	0	0	2	2	0
Centreville	0	3	0	1	0	0	X	4	7	0

Montero (loser), Gross (winner)
Leip—RBI; Leip—3B; Luzansky—SB

The evening game of the doubleheader with the Centreville Colts went differently from the afternoon contest. The Indian bats were muzzled by Centreville hurler Lloyd Gross, who pitched a two-hit, two-run game. The only scoring occurred in the fifth inning for the Indians. Buck Elliott, who just returned from a stint with the Trenton Senators, singled and scored on Leip's scorching triple. Leip scored on the throw-in after Lynn flied out to left field. The Colts crossed the plate three times in the second inning on doubles by catcher Rip Shillingford, second baseman Charles Knapp and center fielder Carroll with a walk to Gross sandwiched in.[41] Montero was knocked out after the fifth inning when he offered up hits to Colts first baseman Wurst, Knapp and Carroll. Revolinsky finished the game giving up just one hit.

Around the town, Indians fans started to voice their displeasure regarding Montero's pitching woes. To quell their concerns, Fred Thomas came to Montero's defense: "All Montero needs is a good rest.

Four—The Climb (June 19–July 31)

They worked him hard at Trenton after he had pitched all winter in Cuba. That's enough to lose any control. In a few weeks, he'll be in form."[42]

Salisbury 10, Pocomoke 1   (19–32) (40–11)   July 18

Salisbury	2	0	2	5	0	0	0	1	0	10	18	2
Pocomoke	0	0	0	1	0	0	0	0	0	1	5	0

Comellas (winner), Scarbinsky (loser)
Trechock (5), Quimby (2), Guerra (2), Reznichak—RBI;
Lynn, Trechock, Elliott—2B; Trechock, Reznichak—HR;
Leip, Lynn—SB

On July 18, the Salisbury Indians traveled to Pocomoke City and trounced the Red Sox 10 to 1. Red Sox relief pitcher Joe Scarbinsky[43] robbed Comellas of his first shutout of the season. In the fourth inning, he drove the ball over the fence for Pocomoke City's lone run. The Indians scored two runs in both the first and third innings. In the initial frame, Lynn started the game with a two-base hit. He advanced to second on Luzansky's groundout to first base. After Trechock's flyout to left field, Reznichak worked a walk. Guerra singled and Quimby drove in Lynn and Reznichak with a base hit. In the third, Lynn and Luzansky opened the inning with consecutive singles. Trechock singled in Lynn and, after Reznichak popped out to Red Sox catcher Dousha, Guerra hit into a fielder's choice that allowed Luzansky to score.

In the fourth inning, the Indians put together a five-run rally. With two outs, Comellas hit a single. Lynn followed with another base hit and Luzansky walked to load the bases. Trechock then blasted a grand slam, his 15th home run of the season, becoming the first Eastern Shore League player to hit a grand slam in the 1937 season. Reznichak then stepped into the batter's box and launched a solo home run. Guerra singled and Quimby struck out to end the inning. The Indians tallied one more in the eighth when Trechock was issued a base on balls and scored on a fielder's choice hit by Guerra.

The game was delayed in the first inning when a ball took a bad hop in left field and injured Halychik's eye. For the game, Salisbury was down a man on their bench. After playing 10 games, James Bergen "jumped" his contract with the team. He left after the protested game against the Crisfield Crabbers on July 15. He later played for the Trenton Senators (NYPL) during the 1937 season. Bergen batted .404 with three RBI, one double and one triple.

Miracle on the Eastern Shore

Salisbury 2, Easton 1 (20–32) (41–11) July 21

Easton	1	0	0	0	0	0	0	0	0	1	4	3
Salisbury	0	0	0	0	0	1	0	0	1	2	7	2

Kohlman (winner), Zarowsky (loser)
Quimby—RBI; Trechock—2B; Reznichak, Leip—SB

On July 21, Joe Kohlman performed a feat that had not occurred so far that season in the Class D Eastern Shore League. While pitching a four-hitter, where two hits were flukes, and striking out 11 batters, he did not issue a walk in a nine-inning game. In a 2–1 defeat, Easton pitcher William Zarowsky[44] had an above-average day scattering the Indians' seven hits.

Easton started the scoring in the first inning when Zimmerman was safe on an infield dribbler. Stiles doubled to left and Zimmerman scored on Beidleman's grounder to first baseman Frank Deutsch,[45] a new recruit trying out with the Salisbury baseball club.

The Allentown, Pennsylvania, native was discovered on July 17 while his team, the Easton Fleas, battled the East Greenville Tigers. Scouts for the Washington Senators were at the Eastern Pennsylvania League contest to look over several East Greenville players. The 22-year-old Deutsch impressed them so much that they offered him a contract, which he signed. After a short stint with the Baltimore Orioles (IL), he was sent to Salisbury.

In the second inning, Salisbury's scoring opportunity fell short. Guerra skied a fly ball that Stiles dropped, allowing Guerra to end up at second base. Deutsch got hit by a pitch. With Quimby at bat, Flowers stepped out of the bullpen and flashed the "hit-and-run" sign but Quimby lifted a weak infield fly and Guerra was doubled off at second base.

In the third inning, the Indians collected a hit but nothing came of it. In the fourth inning, the Indians stranded the bases full. Quimby started with a groundout. Leip, after drawing a walk, stole second base while Kohlman struck out. Lynn and Luzansky both worked a walk to load the bases. Trechock ended the inning by grounding out.

In the sixth inning, the Indians finally evened the score. Reznichak walked and Guerra sacrificed him over to second base. After Deutsch grounded out, which allowed Reznichak to move to third, Quimby drove a two-bagger to deep center that scored Reznichak.

In the seventh inning, the Browns robbed the Indians of a run with a pretty piece of fielding. After Kohlman hit safely, Lynn attempted to

Four—The Climb (June 19–July 31)

sacrifice Kohlman over. Instead, while Lynn was trying to bunt, the ball popped up five feet from home plate and five feet high in the air. The Easton catcher, Weimer, dived out and caught the ball before it touched the ground. Luzansky struck out, Trechock connected with a two-base hit and Reznichak flied out to left field.

In the eighth inning, the Indians returned the favor with their own smart fielding to keep the game tied. Eck hit a single and took second base on Reznichak's throwing error. Weimer placed down a sacrifice bunt to move Eck over to third and was safe at first on Guerra's throwing error. Zarowsky was next up and hit a hot shot to shortstop. Trechock snared the grounder and instead of starting a routine double play, he threw the ball to the plate and Guerra tagged Eck out. Zimmerman and Stiles struck out to end the inning.

In the ninth inning with two outs, Lynn hit a grounder to shortstop. Zimmerman overthrew first base, which led to Lynn advancing to second. Trechock hit a shot to third. Eck gathered the ball but threw it

The Indians' infield (from left): Jerry Lynn (2B), Frank Trechock (SS), Frank Deutsch (1B) and Ed Leip (3B) (courtesy Eastern Shore Baseball Hall of Fame Museum).

Miracle on the Eastern Shore

into the ground at first, which allowed Lynn to score the game-winning run.

On this day, the *Daily Times* reported that Joseph Reznichak and his wife, Joann, agreed to housesit for the Salisbury mayor Truitt while the mayor and his wife embarked on a European tour with plans to return home by August 22.

Before the season, young men approached their employers to receive a leave of absence so they could have the opportunity to try out for a professional baseball club in hopes that they could live out their dreams as a professional baseball player. A few players had spouses who traveled with them. One such player, Thaddeus "Doc" Cash, tried out to be the Indians' third baseman. The story has it, while at Salisbury, he and his wife, Dorothy, lived on the cheapest food on the peninsula—a pound of shrimp a week.

Salisbury 2, Federalsburg 0 (21–32) (42–11) July 22

Salisbury	1	0	0	0	0	0	1	0	0	2	6	0
Federalsburg	0	0	0	0	0	0	0	0	0	0	5	0

Bassler (winner), Ratterree (loser)
Trechock—RBI; Lynn, Trechock—2B; Luzansky—SB

Bassler shook off his jinx and pitched a five-hit 2-0 shutout in the Federalsburg Athletics ballpark. Both teams played errorless ball. The Indians scored in the first inning on two doubles by Lynn and Trechock. The second run came in the seventh inning when Deutsch singled and moved to second on Quimby's walk. He scored when A's catcher Short allowed one of Ratterree's fastballs to get past him. The rest of the game was a pitchers' duel with Bassler striking out five batters by mixing speed with curves. Ratterree pitched a six-hit game, striking out eight Indians.

Lynn displayed his excellent fielding prowess when he sprinted to his right to snag A's second baseman Choc Millman's[46] hot shot right up the middle. After making a backhand stop, he wheeled around and rifled the ball to Deutsch to gun down Millman. Deutsch, the Allentown native first baseman, saved Guerra from an error. A's third baseman Manczak hit a slow roller down the third baseline. Guerra, from behind the plate, sprang up and gathered the ball and threw off-balance. Deutsch went down in the dirt to block the throw and retired Manczak. Deutsch made another stop when A's center fielder LeGates drove a

Four—The Climb (June 19–July 31)

smash down the first baseline. He knocked it down and beat the runner to the bag. In the outfield, Quimby sprinted parallel to the left field fence to snag a liner and Luzansky collided into the center field fence when catching A's right fielder Boyce's long drive.

Since the forfeiture of their wins, the Salisbury Indians had been on a blistering pace with a record of 20–6, almost identical to the first 26 games of the season. Along with their success on the field, the team was having fun off it. While traveling to Federalsburg, several players played a practical joke on their skipper. Flowers dozed off on the bus and they snuck up and gave him a hot foot.

Sometime after July 22, the team bus, which had a lot of miles on it, became inoperable. Clifford H. Duffy, the local taxi cab proprietor, lent his fleet of cabs to the team to travel to the other towns in the loop. To get to the games, five or six players would cram into a cab.

Over the weekend, it was reported that several of Joe Cambria's scouts signed a first baseman from the Hamilton Watch Ten softball team to a contract to try out for the Salisbury Indians. Paul "Peepie" Martin was playing a night game in Baltimore when several scouts noticed his "good brand of ball playing."[47] After the game, the scouts approached him and asked if he ever played baseball. Martin replied that he had some years ago. They inquired if he would like to try out and presented him with a contract to sign. Since late June, the scouts had been searching for Bob Brady's replacement at first base.

From around the league, news came out that after a Cambridge-Centreville game during which umpire Carrington made a ruling that the fans disliked, his automobile mysteriously had three flat tires. On that day, the *Daily Times* began a column entitled "Tribal Trends," which focused on the exploits of the Salisbury Indians.

Salisbury 11, Federalsburg 3   (22–32) (43–11)   July 23

Federalsburg	1	0	0	0	0	2	0	0	3	11	3
Salisbury	6	1	0	0	1	0	1	2	X	11	12	1

Comellas (winner), Zschau (loser)
Trechock, Quimby, Thomas (3), Luzansky (2), Lynn, Leip—RBI;
   Trechock, Leip—2B; Trechock, Quimby, Leip (2)—SB

On July 23, the Salisbury Indians hosted the Federalsburg Athletics and, with a slight advantage in the hits column—12 to 11—they came out victorious, 11 to 3. George Comellas won his 15th consecutive victory, striking out 13 batters and issuing only one base on balls. The Indians started fast with a six-spot in the first inning. Lynn singled and was brought in by a two-base hit by Trechock. Luzansky advanced to third base on Trechock's double and scored on Quimby's single. Trechock advanced to third on the base hit. With Leip at the plate, Trechock took his lead off third base and danced back and forth along the line. As he extended his lead, he took off for home, and scored before A's pitcher Zeke Zschau[48] could complete his delivery. This was the first time this season that a base runner stole home at Gordy Park. During the play, Quimby stole third base. After Leip walked, Thomas's single brought Quimby home and Leip took advantage to score on the same play when Feds catcher Short mishandled shortstop Michael Milici's[49] throw to home plate. Comellas and Lynn drew walks to load the bases. Luzansky worked a walk to force in Thomas. Trechock grounded out to end the inning.

In the second, the Indians scored their seventh run on two errors and a single. They scored another run in both the fifth and seventh innings. In the eighth inning, they tallied two more runs.

Federalsburg scored in the first inning on two singles and a sacrifice. In the seventh, they manufactured two more runs on two Texas Leaguers, a stolen base and a double to left field by Feds center fielder LeGates.

Salisbury 10, Centreville 3   (23–32) (44–11)   July 24

Centreville	3	0	0	0	0	0	0	0	3	X	X
Salisbury	3	2	3	0	0	2	0	0 X	10	X	X

[Box score not found]
Kohlman (winner), Lomas (loser)

July 24 was designated Father and Son Night at Gordy Park with any boy under 15 years old able to enter the ballpark free of charge when accompanied by his father.

Suffering from an upset stomach, Leon Revolinsky allowed three runs in the first inning on two singles, two hit batters and two walks. He left the game in the second inning after Colts second baseman Knapp singled, center fielder Carroll flied out and left fielder Pitko doubled. Kohlman replaced him and struck out shortstop Feinberg and forced right fielder Rist to ground out. Kohlman finished the last 7⅔ innings game, allowing only three hits.

Four—The Climb (June 19–July 31)

The Indians got on the scoreboard in the bottom half of the first inning. Lynn drew a walk and advanced to second on Luzansky's single. Trechock hit a liner to center that scored Lynn. Reznichak doubled to right, bringing in Luzansky and Trechock. Following that, Harold Lomas,[50] the Colts' starting pitcher, was replaced by Ogden.

In the second, the Indians added two runs on singles by Kohlman and Lynn, a passed ball and a fielder's choice. In the third, Deutsch launched a three-run blast over the left field fence, scoring Guerra and Quimby. In the sixth, the Indians put across two more runs on a walk and two singles.

On the injury front, Ed Leip was still nursing his bad leg. Diagnosed as a charley horse, he suffered the injury sometime around a month ago.

Salisbury 7, Centreville 0   (24–32) (45–11)   July 27

Centreville	0	0	0	0	0	0	0	0	5 1
Salisbury	2	0	4	0	0	1	X	7	7 1

Montero (winner), Smyth (loser)
Guerra (2), Trechock, Quimby (2), Leip—RBI;
   Guerra—3B; Trechock—HR; Leip, Trechock—Sac

The next day the Indians played a twin bill against the Centreville Colts. Juan Montero, the Indians' Cuban "fireball artist," dominated the afternoon game, shutting out the visitors 7 to 0 by holding the Colts to only five hits. He struck out three but displayed wildness with seven walks. The Colts almost took the shutout away from Montero with a late rally in their half of the seventh inning. With the bases loaded and one out, the game was paused for one hour due to the darkness, then Rist hit a slow dribbler back to Montero, who flipped the ball to Guerra for a force-out at home plate. Guerra quickly pivoted and delivered a bullet to first baseman Deutsch for a 1–2–3 double play, ending the game.

The Indians' scoring began in the first inning with two outs. Trechock singled and moved to second base when Reznichak was hit by a pitch. Guerra drove a shot to deep right field for a triple, scoring Trechock and Reznichak. In the third, Trechock smashed his 16th home run of the season. The ball landed on the factory roof in left center. Centreville hurler Buck Smyth lost the strike zone and walked three consecutive batters (Reznichak, Guerra and Deutsch). Harold Lomas, his relief, gave up a two-RBI single to Quimby. Another run came when Leip hit into an infield double play, which allowed Deutsch, who was at third

Miracle on the Eastern Shore

base, to hustle down the third baseline and cross home plate before the third out was registered. In the sixth, the Indians added their final run with a walk, single and error.

Salisbury 7, Centreville 2   (25–32) (46–11)   July 27

Centreville	1	1	0	0	0	2	6	2
Salisbury	0	2	0	0	5	7	5	0

Bassler (winner), List (loser)
Leip, Reznichak, Thomas—RBI; Quimby (2)—SB

For the nightcap, the Salisbury Indians defeated the Centreville Colts by a 7-2 score in a rain-soaked shortened contest. The Colts scored a run in the first two innings. The Indians evened up the score 2–2 in the bottom of the second with two consecutive hits. Five more runs were added in the fifth by the Indians on a pair of singles. Bassler, the victor for the Indians, struck out four and walked four while pitching a six-hit game. In the bottom half of the sixth inning, the game was called when a heavy shower soaked the diamond.

Centreville 9, Salisbury 4   (25–33) (46–12)   July 28

Salisbury	0	0	0	0	3	1	0	0	0	4	4	2
Centreville	0	2	4	0	0	1	2	0	X	9	12	0

Revolinsky (loser), Ogden (winner)
Luzansky (2), Reznichak, Bassler—RBI; Lynn, Thomas—2B; Luzansky—3B; Luzansky—SB

The Centreville Colts had their revenge after losing two straight games against the Salisbury team. Colts pitcher Tom Ogden held the Indians to four hits, all in the fifth and sixth innings. He struck out four and issued four walks. The Colts' defense was flawless. Offensively, the Colts' bats came alive against two Indian pitchers, Revolinsky and Bassler. Revolinsky, who started the game, lasted only 2⅓ innings, giving up only three hits but allowing five runs to cross the plate. Revolinsky pitched a scoreless first inning but became wild in the second. He walked Colts right fielder Rist and third baseman Miller. He then hit first baseman Wurst with a pitch to load the bases. Second baseman Knapp drove in the two runners with a two-bagger. In the third, a single by shortstop Feinberg and walks to Rist and catcher Shillingford ended Revolinsky's night. Bassler came in and allowed the fourth run of the

Four—The Climb (June 19–July 31)

inning when Miller greeted him with a two-base hit and Ogden brought Miller in with a single. The Colts lit up Bassler for nine hits. Left fielder Pitko hit a home run in the fifth and the Colts added two more runs in the seventh on Leip's throwing error that went all the way to the center field fence and a single by Wurst.

Trechock had a target on his back during the game. In the fifth inning, he was hit in the arm and was awarded first base. Reznichak hit into a fielder's choice and Trechock advanced to second. Ogden threw a wild pitch so Trechock took off for third base. Shillingford retrieved the ball and rifled it to third in an attempt to peg Trechock out but threw wide and hit Trechock just below the eye. The Indians scored three runs on a double by Lynn and a triple by Luzansky. In the sixth, Thomas doubled to right center and scored on Bassler's line drive up the middle.

The local newspaper christened Luzansky and Lynn the "hustle twins" for their extraordinary play on the field throughout the season. After the game, the Indians moved out of the cellar into seventh place, when the Dover Orioles lost both games of the twin bill against the Cambridge Cardinals.

Before the game, the businessmen of the town of Centreville hosted the first of a series of Booster Days with a semi-serious four-inning ball game between the Good Will Firemen and the Pioneer Pointers. The festivities started around 2 p.m. with the Pointers marching onto the field in overall shorts, bandanna kerchiefs, green straw hats, long underwear and other humorous articles of wardrobe. The Firemen's attire included white knickers and light sweaters of red, blue and yellow with fabric helmets. The Firemen won the game 12 to 7.

Salisbury 21, Cambridge 1   (26–33) (47–12)   July 29

Cambridge	0	0	0	0	0	0	0	1	0	1	7	7
Salisbury	5	1	1	0	0	5	1	8	X	21	24	1

Comellas (winner), Koons (loser)
Trechock (3), Guerra (2), Deutsch (4), Reznichak, Comellas, Leip—RBI; Lynn (2), Luzansky—2B; Trechock—3B; Trechock—HR; Deutsch, Leip—SB

A sports reporter declared the July 29 game against the Cambridge Cardinals "a slugfest to end all slugfests." The Salisbury Indians collected 24 hits, a new league record, along with scoring 21 runs.

Miracle on the Eastern Shore

The Cambridge starting pitcher, Michael Koons, did not last an inning. His replacement, David Tomlinson,[51] reached near exhaustion from the pounding he absorbed and required assistance when leaving the field at the end of the eighth.

The Indians began the scoring in the first inning when the first five men hit consecutive singles (Lynn, Luzansky, Reznichak, Trechock and Guerra). They added another single along with two Cardinal errors and a wild pitch that allowed five runs to cross home plate. In the second inning, Trechock dented the center field factory roof with his 17th home run. In the third, the Indians added another run on two hits, a walk and an error. In the sixth inning, the Indians piled on with five more runs on three singles, doubles by Lynn and Luzansky, a triple by Trechock and a Cardinal error. In the eighth inning, the Indians added eight more runs on seven hits and a double steal.

Salisbury's Cuban mound man, Comellas, lost his bid for a shutout in the eighth when with one out Cards first baseman Iwanicki, who went three for four, hit a single, left fielder Johnson worked a walk and third baseman Frank Gunkel[52] connected for a base hit to load the bases. During the next at-bat, the Cardinals put on a hit and run. Right fielder Austin O'Donnell[53] hit a smash to Leip, who stepped on third base to force Johnson out. Leip wheeled and threw a bullet to Deutsch at first base but the throw was short and wide. Deutsch, being off the bag, swiped at O'Donnell. While applying the tag, Deutsch blocked O'Connor, the umpire covering first base, who was unable to see the play clearly and called him safe. During the play, Iwanicki scampered home and scored. After the game, a reporter asked Deutsch about the play and he answered honestly that he missed the runner by several inches and he was safe.

Comellas allowed seven hits, struck out 13 batters and walked five. Frank Trechock went five for six with a home run and triple, driving in three runs and scoring four runs himself. Deutsch went four for six with four RBI. Luzansky went four for six with a triple and three RBI and Lynn three for five with two doubles and four runs scored. Leip exhibited superb fielding while dealing with a sore leg, handling several hard-hit infield grounders. Luzansky made an outstanding running catch in center. Cardinal center fielder Jackson robbed Deutsch of a double with a catch against the factory wall.

Four—The Climb (June 19–July 31)

Salisbury 2, Cambridge 0   (27–33) (48–12)   July 30

| Salisbury | 0 | 1 | 0 | 0 | 0 | 0 | 1 | 0 | 0 | 2 | 7 | 1 |
| Cambridge | 0 | 0 | 0 | 0 | 0 | 0 | 0 | 0 | 0 | 0 | 2 | 1 |

Kohlman (winner), Raffensberger (loser)
Quimby, Kohlman—RBI; Kohlman—2B; Lynn—SB

After scoring 21 runs against the Cambridge Cardinals the night before, the Indians could register only two runs against the Dorchester County team. Fortunately for them, Joe Kohlman was on the hill and continued his brilliant pitching with a two-hit 2–0 shutout. He struck out nine batters and walked two. He pitched a no-hitter until the seventh inning, when he issued a base on balls to Iwanicki. Next up, Johnson hit a slow roller to Kohlman. Kohlman fielded the ball and began to wheel toward second but Iwanicki had nearly reached second so Kohlman quickly turned toward first base so he could nab Johnson hustling down the basepath. Unfortunately, Deutsch had drifted off the base to watch the play at second and was not in a position to receive the throw. Kohlman held on to the ball and all runners were safe. Kohlman allowed another hit in the ninth.

The Indians got on the scoreboard in the second inning. Reznichak struck out. Guerra hit a long fly to deep center field that Jackson dropped and Guerra hustled to third base. Flowers then called for a squeeze play, which completely crossed up the Cardinals. Quimby laid down a perfect bunt that allowed Guerra to score.

The Indians added their second run in the seventh. Quimby and Deutsch singled. Deutsch was picked off at first base during a failed hit and run. Quimby advanced to third. Leip walked and Kohlman drove Raffensberger's first pitch to right center for a two-base hit. Quimby scored and Kohlman was thrown out attempting to stretch the double into a triple.

For the Cardinals, Raffensberger equaled Kohlman's performance by allowing only seven hits, striking out seven and walking two. Defensively, Luzansky had one of his busy nights in center field. He made three nice catches while battling the shadows on the field.

During the day, it was reported that there would be a managerial change for the Dover Orioles. Their manager, Ed Roeltz, was recalled up to the Baltimore Orioles. While there, he was expected to be a pinch hitter and reserve infielder. E.A. "Jiggs" Donahue,[54] who managed the Dover ball club during the old loop, took the helm as skipper.

Miracle on the Eastern Shore

Salisbury 15, Federalsburg 0   (28–33) (49–12)   July 31

Federalsburg	0	0	0	0	0	0	0	0	0	0	6	9
Salisbury	2	2	1	0	3	0	2	5	X	15	13	0

Montero (winner), Hudson (loser)
Guerra (6), Reznichak (2), Trechock, Quimby—RBI; Trechock (2), Guerra—2B; Guerra, Leip—SB

The last day of July was again designated Father and Son Night at Gordy Park. Fans witnessed total domination by their local team as the Salisbury Indians defeated the Federalsburg Athletics 15 to 0.

Montero, who shut out the Centreville Colts 7 to 0 on July 27, pitched a six-hit shutout where he struck out four and walked one. The A's had two opportunities to rob Montero of a shutout. In the sixth inning, the A's left two men on the basepaths, and in the ninth inning, they stranded one runner on third base. Trechock and Lynn exhibited airtight fielding to aid Montero.

The Salisbury batters collected 13 hits and, aided by nine Federalsburg errors, accumulated 15 runs. They scored in every inning except for the fourth and sixth. Guerra had a special game, going three for five and driving in six runs. Also, Reznichak went three for five with two runs batted in.

At the end of July, the standings stood:

Easton Browns	37–25
Federalsburg Athletics	34–29
Cambridge Cardinals	33–31
Centreville Colts	33–32
Crisfield Crabbers	31–34
Pocomoke City Red Sox	30–34
Salisbury Indians	28–35
Dover Orioles	27–34

After June 19, the Salisbury Indians played a stretch of .750 baseball, compiling a 27–9 record. Comellas (15–0, 147 strikeouts) and Kohlman (15–1, 165 strikeouts) led the league in pitching while Trechock continued to set the pace for sluggers with a .368 batting average and 17 homers. Lynn trailed with a .365 batting average.

Five

Domination on the Diamond (August 1–31)

Crisfield 5, Salisbury 1   (28–34) (49–13)   August 1

Salisbury	0	0	0	0	1	0	0	0	0	1	6	3
Crisfield	0	1	0	0	2	1	0	1	X	5	11	1

Bassler (loser), Rife (winner)
Reznichak—RBI; Reznichak—2B; Bassler—SB

    The start of the month of August had another showdown between Bassler and Rife. The first contest went to Rife with a score of 3 to 1. This time Rife led the Crabbers to a 5-1 victory over the Indians. Although Bassler scattered 11 hits, timely hitting, coupled with a few close decisions that went against the Indians, amassed five runs. Rife pitched a six-hit game, striking out five and walking four. He hunkered down when he needed to, stranding 10 Indians on the basepaths. The Indians scored their only run in the fifth inning. Bassler and Lynn hit consecutive singles. After Luzansky flied out to third, Trechock grounded to second, forcing out Lynn and advancing Bassler to third. Reznichak smashed a line drive to center field that scored Bassler. Guerra flied out to end the inning.
    The Crisfield ball club was recently experiencing what would be called little injury jinxes. Not so long ago, the Crabbers were only one game out of first place before things began to go south. Since mid–July, catcher Myers suffered a broken nose and a split finger, first baseman Gilmartin was out with strained leg muscles, second baseman Urban got spiked, left fielder Riggin and utility player Hudson sprained their ankles, right fielder Millar was out for several days with multiple leg injuries and pitcher Buzz Mahrer was out for a time with a sore arm.

Miracle on the Eastern Shore

Salisbury 11, Dover 2   (29–34) (50–13)   August 3

Dover	2	0	0	0	0	0	0	0	0	2	3	1
Salisbury	2	4	1	1	0	3	0	0	X	11	14	5

Comellas (winner), Killen (loser)
Reznichak (2); Lynn (2); Trechock, Thomas (2), Quimby (2), Leip—RBI; Reznichak, Quimby—2B; Trechock, Luzansky, Leip—SB

    The Salisbury Indians returned home and hosted the lowly Dover Orioles. Flowers sent Comellas to the mound and he hurled a three-hitter for his 17th consecutive victory as the Indians overpowered the Orioles 11 to 2. He struck out six and made the Dover batters look silly popping up weakly throughout the infield. Only five batters sent balls to the outfield and three were caught. The Indian batsmen collected 14 hits against two Dover pitchers (Killen and Thomas Taylor). Lynn had three singles in four at-bats; Fred Thomas went two for three; Luzansky and Reznichak, who snapped out of his batting slump, went two for four; and Deutsch went two for five. Reznichak had been struggling at the plate, hitting just .159 during the last half of July. Lynn continued to play at a high level defensively. A staff writer remarked that Lynn "fielded like a demon—going to left and right a la Gehringer."[1]
    The Orioles scored their only two runs of the game in the first inning. Dover leadoff hitter and second baseman Archer reached first base on Trechock's error. Archer was forced out at second when Orioles left fielder Weatherlow bunted to Comellas. It should have been a double play but Trechock overthrew first base. Lynn retrieved the ball and wildly threw it into left field. Quimby chased down the ball and overthrew third. With those throwing errors, Weatherlow sprinted around the horn and scored Dover's first run. Dover shortstop Vandegrift then tripled to right field and scored on the relay throw when Trechock overthrew third base. When the inning was over, the Indians had committed five errors.
    The Indians tied the game in their half of the first inning when they loaded the bases on singles by Lynn and Luzansky and a walk to Trechock. Lynn and Luzansky scored on Reznichak's double. Killen steadied himself and struck out the next three batters (Thomas, Quimby and Deutsch). But the Indians were relentless and sent Killen to the showers when they scored four runs on three hits in the second inning. The Indians also scored a run in the third and fourth innings and three more in

FIVE—Domination on the Diamond (August 1–31)

A casual photograph of three Indians infielders before a game: (from left) Frank Trechock, Frank Deutsch and Ed Leip (Walter Thurston Photograph Collection, Edward H. Nabb Research Center for Delmarva History and Culture, Salisbury University).

the sixth inning. The win moved the Indians into a tie with Pocomoke City for sixth place.

Salisbury 6, Dover 1   (30–34) (51–13)   August 4

Salisbury	1	0	0	0	0	2	0	3	0	6	5	2
Dover	0	0	0	0	0	0	0	0	1	1	5	3

Kohlman (winner), Wittig (loser)
Luzansky, Reznichak (2), Guerra, Deutsch, Leip—RBI; Luzansky—HR; Luzansky—SB

Salisbury then traveled to Delaware's capital and defeated the Orioles by the score of 6 to 1. Joe Kohlman pitched an outstanding game, holding the Orioles to a single run on five hits. He struck out nine and walked one. Kohlman was pitching a shutout until the ninth inning, when with one out, Orioles center fielder James McInerney[2] doubled in Dover's only run.

The Indians scored in the first inning when Luzansky looped a long fly down the left field line. Orioles left fielder Jake Outwin[3] went back

Miracle on the Eastern Shore

to catch the ball but misjudged it and the ball caromed off the fence and rolled alongside it away from Outwin. Luzansky hustled around the bases and slid home ahead of the throw for an inside-the-park home run. After that, Wittig, Dover's starting pitcher, settled in and pitched no-hit ball until the sixth inning when, after striking out Kohlman, he walked Lynn. Luzansky singled, followed by Trechock working a walk. Reznichak hit a two-run single. Trechock was thrown out at third by center fielder McInerney and Guerra struck out to end the inning. In the eighth inning, Wittig walked Luzansky and Reznichak. Luzansky scored on Guerra's single. Quimby walked to load the bases and Wittig then walked Deutsch, forcing in Reznichak. Finta relieved Wittig and walked Leip, forcing Guerra across the plate. Kohlman grounded out to second baseman Archer to end the inning.

After the game, President Kibler announced his ruling relating to the protested game on July 15 that was won by Crisfield. The game would be replayed. Scheduled for August 16, it would start in the bottom half of the third inning with the score 3 to 1 in favor of the Dover Orioles. For the Indians, Revolinsky would be on the mound.

Salisbury 10, Pocomoke 8   (31–34) (52–13)   August 5

Salisbury	2	0	3	0	0	4	0	0	1	10	11	2
Pocomoke	0	0	0	1	5	0	0	1	1	8	14	1

Comellas (winner), Baumann (loser)
Trechock (3), Guerra (2), Luzansky (3), Leip, Reznichak—RBI; Trechock, Luzansky, Deutsch—2B; Luzansky, Guerra, Reznichak—HR; Guerra (2), Comellas—SB

Pocomoke City and Salisbury engaged in a slugfest in the Worcester County town with the Indians edging out the Red Sox by a 10-8 score. The Indians started the scoring in the first inning. After Lynn grounded out to third, Luzansky walked and scored on Trechock's double. Trechock advanced to third and scored when Guerra reached first on third baseman Henry Schluter's error. In the third inning, the Indians scored three more runs. Lynn hit a single and scored when Luzansky crushed a long high fly over the right field fence. After Trechock and Reznichak grounded out to third, Guerra hit a blast over the left field fence. In the sixth inning, the Indians scored four times. With two outs, Deutsch doubled and Leip singled him in. After giving up a base hit to Comellas, Red Sox starting pitcher Al Baumann[4] was relieved by Scarbinsky, who

Five—Domination on the Diamond (August 1–31)

walked the next two batters, Lynn and Luzansky. The latter forced in Leip. A single by Trechock brought in Comellas and Lynn. In the ninth inning, the Indians added another run when Reznichak blasted a shot over the center field fence, his eighth homer of the season.

Trechock hit three singles, which indicated that he was breaking out of his hitting slump. For the past week and a half, he was batting .233. Defensively, Deutsch snagged a hot shot from Scarbinsky that was hit so hard that the fans could not believe he had a chance to glove it.

Pocomoke City's first run, a home run by right fielder Jester, came in the fourth inning. In the fifth, the Red Sox manufactured five runs on a double, three singles and a walk. After Red Sox pitcher Baumann grounded out to Lynn, second baseman Jones singled. Shortstop Frank LeRoy flied out to center field.[5] Next, center fielder Dugan and Jester connected on consecutive singles, with the latter bringing in Jones, then third baseman Schluter worked a walk. Trechock committed an error that allowed left fielder Casper Clough[6] to reach safely. Dugan and Jester scored on the play. First baseman "Zulu" Gray[7] walked and catcher Dousha hit a double off Comellas, who relieved Montero, that allowed Schluter and Clough to score. The Red Sox scored one run each in the eighth and ninth innings. Dousha scored on LeRoy's single and Schluter, after hitting a double, scored on Dousha's base hit. The Pocomoke batters blasted Montero with eight hits in 4⅔ innings.

The Indians, in turn, pounded Baumann for nine hits and eight runs. After relieving Baumann in the sixth inning, Scarbinsky quieted the Indian bats, allowing only two hits, one being the home run by Reznichak.

On this day (August 5), the *Wilkes-Barre Record* reported that Plymouth Township, Pennsylvania, native Mike Depko, who was picked up by the Trenton Senators and optioned to Salisbury on June 23 for further seasoning, had been recalled to the Senators. The 19-year-old hurler appeared in the June 14 exhibition game against South Philadelphia. By June 26, he was pitching for the Rome Colonels (CAML) and, for the rest of the season, compiled a 4–5 record in 10 appearances.

Salisbury 2, Pocomoke 0   (32–34) (53–13)
August 6 afternoon   (7 innings)

Pocomoke	0	0	0	0	0	0	0		5	2
Salisbury	0	0	0	2	0	0	X	2	5	0

Revolinsky (winner), Baumann (loser)
Revolinsky, Lynn—RBI; Leip—2B

Miracle on the Eastern Shore

Leon Revolinsky dominated the Pocomoke City team in the afternoon game of a doubleheader for a 2-0 victory. He scattered five hits in the seven-inning game. Twice during the game, he bore down with two base runners on and denied them to reach third base. An incident occurred that caused the acting Red Sox manager, Hank Harris, to file a formal protest during the game. The play in question was as follows: Quimby slashed a base hit and advanced to second base when Deutsch was safe at first on third baseman Schluter's throwing error. Leip drew a walk to load the bases. While Quimby was jogging to third base, he turned his ankle and fell near the bag. Umpire Toach, at home plate, seeing Quimby in distress, threw up both hands to signal "time" to suspend the game. Pocomoke catcher Dousha, apparently not seeing the umpire's signal, threw to third base, where Schluter tagged Quimby out as he lay on the ground clearly in some discomfort near the base. The umpires conversed and ruled that Quimby was entitled to third and, by virtue of the base on balls issued to Leip, called Quimby safe.

Pocomoke 8, Salisbury 3 (32–35) (53–14) August 6 night

Pocomoke	0	0	0	0	0	2	6	0	0	8	10	1
Salisbury	3	0	0	0	0	0	0	0	0	3	4	2

Bassler (loser), Gray (winner)
Luzansky, Quimby, Thomas—RBI; Lynn—2B; Luzansky—3B; Luzansky, Guerra—SB

In the night game of the Pocomoke City-Salisbury twin bill, "Hard Luck Lefty" Bassler had a solid game until the sixth inning, when a costly error by Lynn allowed Pocomoke City to score two runs. In the seventh inning, Bassler fell to pieces when he loaded the bases and walked in the tying run. Leip then committed a fielding error. Flowers called on Kohlman to relieve Bassler to stop the rally but he was ineffective for the first time in the season. He walked in the winning run that was credited to Bassler, then Red Sox center fielder Dugan doubled and right fielder Jester singled to bring in two more runs. When the inning ended, Pocomoke City had scored six runs. For the last two innings, Revolinsky pitched a one-hitter to end the onslaught.

The Indians looked like they were cruising for a comfortable win when they scored three runs in the first inning on Lynn's two-base hit, Luzansky's triple, Quimby's sacrifice and Thomas's long fly to right field. Pocomoke hurler "Zulu" Gray, the Dagsboro, Delaware, "pitching

Five—Domination on the Diamond (August 1–31)

demon," allowed four hits in the first two innings and then held the Indians hitless for the rest of the game.[8]

"Papa Joe" Cambria, while attending a Trenton Senators game, commented that "Little Bill" Luzansky's "a great prospect, that boy and he thinks [Luzansky] will be ready for Class A ball next year."[9]

After splitting the doubleheader, the Salisbury ball club moved into fifth place in the standings.

Salisbury 8, Cambridge 3   (33–35) (54–14)   August 7

Salisbury	3	1	3	0	0	1	0	0	0	8	9	0
Cambridge	2	0	0	0	0	0	0	0	1	3	6	3

Montero (winner), Klepper (loser)
Thomas, Guerra (3), Luzansky (2), Deutsch—RBI; Guerra, Luzansky, Deutsch and Lynn—2B; Thomas, Lynn, Trechock—SB

In the town of Cambridge, the Indians stomped on the Cardinals' new pitcher, Allen Klepper,[10] for seven runs on five hits through the first three innings. Klepper was relieved by Michael Koons, who held the Indians to only one run on four hits over six innings. Montero displayed his greatest control of the season as he limited Cambridge's batters to six hits, while also dishing out three strikeouts and three walks. The Cardinal batters either topped Montero's curveball or undercut his submarine balls, resulting in weak pop flies and soft grounders.

Lynn started the initial inning with a walk. He advanced to second on a wild pitch from Klepper. The next batter, Thomas, singled, which scored Luzansky. Lynn walked and Thomas and Lynn executed a double steal. After Trechock struck out, Reznichak hit into a fielder's choice with Thomas being thrown out at home plate. Guerra doubled, bringing in Lynn and Reznichak. During the play, Guerra was thrown out trying to stretch a double into a triple.

In the second inning, with two outs, Montero walked and scored on Luzansky's double. In the third stanza, Lynn grounded out to the pitcher and Trechock walked. Reznichak followed with another base on balls. Guerra singled in Trechock and Deutsch hit a two-run single, bringing in Reznichak and Guerra. In the sixth inning, Deutsch smashed a two-base hit and, after two groundouts by Leip and Montero, Luzansky singled Deutsch in for the Indians' eighth and final run.

The Cardinals scored two runs in the first stanza when second

Miracle on the Eastern Shore

baseman Murtaugh and left fielder Johnson walked and right fielder Healy brought them both in with a single. In the ninth, third baseman Gunkel drove in Healy with a base hit.

During the eighth inning, Salisbury's first baseman, Frank Deutsch, suffered a spiked ankle. Charles Quimby replaced him at first in the ninth inning. The gash, although deep, wasn't believed to be that serious, however Flowers chose to take him out of the lineup for a few days out of caution.

Salisbury 7, Crisfield 0   (34–35) (55–14)   August 8

Salisbury	1	0	0	4	0	0	0	1	1	7	11	0
Crisfield	0	0	0	0	0	0	0	0	0	0	4	5

Kohlman (winner), Rife (loser)
Luzansky (2), Lynn, Guerra, Quimby (2), Leip—RBI; Trechock, Lynn—2B; Lynn—HR

For the next game, Salisbury journeyed down to Crisfield and sent Kohlman to the mound, where he pitched a four-hit shutout in a 7-0 victory, his fourth of the season. The Crabbers helped the situation by committing five errors during the contest. Kohlman was on top of his game, not allowing a Crabber to reach third base and only two to reach second base. He gave up two hits to Webb, the Crabbers' center fielder, and one hit each to Sterling and Reba, Crisfield's starting first baseman and shortstop, respectively.

The Indians began their scoring with a home run from Lynn in the first inning. They put up a four-spot in the fourth inning. Trechock reached first base on an error by Crisfield first baseman Sterling. Reznichak worked a walk and Guerra singled in Trechock. Next up, Quimby drove in Reznichak with a base hit. Leip's fielder's choice allowed Guerra to score, and Luzansky flied out to right field and Quimby scored.

In the eighth inning, Quimby walked and, after a successful sacrifice by Kohlman, Quimby scored on Luzansky's flyout to center field. In the ninth, Trechock reached safely on an error by Crabbers third baseman Marinelli and came around to score on Quimby's single.

The Indians had been busy with their roster. Manager Jake Flowers announced that Jose Salazar,[11] another one of Cambria's Cuban recruits, who reported to the team on August 2, had not signed his contract yet. Without a signed contract, Flowers could not officially put Salazar into the rotation. Comellas spent 10 minutes with the *Daily Times* staff to

FIVE—Domination on the Diamond (August 1–31)

teach them how to pronounce the new Cuban pitcher's name. Spelled Salazar, it was pronounced "Thalathar" with a faint "z" sound in each "th." The easiest way to say it was with a lisp. Comellas also informed the staff that Salazar spoke even less English than Guerra and had a zip on his fastball that equaled Montero's speed.

Flowers also shared some unfortunate news about Reznichak. He would be out of the lineup for approximately three weeks with the goal of returning before the playoffs. Since June 24, Reznichak had been playing with a fractured ankle. He was sent to the doctor to put his ankle into a cast. Miraculously, while playing on that badly injured ankle, Reznichak batted .280 with eight doubles, one triple, four home runs and 28 RBI. For the past couple of months, Jerry Lynn had been covering second base, as one sports reporter described, like Charlie Gehringer and hitting like Joe DiMaggio.[12] In addition, he had been assisting Reznichak in covering some sectors of right field that the right fielder's limited mobility prevented him from reaching.

A rare group photograph of the 1937 Salisbury Indians team along the first base line at Gordy Park. Back row, from left: Juan Montero, Jose Salazar, Joe Garliss, Leon Revolinsky, Joe Kohlman, Ed Leip, John Bassler and Bill Luzansky; front row, from left: Mike Guerra, Jerry Lynn, Charles Quimby, Jake Flowers, Frank Trechock, Fred Thomas and Jorge Comellas. Note: The image has been digitally enhanced owing to the original photograph's poor quality (courtesy Mary Jane [Revolinsky] Martinez).

Miracle on the Eastern Shore

News from around the league announced the outright release of Federalsburg player-manager George Short from the team. Replacing him was 44-year-old NYPL circuit veteran Johnny Tillman,[13] who took over the management in a twin bill against Dover. Federalsburg won the first game 10–8. After playing three and a half innings, the second game was called to avoid violating Delaware's law prohibiting play after six o'clock on Sundays.

Salisbury 7, Crisfield 1   (35–35) (56–14)   August 10

Crisfield	0	0	0	0	0	1	0	0	0	1	7	2
Salisbury	0	0	1	0	4	0	0	2	X	7	8	2

Comellas (winner), Decker (loser)
Guerra, Lynn, Quimby, Comellas, Thomas—RBI; Comellas—2B; Thomas, Luzansky—SB

The Salisbury Indians next hosted the Crisfield Crabbers, who had taken the last three contests from the Indians. Behind their lanky Cuban slant thrower, the Indians defeated the visitors 7 to 1. It was Comellas's 19th consecutive victory of the season, which tied the major league record set in 1912 by Rube Marquard,[14] the New York Giants hurler. The victory also brought the Indians' league standing to exactly .500 with a 35–35 record. Comellas again missed out on his first shutout of the year when two errors and a wild pitch in the sixth inning accounted for Crisfield's lone tally. He ended the game by allowing seven hits while striking out 11 Crabbers and walking two. Fans introduced a new chant for Comellas when there were two strikes on the batter—"give him the 'adios' ball, George."[15] In most cases, Comellas obliged.

The Indians started the scoring in the third inning. Luzansky singled. After Thomas flied out, Lynn and Trechock drew walks to load the bases. Guerra hit a long flyout to center that allowed Luzansky to score. Quimby popped out to second to retire the side. In the fifth inning, the Indians scored four more runs. Luzansky drew a walk and Thomas hit a grounder to third base and was safe due to Crisfield third baseman Urban's throwing error. Next up, Lynn placed a perfect bunt down the third baseline and was safe at first base. Luzansky, hustling around the diamond, scored when Marnie dropped the throw at first base. Thomas scored on Trechock's single to left field. Guerra sacrificed Lynn and Trechock over and Lynn scored on a wild pitch. Quimby flied out to right field and Trechock tagged up and scored on the catch.

FIVE—Domination on the Diamond (August 1–31)

In the eighth inning, the Indians scored two more runs on three hits and a long flyout.

Defensively, Leip, Trechock and Deutsch made spectacularstops on hot shots that robbed several Crabbers of base hits. Deutsch made a beautiful backhand stop and tossed the ball to Comellas, who beat the runner to the bag. Thomas, playing in right field on account of Reznichak, the Indians' regular right fielder, being out indefinitely with an ankle injury, made a shoestring catch on a fly ball and then rocketed it to third base to nail Crisfield hurler Ralph Decker,[16] who tried to advance after the catch. Trechock gathered up a scorching grounder by Reha and made an off-balance throw to Deutsch to beat him.

Across the nation, chatter about another East Coast minor league baseball club's exploits began to spread. During the 1937 baseball season, the Newark Bears were tearing up the Class Double A International League. Behind a potent lineup of soon-to-be major leaguers, the New York Yankees farm club was playing .737 ball, with 84 games won and 30 losses. Because of this feat, many sportswriters opined if the ball club should belong in the major leagues. A local sportswriter then contemplated the comparison between the Newark Bears and the Salisbury Indians. If the Bears belonged in the majors, could the Indians prosper in a Class A or Class Double A league? The Indians were playing .800 ball, with 56 games actually won and 14 lost. Their pitching staff was extraordinary—Comellas (19–0), Kohlman (17–1), Revolinsky (7–2) and Montero (4–1). The Indians had one of the best aggregation of hitters in the minors, led by Lynn (.365), Trechock (.356) and Luzansky (.321). At the helm, they possessed the smartest manager in the league or possibly the entire minor leagues, D'Arcy "Jake" Flowers. And the final factor that made the Salisbury Indians equal to or possibly better than the Newark Bears was their determination not to be beaten after suffering catastrophic adversity—the unbelievable forfeiture of 21 victories.[17]

Salisbury 7, Easton 2   (36–35) (57–14)   August 12

Salisbury	0	0	0	0	0	0	0	3	4	7	14	0
Easton	0	0	0	2	0	0	0	0	0	2	10	1

Kohlman (winner), Cantwell (loser)
Guerra (2), Deutsch—RBI; Luzansky (2), Guerra (2)—2B

On August 12, the Salisbury Indians manufactured a come-from-behind victory against the Easton Browns by a score of 7 to 2. Starting

Miracle on the Eastern Shore

pitcher Juan Montero pitched airtight ball, scattering 10 hits for seven innings while yielding one walk and striking out one. The only real damage Easton delivered against Montero came in the fourth inning when they scored their runs. After Mikus's double and Vernon's single, Eck brought them in with a base hit.

In the eighth inning, Easton manager George Jacobs sent Browns ace hurler Kuntashian into the game to relieve Walt Cantwell,[18] who was shutting down the Indians for seven innings, scattering nine hits. Flowers responded to Jacobs's move by ordering Kohlman to start warming up as he wanted to fight fire with fire. In the Indians' half of the eighth inning, Cantwell walked Lynn to start it off, followed by a single from Trechock. Guerra squared up like he was placing down a bunt but instead drove a two-base hit to the left field fence, scoring Lynn and Trechock. Kuntashian entered the game and made Quimby fly out to deep center field, which allowed Guerra to advance to third after the catch. Deutsch tapped an infield dribbler that allowed Guerra to score and Leip flied out to center to retire the side.

In the bottom of the inning, Montero served up a double to Leroy Mikus.[19] Flowers signaled for Kohlman to relieve him. Kohlman struck out Easton first baseman Vernon, walked center fielder Stiles and made catcher Lenzi pop out to Quimby. Next up was third baseman Eck, who was gunned down at first on a beautiful stop and toss by Trechock to end the inning.

In the ninth inning, Kuntashian struck out Kohlman. Luzansky hit a ground-rule double that bounced over the left field fence and Thomas worked a walk. Lynn hit a fielder's choice to second baseman Pultz, who tried to force out Thomas at the bag but his throw was dropped by shortstop Weimer. Luzansky sprinted home during the play while Thomas and Lynn were safe at first and second. Trechock grounded out to first, advancing both runners. Guerra bounced a ground-rule double over the left field fence, scoring Thomas. Quimby drove in Lynn with a single to center and Deutsch hit a single to the same spot to score Guerra while Quimby advanced to third. Leip weakly tapped a slow roller back to the mound to end the inning.

Kohlman finished the game by striking out pinch hitter Zimmerman, walking Weimer and having both Pultz and Beidleman, the Easton right fielder, fly out to center field. For Pultz's out, Luzansky made a running shoestring catch on his low line drive.

Charley Quimby had a great game after struggling for two weeks while dealing with injuries. He collected three clean singles and made

Five—Domination on the Diamond (August 1–31)

a pair of pretty catches in left field. A reporter indicated that Leip patrolled third base like Pie Traynor.[20] Guerra hit two doubles and a single and played flawlessly behind the plate. In the fourth inning, Thomas threw a near-perfect strike to home plate on first baseman Vernon's line single to right field, stopping left fielder Mikus at third, who was on second base before the play. With Comellas and Kohlman being so dominant, local newspapers had crowned them the "Win Twins."

In the August 12, 1937, issue of the *Queen Anne's Record-Observer*, Harpel Moore,[21] the Cambridge Cardinals' scorekeeper, remarked on the apparent difference between the Salisbury and Cambridge teams. "In comparing the two teams (Salisbury and Cambridge) the outstanding difference is the ages of the ballplayers where Cambridge players' ages will average from 19 to 22, the Salisbury Indians' ages will average from 22 to 25. That difference from two to three years' experience is the secret of Salisbury's success throughout the League. I'll venture to say that three years from now the majority of our boys will be in higher baseball drawing more money or will find another occupation more profitable."[22]

Was Moore's analysis correct? Did their ages play a role in their dominance? When the op-ed appeared, the elder statesman on the Salisbury team was Ed Leip at 27 years old and the youngest Charlie Quimby at 20 years old. Salisbury's roster averaged 23 years of age. Comparably, Cambridge's oldest players were Reds Hoffner and former Federalsburg player-manager George Short at 26 years old and its youngest, Chip Marshall, at 18 years old. Cambridge's roster averaged 22.75 years. Cambria had assembled this baseball juggernaut by signing players with a variety of experiences. A few players attended institutions of higher education while most of them were just semipro sandlot ballplayers who were either high school standouts or neighborhood heroes. Combined with non-English-speaking Cuban ballplayers and the four individuals with previous professional experience that every team in the league possessed, the ability of the manager to precisely identify and mature these unique and varying talents to create a cohesive team was the key ingredient to Salisbury's success.

Salisbury 5, Easton 0   (37–35) (58–14)   **August 13**

Easton	0	0	0	0	0	0	0	0	0	0	4	0
Salisbury	0	0	1	0	1	1	1	1	X	5	11	3

Kohlman (winner), Zarowsky (loser)
Thomas, Luzansky, Trechock, Leip, Deutsch—RBI;
  Luzansky, Leip—SB

Miracle on the Eastern Shore

After shutting down the Easton Browns in a relief effort the night before, Kohlman took the mound and pitched a four-hit shutout against them, his second consecutive shutout and fifth of the season. In the 5-0 victory, the Browns were completely baffled by Kohlman's control and speed as he struck out seven men and walked three. The only hits came from Zimmerman, Pultz, Mikus and Vernon; the latter doubled. The victory was Kohlman's 19th consecutive game, which tied Rube Marquard's 25-year-old major league record. Kohlman's teammate George Comellas accomplished this feat on August 10.

The Indians started the scoring in the third inning when Kohlman crushed a two-bagger to right center field. Luzansky sacrificed him to third base. Kohlman scored when Thomas singled to right field. The Indians scored a run in the fifth, sixth and seventh innings. In the eighth inning, Deutsch broke out of his hitting slump when he crushed one of Zarowsky's fastballs over the left field fence with some 15 yards to spare. For 10 games, Deutsch was hitting a lowly 5 for 35 (.142).

Defensively, there were several outstanding plays. Browns left fielder Mikus in the first inning made a running backhand catch on a ball that Luzansky tagged for a potential two-base hit. For the Indians, Trechock, who was positioned in deep short at the start of the play, ran to the infield grass to make a falling shoestring catch of Stiles's short looping liner. The Indians also performed an unusual double play. With Zimmerman on second base and Pultz on first base, Beidleman struck out. Thomas whipped the ball to Deutsch at first base with Pultz off the sack. Deutsch started a rundown. Meanwhile, Zimmerman took off for third. Seeing this, Deutsch whipped the ball across the diamond to Leip, who tagged Zimmerman out before he started his slide.

Frank Thomas had both joints of the little finger on his right hand dislocated by a foul tip but he never left the game. Only Ed "Jap" Hullings[23] of Burlington, New Jersey, a newcomer trying out for the vacancy in right field, went hitless.

Desperately searching for a replacement for their starting right fielder, Joe Reznichak, who was lost for the season, Salisbury's management quickly signaled the Trenton Senators of an urgent need for a "reliable and sturdy flychaser," who in turn phoned El Robbins, a well-known Florence, New Jersey, baseball leader, who then contacted Frank Bertino, the manager of the semipro Beverly Reelers of the Burlington County League.[24] Bertino reached out to his star outfielder, who was batting over .500 for the season, and offered him a chance to play

FIVE—Domination on the Diamond (August 1–31)

for a professional ball club. Hullings agreed and jumped on the first bus to the Eastern Shore.

The Burlington Township High School graduate became the third Burlington County representative to play in the Eastern Shore League that season. Alex "Spunk" Pitko, an outfielder with the Centreville Colts, and Tommy Daddino, the first baseman with the Pocomoke City Red Sox, were the others.

Salisbury 11, Dover 3   (38–35) (59–14)   August 14

Salisbury	0	1	2	2	2	2	0	2	0	11	12	1
Dover	3	0	0	0	0	0	0	0	0	3	4	2

Revolinsky (winner), Killen (loser)
Trechock 4, Revolinsky 2, Hullings 2, Lynn, Guerra, Quimby;
  Guerra—2B; Trechock, Revolinsky—HR; Quimby—SB

On August 14, the Indians traveled up to the Blue Hen state capital and thumped Dover 11 to 3 behind Revolinsky's strong four-hit outing. The Orioles started strong when they tallied three runs in the first inning. After that, Revolinsky "took a fresh chew, bore down" and retired 24 consecutive batters.[25] Revolinsky helped his cause offensively by contributing three of the 12 hits, including a "Herculean" home run.[26] Trechock crushed his 18th home run to the deepest part of the park. The victory allowed the Salisbury ball club to move past Centreville and take possession of fourth place.

In the first inning, after left fielder Heim[27] grounded out to second, first baseman Swoboda hit a double. Shortstop Archer grounded out to the pitcher and right fielder Marnie reached on an error by Trechock. Center fielder McInerney then walked and second baseman Anderson[28] hit a two-run double. Third baseman Ed Taylor[29] singled in another run.

In the second inning, the Indians got on the scoreboard when Guerra started with a double and was brought in on Quimby's single. In the next inning, the Indians tied the game with two runs. Revolinsky began the inning with a single. After Luzansky reached on an error and Lynn walked, Trechock flied out to center field to bring in Revolinsky. Guerra followed with an RBI single. The Indians took the lead in the fourth. After Quimby flied out to first base, Deutsch singled. Leip hit into a fielder's choice, advancing Deutsch. Revolinsky then hit a two-run home run.

In the fifth inning, Scrap Theurer[30] relieved Howard Killen, Dover's

Miracle on the Eastern Shore

starting pitcher, who surrendered six hits and a walk in four innings. Theurer walked the first batter he faced, Lynn. After Trechock struck out, Guerra worked a walk. Hullings drove Lynn and Guerra in with a two-base hit. Quimby grounded out to second base and Deutsch flied out to left to end the inning. In the next inning, Leip and Revolinsky singled. Luzansky sacrificed the runners over. Lynn followed with an RBI single. Revolinsky scored on Trechock's groundout. The Salisbury ball club finished their scoring in the eighth inning. After Luzansky grounded out to Theurer, Lynn walked and Trechock followed it up with a two-run homer. Theurer finished the game dealing out six hits and four bases on balls while striking out two.

Salisbury 7, Federalsburg 1   (39–35) (60–14)   August 15

Salisbury	2	0	0	2	0	0	2	0	1	7	11	0
Federalsburg	0	0	1	0	0	0	0	0	0	1	11	1

Bassler (winner), Ratterree (loser)
Trechock, Guerra, Quimby, Deutsch (2), Bassler—RBI; Luzansky—2B

On August 15, at the ballpark in Federalsburg, Bassler held the Athletics to 11 hits, mostly harmless singles. Bassler copied Revolinsky's league record (of sorts) by pitching a full nine-inning game without delivering a strikeout or issuing a base on balls.

Ratterree, the Federalsburg ace, got pounded for 10 hits through seven innings. Frank Trechock led the charge by going three for four with one run batted in while Frank Deutsch went three for five with two runs batted in. The Salisbury Indians scored two runs in the first, fourth and seventh innings off Ratterree and another in the ninth inning off Larry Burdsall,[31] who relieved Ratterree in the eighth inning. Bassler's win pushed the Salisbury Indians into third place.

In the first inning, Luzansky and Lynn started with consecutive base hits. Trechock's base hit allowed Luzansky to cross home plate and Guerra knocked in Lynn. In the fourth inning, Quimby worked a walk, followed by Deutsch's base hit that allowed him to score. Leip hit into a fielder's choice. Bassler then brought in Leip. In the seventh inning, Trechock and Hullings scored. In the ninth inning, Hullings scored for the second time on Deutsch's base hit.

For the Athletics, their only run occurred in the third inning when first baseman Garrett Grier[32] scored on third baseman Manczak's blooper.

On this day, Tom Ogden, the 20-year-old right hander for the

Five—Domination on the Diamond (August 1–31)

Centreville Colts, pitched a no-hit, no-run game, shutting out the Cambridge Cardinals 2 to 0.

Salisbury 6, Crisfield 5   (40–35) (61–14)   August 16
Replay of Protested Game

Crisfield	0	2	1	0	0	0	0	1	1	5	4	1
Salisbury	0	1	4	0	1	0	0	0	X	6	10	4

Revolinsky (winner), Barnes (loser)
Reznichak, Quimby, Guerra—RBI; Deutsch—2B; Reznichak, Quimby—HR; Guerra (2)—SB

In the afternoon of August 16, Salisbury hosted Crisfield to finish the protested game that started 32 days earlier on July 15. The game started in the bottom half of the third inning with the Crabbers holding a 3-1 advantage. The issue came in Crisfield's half of the third inning, when the runner, Barnes, missed touching third base and was ruled out, which retired the side. Crisfield believed he touched the bag and continued the game under protest. For the Indians' only score, Reznichak hit a solo shot that landed on the factory roof in the second inning.

The Indians had a hard time keeping close to the same lineup used in July. For the outfield, Jim Bergen was in left field and Reznichak was in right field. Leip was also out of the game dealing with a charley horse. Quimby was the first baseman and Guerra started at third base while Thomas was behind the plate.

The afternoon lineup included Deutsch taking first-base duties while Quimby moved back to left field, replacing Bergen, who reportedly "jumped" his contract with the club and traveled north to be with the Trenton Senators. Flowers assigned Hullings to patrol right field in place of Reznichak. Leip took his position at third base, placing Thomas on the bench. The pitching matchup still had Revolinsky, who relieved Montero during the previous game, on the hill for the Indians and Barnes for the Crabbers.

In the bottom half of the third inning, Luzansky hit a blooper and Deutsch safely reached first base on a fielder's choice. Trechock and Hullings flied out weakly to short. Luzansky and Deutsch advanced on Barnes's wild pitch. Guerra's single scored Luzansky, then Quimby clubbed a high fly ball over the left field fence for a three-run home run, his fifth of the season. The Indians scored another run in the fifth inning when Guerra scored.

Miracle on the Eastern Shore

In the ninth inning, Revolinsky put two on with no outs. Flowers sent in Kohlman to relieve him. One man scored when Trechock botched the relay throw to first base on a double play. Kohlman struck out the next two batters to end the game.

During the game, Luzansky snow-coned Crisfield right fielder Millar's line drive to left center field. Sprinting, he barely caught the ball with the tips of his fingers. A reporter remarked, "It was enough to make Tris Speaker green with envy."[33]

Salisbury 10, Crisfield 3   (41–35) (62–14)   August 16

Crisfield	2	1	0	0	0	0	0	0		3	4	5
Salisbury	0	1	0	5	0	1	0	3	X	10	10	5

Comellas (winner), Decker (loser)
Quimby (2), Lynn (2), Trechock (2), Guerra—RBI; Lynn—SB

In the nightcap of this unique twin bill at Gordy Park, George Comellas won his 20th consecutive victory with a 10-3 win over the Crisfield Crabbers, a new professional baseball record. The moment seemed to be bigger than the jittery Cuban realized. He had difficulty finding the plate through the first few innings, walking five batters to give the Crabbers a three-run margin. Eventually, he settled down to pitch a four-hit contest. He walked nine men and struck out only four batsmen. The Indians' infield came to Comellas's defense. For the first four innings, they pulled a double play in each inning to rob the Crabbers of potential runs.

Decker, the Crabber hurler, proved ineffective. He walked six men, struck out three and, when men were on the basepaths through walks or Crabber errors, he yielded 10 hits. Four times during the nightcap, Barnes strolled down to the bullpen in preparation to come into the game to relieve Decker. Each time, the Indians finished their rally by the time he traveled a hundred yards and he would turn around and return to the dugout.

Following the game, M.E. Murphy, the Indians' business manager, was transported to Peninsula General Hospital to receive treatment for blood poisoning in his right leg. Murphy believed the blood poisoning was developed from mosquito bites. Dr. Philip A. Insley,[34] who was treating Murphy, reported that his condition was not too serious.

FIVE—Domination on the Diamond (August 1–31)

Salisbury 10, Federalsburg 1   (42–35) (63–14)   August 17

Federalsburg	0	0	0	0	0	0	1	0	0	1	1	5
Salisbury	0	0	3	3	2	0	0	2	X	10	16	4

Montero (winner), Burdsall (loser)
Lynn, Montero, Trechock (3), Deutsch (2), Guerra,
   Quimby—RBI; Leip, Guerra, Lynn, Hullings, Luzansky—2B

Juan Montero was next up in the rotation and he did not disappoint. The Cuban speed king limited the Federalsburg bats to a single hit, the second one-hit game of the season in the Eastern Shore League, for a 10-1 victory that extended the Indians' win streak to 10. He had nearly perfect control of his "fireball," allowing him to strike out eight men while walking just one. He carried a no-hitter into the eighth inning, when A's left fielder James Scully[35] dumped a humpback liner along the right field foul line. The Athletics scored in the seventh inning thanks to two errors and a wild pitch.

The Salisbury bats collected 10 hits off Burdsall in five innings and six hits in three innings from the relief pitcher, Robert Stant. Leading the slugfest, Lynn and Guerra each garnered three hits in five at-bats. One of Lynn's hit was a double. Deutsch hit a double and a single in four at-bats. Leip had a double and two walks in four at-bats. Trechock's two singles drove in three runs. Four short days ago, the Indians were in fifth place. On August 17, they were in second place, just one game behind league-leading Easton Browns.

Baseball players are creatures of habit, especially if it appears to be benefiting them at the plate. These superstitious rituals could include consuming the same meal before a game, dressing oneself in a particular order and performing repetitive movements while pitching or hitting. For one Salisbury batsman, his lucky charm was visiting the local medical institution, the Peninsula General Hospital. Guerra had been a daily visitor at the hospital, visiting a patient (probably Indians business manager Melvin Murphy). After two such visits, he had a three-hit game.

Salisbury 13, Federalsburg 2   (43–35) (64–14)   August 18

Federalsburg	2	0	0	0	0	0	0	0	0	2	9	3
Salisbury	0	0	2	8	0	0	3	0	X	13	12	1

Bassler (winner), Zschau (loser)
Guerra (2), Quimby (2), Bassler, Trechock (3), Deutsch,
   Hullings—RBI; Guerra, Quimby—2B; Hullings—3B;
   Leip (2), Guerra—SB

Miracle on the Eastern Shore

After a 10-1 defeat the night before, the Federalsburg Athletics returned to Gordy Park and suffered another crushing loss by a score of 13 to 2. Salisbury portside hurler Bassler, whose fans nicknamed him "Hard Luck Lefty," pitched a solid game, scattering nine hits and, after surrendering two runs in the first inning, bearing down to pitch shutout ball for the rest of the game. The Athletics' runs occurred on a single, an error and a triple by right fielder Edward Lane.[36]

Salisbury had to wait until the third inning to get a run on the board. With two outs, Trechock singled and Guerra drove him in with a two-base hit. Quimby then singled in Guerra. In the fourth inning, the floodgates opened and Salisbury sent eight baserunners across the plate on five hits, two walks and three fielding errors that sent Zschau, the A's starting pitcher, to the showers. Bassler delivered the game-winning hit that brought in Leip. Each batter for the Indians had a hit during the contest. The Indians scored three more runs in the seventh inning on two hits, three walks, an error and a wild pitch.

During the Athletics' half of the seventh inning, Leip showcased his superb fielding ability by making a running backhand stop on a scorching grounder by A's third baseman Manczak down the third base-line and rifled a bullet to first base for the putout.

William Needham, Associated Press staff writer, offered a regional allegory while describing the experience of Salisbury's opponents: "Nobody's ever figured out how a chicken feels on the chopping block but the chicken's experience must be something akin to the reactions of an Eastern Shore League team playing against Salisbury. A few squawks and it's all over. The Federalsburg Athletics got in enough squawks to account for two runs against the Indians last night but the axe fell just the same."[37]

Salisbury 9, Centreville 1   (44–35) (65–14)   August 19

Centreville	0	0	0	1	0	0	0	0	0	1	7	5
Salisbury	1	1	0	0	5	0	0	2	X	9	9	1

Kohlman (winner), Lomas (loser)
Guerra, Deutsch, Quimby, Garliss, Leip, Kohlman (2), Lynn—RBI; Deutsch—2B; Deutsch, Guerra, Lynn—SB

Joe Kohlman chalked up his 20th consecutive victory, becoming the second pitcher, albeit on the same team, to break a 25-year-old record by Giants Rube Marquard. The victim, the Centreville Colts, was held to

FIVE—Domination on the Diamond (August 1–31)

one run on seven hits for a 9-1 defeat. He struck out 16 Colts and walked two while establishing another league record by pitching 24 consecutive innings of shutout ball before the Colts scored in the fourth.

The Indians started their scoring with a run in the first inning. Lynn and Trechock singled, then advanced on a wild pitch by Colts starting pitcher Lomas, and Lynn scored on Guerra's long fly to left field. In the second inning, the Indians added another run on singles by Joe Garliss,[38] the new 21-year-old right fielder who played for the Charlotte Hornets (PIED) earlier in the year, and Deutsch. Garliss scored on a fielder's choice by Leip. In the fifth inning, five Indians crossed the plate on a single hit and three Colts errors. In the eighth inning, the Indians scored two runs on three hits and an error.

During the 12-game winning streak, the Indians outscored their opponents 100–22. During his first game for Salisbury, Garliss attempted a nearly impossible shoestring catch, missing the ball by inches but still keeping it from getting past him. He also showed off a cannon of a throwing arm. For Leip, the Eastern Shore watermelon had been his superfood. The more of them he ate, the better ball he played. The local writers all agreed that Deutsch was the best-fielding first baseman in the league. Deutsch had made some nice plays around first base with his excellent footwork. *The Daily Home News* reported that Reznichak, on the injury list, accepted an appointment as head football coach for the Panzer College of Physical Education and Hygiene.

Centreville 2, Salisbury 1   (44–36) (65–15)   August 20

Salisbury	0	0	1	0	0	0	0	0	0	1	7	1
Centreville	0	2	0	0	0	0	0	0	X	2	7	0

Comellas (loser), Ogden (winner)
Lynn—RBI; Leip, Luzansky—SB

On August 20 at the Centreville ballpark, several streaks came to end. First, the 12-game winning streak that catapulted the Salisbury Indians from sixth place to second place. Second, George Comellas, the ace Cuban pitcher for the Indians, saw his incredible winning streak of 20 games snapped in a heartbreaking 2-1 defeat. The game was impacted by several close decisions that did not go the Indians' way.

To start the game, both sides were retired in order in the first inning. In the top of the second inning, Leip worked a walk with two outs but Deutsch struck out to end the inning. In the bottom of the

Miracle on the Eastern Shore

inning, Colts shortstop Feinberg started off with a single and advanced on right fielder Rist's scratch single to short. Catcher Shillingford placed a perfect sacrifice down the third baseline. Comellas became a little flustered and threw a wild pitch that allowed Feinberg to score. Rist went to third. Third baseman Miller slapped a scratch single down the first base foul line, scoring Rist.

After the inning, Comellas calmed down and allowed only a single by Ogden, the Colts' hurler, in the fifth, a single by Feinberg in the sixth and successive base hits by Miller and first baseman Wurst in the seventh. Ogden hit into a double play to end the threat in the seventh inning. In the eighth inning, left fielder Pitko hit a triple but did not score.

The Indians scored their only run in the third inning. Thomas singled, Comellas flied out to right field and Luzansky was hit by a pitch. Thomas and Luzansky attempted a double steal but Thomas was pegged at third on a very close call by the base umpire, O'Connor. Luzansky scored on Lynn's single. Luzansky was so fast around the bases that he crossed home plate and was halfway to the dugout before the catcher caught the throw from the outfielder. Trechock was hit by a pitch and Garliss grounded into a fielder's choice to end the inning.

In the fourth inning, the Indians wasted two singles. Feinberg threw out Quimby trying to score on a grounder to short. After that, Pitko made a spectacular one-handed catch on a lazy fly and doubled up Leip, who was halfway to third. In the fifth inning, Luzansky smashed a scorching liner over the right field fence, which appeared to the fans in the stands to had snuck just inside the foul pole. As Luzansky began his home run trot around first base, umpire Boyer called it foul. A heated argument ensued at first base. They brought in umpire O'Connor, who indicated that the ball was fair but Boyer refused to reverse his call.

Garliss started off the sixth inning with a single and advanced on Quimby's fielder's choice. Leip was hit by a pitch. Deutsch singled to center field and Garliss tried to score from second base. Colts center fielder Carroll's throw to the plate was high and Garliss slid under Shillingford as the Colts' catcher tried to apply the tag but dropped the ball. It trickled into the infield. However, umpire Boyer called Garliss out. In the seventh inning, Luzansky singled for the Indians.

Centreville's 21-year-old ace right hander, Thomas Ogden, continued his brilliant pitching. In his last outing on August 15, he pitched a no-hit, no-run game against the Cambridge Cardinals. Throughout

FIVE—Domination on the Diamond (August 1–31)

the game, his teammates helped him out immensely. Rip Shillingford, catching in place of the injured Knapp, twice threw out the lead runner in a double steal at third base.

As for Comellas, he kept seven hits well scattered, walking none and striking out five.

On August 5, it was reported that the Centreville baseball team for the first time in the 1937 season had use of hot water for their showers at the Centreville baseball park. A heater, an 80-gallon tank and about 60 feet of pipe were installed by Johnny Rozier,[39] a Centreville plumber and an ardent Colts fan.

Salisbury 1, Dover 0   (45–36) (66–15)   August 21

Dover	0	0	0	0	0	0	0	0	0	0
Salisbury	0	0	0	0	0	0	1	1	4	0

Revolinsky (winner), Killen (loser)
Leip—RBI; Thomas—2B

On August 21, Leon Revolinsky entered the minor league history book when he pitched a no-hit, no-run 1–0 seven inning game over the Dover Orioles in the first game of a doubleheader at Gordy Park. He walked six batters and struck out two. On the other side, Dover hurler Howard Killen held the Indians to four hits and kept them scoreless until the seventh.

In the seventh inning, Thomas doubled to left field and Leip grounded to shortstop. While Leip was beating out the throw at first base, Thomas scored from second base.

Salisbury 5, Dover 4   (46–36) (67–15)   August 21   (12 innings)

Dover	X	X	X	X	X	X	X	X	1	0	0	0	4	X	X
Salisbury	X	X	X	X	X	X	X	X	1	0	0	1	5	X	X

Kohlman (winner), Wittig (loser)
[Box score not found]

In relief of starting pitcher Juan Montero, Joe Kohlman chalked up his 21st consecutive victory. Kohlman came in to start the 10th inning and pitched no-hit ball for three innings. He struck out four of the 10 batsmen he faced. This was the third time he received a victory as a reliever. Montero and Orioles ace John Wittig hurled a pitchers' duel.

Miracle on the Eastern Shore

In the early innings, Salisbury scored three runs. Hard luck fell on Montero in the ninth inning when Dover took a one-run lead. The Indians responded in their half of the ninth inning when two walks and an error led to Guerra, pinch-hitting for Montero, lifting a long fly to the outfield to knot up the game four all.

In the 12th inning, Trechock tripled and scored on Garliss' single.

In his first three at-bats, Luzansky tripled, singled and doubled. After that, Dover decided to intentionally walk him until the 11th inning.

Salisbury 10, Federalsburg 5   (47–36) (68–15)   August 22

	1	2	3	4	5	6	7	8	9	R	H	E
Salisbury	1	0	0	0	5	1	0	2	1	10	13	1
Federalsburg	0	0	0	0	0	1	3	1	0	5	12	5

Bassler (winner), Moran (loser)
Luzansky (4), Lynn, Trechock, Quimby (2), Leip, Thomas—RBI; Lynn, Revolinsky—2B; Luzansky—HR

On the afternoon of August 22, the Salisbury Indians and the Federalsburg Athletics met in the Caroline County town to engage in a free-for-all slugging contest with Salisbury winning by a score of 10 to 5. A total of 25 hits were given out with Luzansky and LeGates hitting home runs. Luzansky drove in four runs. For six-plus innings, Bassler held the Athletics to one run while scattering 11 Athletics hits. In the seventh inning, Revolinsky came in to preserve the lead, allowing one hit in 2⅓ innings.

Luzansky led off the contest with a homer. The Indians added five more runs in the fifth inning. After Thomas grounded out to third baseman Manczak, Bassler walked. Luzansky popped out to Manczak and Lynn followed with a double that allowed Bassler to scamper around the bases and score. Trechock singled in Lynn and Garliss tallied his own base hit. Quimby welcomed Zschau, who relieved starting pitcher Moran, with a two-run two-base hit that allowed Trechock and Garliss to score. Quimby came in to score on Leip's double and Deutsch grounded to second baseman Johnson to end the inning.

In the sixth inning, one run crossed the plate for the Indians when Thomas worked a walk, advanced to second on a passed ball, was sacrificed to third by Bassler and scored on Luzansky's flyout to left field. In the eighth, the Indians tallied two runs when Thomas singled and Revolinsky crushed a double. Luzansky brought them in with a well-hit

Five—Domination on the Diamond (August 1–31)

single. The Indians finished their scoring in the last inning when Garliss scored on Thomas's base hit.

The Athletics got on the board in the sixth inning when a double by center fielder LeGates brought in right fielder Stant. In the next inning, the Athletics put up a three-spot. Bassler offered up three hits to shortstop Milici, Boyce and Zschau, with the latter bringing in Milici. The next batter, first baseman Grier, crushed a two-run double. Indians manager Flowers signaled for Revolinsky to replace Bassler on the mound, and he delivered. He struck out Manczak and made Stant fly out to center field to end the rally. Federalsburg added one more run when,

> Salisbury, Md.
> Aug. 22, 1937.
>
> Johnny Bassler!—
>   It has long been an established fact that man cannot serve two masters (or should I say two mistresses?) Your game today showed the effects of too much night life. Also, it's looks perfectly ridiculous to see you constantly smirking at the occupants of the grandstand. I sincerely hope you will accept this criticism in the spirit in which it is sent.
>   Always A Bassler Fan.

A fan letter to Indians southpaw pitcher John Bassler, August 22, 1937. A fan expresses some concerns that Bassler's after-game activities were adversely affecting him on the mound. Bassler gave up 11 hits over 6⅓ innings to the Federalsburg Athletics in a 10–5 victory. Also, the fan finds his pleasant interactions with spectators in the grandstand during the game unbecoming (courtesy Bonnie and Mark Briese).

Miracle on the Eastern Shore

in the eighth inning, LeGates lifted one of Revolinsky's offerings over the fence.

Salisbury 8, Dover 1 (48–36) (69–15) August 26

Dover	0	1	0	0	0	0	0	0	0	1	5	3
Salisbury	3	3	0	1	0	0	1	0	X	8	14	2

Kohlman (winner), Taylor (loser)
Garliss (2), Guerra, Quimby, Kohlman, Luzansky, Trechock, Quimby—RBI; Quimby, Kohlman, Garliss—2B

For three straight days, all games in the Eastern Shore League were rained out. The league directors voiced some concerns regarding each ball club's ability to complete all 100 scheduled games. It was discussed that a series of doubleheaders would occur during the last two weeks of the season.

The night game slated for August 25 versus the Cambridge Cardinals in the Dorchester County town was postponed due to wet grounds. The game was officially designated as "Jake Flowers Night" to honor the Salisbury Indians manager and hometown hero. Mayor Howard W. Jackson[40] of Baltimore, along with other mayors and city councilmen from nearby towns, were invited to attend.

While waiting for the next game, Flowers went fishing that Wednesday and caught a mammoth bass in Schumaker's pond. While driving on Park Street on his way to his house, the street caved in under the weight of his car, causing him to crash. The street had just been resurfaced over new sewer lines.

The local newspaper reported that Deutsch attended the smoke-eaters' annual crab feast as a guest of the Salisbury Fire Department a week prior and for two solid hours, he filled up on crabs and Whistle orange soda.

The afternoon before the August 26 game, the grounds crew hastily prepared the flooded baseball diamond by digging drainage ditches between the stands and the field while pumping the outfield. The basepaths were dried by burning 130 gallons of a mixture of gasoline and oil.

Finally, under the floodlights, the Salisbury Indians hosted the Dover Orioles at Gordy Park. The game was promoted as a Wheaties Night. During the 8-1 victory, Salisbury slugged out 14 hits against Dover pitcher Thomas Taylor. The Indians started in the first inning. Luzansky singled and Lynn was hit by a pitch. The runners advanced on

Five—Domination on the Diamond (August 1–31)

a wild pitch as Trechock swung for strike three. Garliss then grounded into a fielder's choice, which allowed Luzansky to score. Lynn scored on Guerra's single to right field. Guerra took advantage of Orioles right fielder James White,[41] who nonchalantly lofted the ball back in, and stretched a single into a two-base hit. Quimby doubled to left center field and brought in Guerra.

In the second inning, Dover scored their only run on an error by Lynn and a single by third baseman Ed Taylor, scoring Swoboda, the Orioles' first baseman.

The Indians scored three more runs in the bottom of the second inning. They added another run in the fourth and one in the seventh.

Kohlman, through the first eight innings, pitched a two-hitter. In the ninth, singles by Hal Marnie, Hal Stock and Scrap Theurer loaded the bases. Dover manager Jiggs Donahue sent Stephen Finta to pinch-hit for Thomas Taylor and Kohlman struck him out to retire the side. In the end, he pitched a five-hit game, striking out 12 Orioles and walking one.

Orioles shortstop Alex Trakimas[42] narrowly escaped being blinded when a wild throw from center field by Marnie, who was retrieving Deutsch's single, hit him in the eye. A gash just below the eye opened up and he was taken to the Peninsula General Hospital to receive two stitches on his cheek.

Guerra continued his hitting spree, collecting 10 hits in 13 trips at the plate (including going four for five in this game). Ever since he started visiting patients in the Peninsula General Hospital, he had been nearly unstoppable.

Salisbury 14, Dover 7   (49–36) (70–15)   August 27

									R	H	E
Salisbury	0	7	4	0	0	0	3	0	0	14	9	1
Dover	0	1	4	2	0	0	0	0	0	7	7	5

Revolinsky (winner), Theurer (loser)
Revolinsky (2), Trechock (2), Garliss (4), Quimby, Lynn (2), Guerra—RBI; Trechock—SB

From June 19 to August 27, the Salisbury Indians climbed out of the cellar after having 21 victories taken away from them to have a share of first place with the Easton Browns. The Indians accomplished this with a winning percentage of .831 in 59 games, losing only 10 games during that span.

The Indians won a weird game in the Blue Hen State capital where

Miracle on the Eastern Shore

Dover Orioles pitchers (Scrap Theurer and Eddie Tantillo[43]) yielded nine singles and issued nine walks. The Orioles committed five fielding errors. This all contributed to the Indians scoring 14 runs.

For the Indians, Revolinsky was off his game, which allowed the Orioles to score seven runs off six hits. By the sixth inning, his inability to find the plate made Indians skipper send Bassler in to relieve him. Southpaw Bassler pitched 3⅔ innings, allowing one hit and one walk while striking out five.

The Indians put up seven runs on two hits in the second inning. Quimby began the inning with a walk. Quimby was removed from the basepaths after Leip's hit into a fielder's choice. Then Leip advanced to second when Deutsch reached safely at first. Next up was Revolinsky, who connected with a two-run single, scoring Leip and Deutsch. Luzansky and Lynn were awarded bases on balls. Trechock reached on a fielding error by center fielder Marnie. Garliss hit a two-run single and Guerra walked. Quimby ended the inning by flying out to center field.

In the next inning, the Indians scored four times on two hits and three walks. Revolinsky, Luzansky, Lynn and Trechock scored. In the seventh inning, the Indians scored three runs on three hits. Deutsch started the inning with a walk and advanced to second when Bassler sacrificed him over. He would score along with Luzansky and Trechock during the inning. Luzansky, Trechock and Garliss each singled.

The Orioles got on the scoreboard in the second inning when Dover's starting pitcher, Theurer, earned a walk and scored on left fielder Trakimas's single. In the next inning, Revolinsky lost the strike zone and walked shortstop Archer, first baseman Swoboda and Marnie. Theurer hit into a fielder's choice that allowed Archer to score. Swoboda was thrown out at third base during the play. Ed Taylor crushed a three-run moon shot. In the fourth inning, left fielder Heim singled and scored on Archer's double. Archer scored on Swoboda's groundout to Lynn.

The player of the game was Reznichak's permanent replacement in right field, Joe Garliss. He registered four putouts and collected three hits in four at-bats with four runs batted in. Trechock made a tremendous play when he speared Heim's hot smash in deep short and threw to Lynn for a force-out at second base.

The next day (August 28), it was announced that Cambria sold the player contracts for the outright sale of Joseph Kohlman, Jorge Comellas, Fermin Guerra, Frank Trechock and Jerome Lynn to the

FIVE—Domination on the Diamond (August 1–31)

Washington Senators in a deal involving a total sum of $10,000. When the season ended, four of the five players joined the Senators.

On the same day, the Official All-Star Eastern Shore League team was announced. The selections were made by the writers of the circuit in cooperation with the National Association of Professional Baseball Leagues. Six Salisbury Indians were named: Jerry Lynn (2B), Frank Trechock (SS), Bill Luzansky (CF), Mike Guerra (C), Joe Kohlman (RHP) and Jake Flowers (manager). Lynn, Trechock and Flowers received unanimous votes. Honorable mentions were Deutsch, Leip, Reznichak, Thomas, Comellas and Bassler.

The other selections were Bob Iwanicki of Cambridge (1B), Henry Schluter of Pocomoke City (3B), Alexander Pitko of Centreville (LF), George LeGates of Federalsburg (RF), Ken Raffensberger of Cambridge (LHP) and Ed Feinberg of Centreville (UTIL).

Pocomoke 4, Salisbury 3 (49–37) (70–16) August 29

Pocomoke	0	0	1	0	0	0	0	3	0	4	9	0
Salisbury	0	0	1	1	0	0	1	0	0	3	8	1

Montero (loser), Gray (winner)
Lynn, Montero—RBI; Luzansky—3B; Guerra, Trechock, Leip—SB

The Pocomoke City Red Sox journeyed to Wicomico County and handed the Indians a 4-3 loss, Salisbury's third loss in the past 20 games. Indians pitcher Juan Montero increasingly weakened throughout the game and gave the contest away in the eighth inning when the Red Sox scored three runs. Pocomoke City opened the scoring in the third inning on a two-base hit by second baseman Jones and a single by catcher Dousha. Salisbury tied it up in the bottom half of the inning when Luzansky tripled to right center field and scored on Lynn's single.

The Indians took the lead in the fourth when Guerra bunted for a base hit, sacrificed to second and advanced to third after a catch of a long fly. Now 90 feet away, the fleet-footed Cuban took his lead. While Gray started his delivery, he sprinted home. It was a close play at the plate but umpire Toach called him safe. From the Red Sox dugout, manager Vic Keen argued the call but it fell on deaf ears.

In the seventh inning, Leip singled, advanced to second on a sacrifice and moved to third on a wild pitch. He scored after the catch of Montero's flyout to center.

Miracle on the Eastern Shore

In the eighth inning, center fielder Dugan grounded out to first base. Montero then issued three consecutive walks to shortstop Hall, pitcher Gray and second baseman Jones. Hall scored on left fielder Denenberg's groundout to first base. Gray and Jones scored on Dousha's single to left field and right fielder Jester hit into a fielder's choice to end the inning.

The fans in the grandstand and bleachers questioned Flowers's decision to leave Montero in the game. Little did they realize that the bullpen was a bit spent. Bassler and Revolinsky had pitched the night before and could scarcely be dependably called on again. Comellas had been recovering from an attack of tonsillitis. Kohlman had just recovered from bronchitis and his stamina was affected. Since coming to Salisbury, Montero had been great in the pinch. Like Revolinsky, he usually pitched better when he had a man or two on bases. This day was not his day.

Montero's teammates worked hard to help him by registering 22 fielding assists. Thirteen Red Sox were stranded on the basepaths. This was one of the few games during the season that the Indians hitters were outslugged by an opponent. The slow curve thrown by Zulu Gray proved to be their Achilles' heel.

In the August 25 issue of *The Daily Times*, Roger H. Pippen, sports editor of the *Baltimore News-Post*, reflected on the Salisbury ball club's amazing comeback as one of the greatest feats in baseball history, even better than the 1914 Boston Braves, who won the National League pennant after being in last place midseason. Most teams' morale, he stated, would be wrecked with such a handicap put upon them but the Indians never let up and they became the talk of the baseball world. Notices of their comeback appeared in newspapers across the nation.

Salisbury 8, Centreville 5   (50–37) (71–16)
August 30 afternoon

Centreville	1	0	0	0	0	2	0	2	5	6	4
Salisbury	1	2	2	1	0	2	0	0	X	8	11	1

Kohlman (winner), List (loser)
Luzansky, Leip, Deutsch, Lynn, Guerra, Quimby—RBI;
   Leip (2)—2B; Luzansky (2), Guerra—SB

August 30 was a full day for the Salisbury Indians at Gordy Park. In the afternoon game, Kohlman kept his winning streak alive at 23

Five—Domination on the Diamond (August 1–31)

consecutive wins with an 8-5 win against the Centreville Colts. Kohlman had recently recovered from a bout with bronchitis and lost 10 pounds. Although not his finest moment, he pitched a six-hit contest, striking out six, walking four and throwing two wild pitches. Luzansky, in the first inning, drew a walk, stole second, advanced to third on a fielder's choice and then stole home. During the game, Gordon Troy, Centreville's second baseman, became the first visiting player to hit a home run in Gordy Park since June 21. He launched a ball that cleared the fence between the foul line and the fence corner.

Salisbury 4, Crisfield 2   (51–37) (72–16)   August 30 night

Crisfield	0	2	0	0	0	0	0	0		2	7	2
Salisbury	1	0	1	0	1	1	0	0	X	4	10	2

Comellas (winner), Barnes (loser)
Lynn, Garliss, Comellas—RBI; Luzansky, Lynn, Trechock—2B; Thomas, Garliss—SB

In the nightcap, the Indian sluggers were zoned in to the pitches thrown by the Crabbers' slowball hurler, Sherwood Barnes, collecting 10 hits, with Lynn and Comellas leading the slugfest with two base hits each. In the first inning, Luzansky started it off with a double. Lynn followed with a double of his own to bring him in. In the second inning, Crisfield took the lead when two runners crossed the plate. Marnie and Myers singled and advanced on a double steal and both scored on center fielder Webb's single. Webb was caught off first base and tagged out in a rundown. It was the first time that season that Webb got caught preparing to steal. Prior to that, he had been successful in 58 attempts.

In the third inning, Trechock doubled and scored on Barnes's wild throw to first base to tie up the score. In the fifth, Salisbury took control of the game when a hit and an error yielded a run. In the sixth inning, a walk, sacrifice and single gave the Salisbury Indians a 4-2 victory. Comellas pitched a solid seven-hit game, striking out nine with no walks.

Salisbury 4, Pocomoke 1   (52–37) (73–16)   August 31

Salisbury	0	0	1	0	2	0	0	1	0	4	8	1
Pocomoke	0	0	0	0	0	1	0	0	0	1	8	2

Bassler (winner), Harris (loser)
Lynn, Trechock, Deutsch—RBI

Miracle on the Eastern Shore

On the last day of August, the Salisbury Indians traveled down to Worcester County and came out victorious with a 4-1 score against the Red Sox. Lefty Bassler gave up eight hits, walked two and struck out nine. When the Red Sox threatened, he delivered his sharp-breaking curveball to close the door. Salisbury made their eight hits count in crucial situations. Salisbury started the scoring in the third inning when Deutsch singled. After Bassler flied out to left field, Luzansky and Lynn hit consecutive singles, with the latter scoring Deutsch. Trechock and Guerra both hit into fielder's choices to end the inning.

They added two more in the fifth. Deutsch struck out and Bassler and Luzansky hit consecutive singles. Lynn worked a walk and Trechock flied out to left field, which allowed Bassler to score. Luzansky scored on a wild pitch. In the eighth inning, Garliss was safe at first on a fielding error by second baseman Jones and advanced to second on a sacrifice by Quimby. After Leip grounded out to third base, Deutsch drove Garliss in with a base hit. Bassler grounded out to second base. Pocomoke City added their lone run in the sixth inning when Dousha hit a double and, after Jester grounded out to third case, Schluter hit a two-base hit that allowed Dousha to score. First baseman Daddino lined out to Deutsch and shortstop Hall struck out to end the inning.

The playing field was somewhat difficult. After a heavy downpour that softened the infield and with the outfield already crisscrossed with drainage trenches, Lynn committed the only Indian fielding error when he fumbled a hot grounder and badly threw the ball over to first base. Jones and Harris committed the two errors for the Red Sox.

Joe Garliss and Ed Leip were the fielding stars of the game. Garliss registered four putouts. Leip easily handled eight difficult chances without committing an error. On one play, Luzansky was nearly under a long fly in right center when he slipped on the muddy grass and Garliss, backing him up, flashed past him to make a running catch. At another moment in the game, Garliss sprinted in from deep right field to snag a near-perfect Texas Leaguer while leaping drainage ditches and puddles. Leip snared a foul fly over his head after running 50 yards.

An anecdote about the laundry duties that Salisbury's batboy, Maurice Fields, performed for the team. During the hot and humid summer months on the Eastern Shore, players would roast in their wool flannel uniforms. After the game, the players would leave their uniforms, all drenched with sweat, with Fields so he could bring them to the cleaners. They would pay Fields a quarter every two weeks. Flowers would

FIVE—Domination on the Diamond (August 1–31)

give him 50 cents every two weeks. If they were playing the next night, which happened most nights, it would be difficult for Fields to send the uniforms out to be cleaned so he would hang the uniforms up to get the stink off them.

By the end of August, the Salisbury Indians were a half game behind the first-place Easton Browns. For the month, the ball club played .862 ball with a 25–4 record and from June 20 on, they played .825 ball with a 52–11 record. From the official compilation of the league that appeared in the August 28 issue of the *Salisbury Daily Times*, Trechock (.360) and Lynn (.344) were perched on top of the league's batting list. Trechock also led in home runs (18) and RBI (73). Guerra was tied for second with 72 RBI. Luzansky was a distant second with 22 stolen bases behind Crisfield's Webb (58). Kohlman (21–1), Comellas (20–1) and Revolinsky (10–2) held the best winning percentages. Kohlman had five shutouts and led in strikeouts with 225.

Six

The Final Stretch (September 1–6)

On September 1, Salisbury added two new recruits after the 14-player deadline passed, Jose Salazar, a Cuban fastball pitcher who finally signed his contract, and John Kruk,[1] a 23-year-old Arlington, New Jersey, first baseman. Joe Cambria personally offered Kruk a contract after seeing him play semiprofessional ball in New Jersey. After Kruk was introduced to the Washington Senators' owner, Griffith proclaimed that he just met the next Hank Greenberg.[2] According to the league bylaws, each team could carry a roster of 18 men to the end of the season. The 18-man limit still prohibited more than two class men and two one-year men.

> **Salisbury 10, Pocomoke 2   (53–37) (74–16)   September 1**
>
> Pocomoke   1 0 0 0 1 0 0 0 0   2   6   1
> Salisbury   2 2 2 0 4 0 0 0 X   10 15   1
>
> Montero (winner), Keen (loser)
> Guerra (2), Montero, Luzansky, Quimby (2), Garliss, Leip, Deutsch—RBI; Guerra—2B; Guerra—HR; Guerra, Leip, Luzansky—SB

More than 3,000 fans attended the game at Gordy Park to pay tribute to the "wonder team" of Salisbury, Maryland. The guest of honor, Clark Griffith, stood on the speakers' stand behind home plate and addressed the fans and the team before the game. "I don't remember ... in my fifty years of baseball a team" (which he termed a miracle team—a team that would not be denied) "which has shown the pluck, grit, and determination these boys have had." He continued, "This celebration tonight is to spur them on. I am happy to congratulate each and every one, manager Flowers and Joe Cambria." He then

Six—The Final Stretch (September 1–6)

credited the fans for their "inspiration that made these boys come from behind."[3]

Flowers then approached the microphone and thanked the fans for their support and interest in the team. Along with Griffith on the speakers' stand stood Mayor Truitt; State Comptroller William S. Gordy; State Attorney General Herbert R. O'Conor; C.R. Hare, the chairman of the Boosters' Committee; and J.S. Reeves, the secretary-treasurer of the committee. To celebrate the season the Salisbury Indians had had so far, the committee presented to the 14 regulars, along with Joe Reznichak, manager Flowers, business manager M.E. Murphy, secretary John Milton and general manager Poke Whalen, a gift of an engraved 10-carat-gold-filled, 17-jewel wrist watch made by Hamilton with an inscription on the watch that included the player's name—*Salisbury Base Ball Club–1937* and a space left for the word *Champions* if they were

On September 1, 1937, the Salisbury Indians Boosters' Committee presented the players and several members of the administration with the gift of an engraved 10-carat-gold-filled, 17-jewel wrist watch made by Hamilton. Pictured is the front of the watch given to Leon Revolinsky (courtesy Mary Jane [Revolinsky] Martinez).

Pictured is the back of the watch given to Leon Revolinsky (courtesy Mary Jane [Revolinsky] Martinez).

victorious after the playoff series. Manager Flowers was gifted a new automobile. Owner Joe Cambria was presented with an engraved loving cup. Jose Salazar, the new Cuban pitcher; Elijah Disharoon, in charge of the center field scoreboard; batboy Maurice Fields; and bus driver Ernest Foskey were presented with other gifts.

Hare remarked: "It will be only a short time until these boys move up to baseball fame.... We want each and every one of them to have something to recall the happy days when he was playing on the 'wonder team.'"[4]

For the game, Flowers sent Montero to the mound and he pitched a six-hit game. He struck out five Red Sox and walked three in a 10-2 victory against Pocomoke City. Mike Guerra led the hitting barrage at the

Indians third baseman Ed Leip posing with his parents, Edgar Sr. and Nellie Leip, before the September 1 game against the Pocomoke City Red Sox (courtesy Eastern Shore Baseball Hall of Fame Museum).

Six—The Final Stretch (September 1–6)

expense of two Pocomoke pitchers (Red Sox manager Vic Keen and Joe Scarbinsky). He collected four hits, including a double and a two-run home run, in five at-bats. He even stole home for the second time for the season. The Salisbury hitters drove Keen off the mound after the third inning when he "gave up the ghost."[5] In a relief role, Scarbinsky was pounded for 10 hits for the next five innings.

After the sixth inning, Griffith exclaimed that "everything I have said about this team goes double."[6] In attendance were the parents of Joe Kohlman and the families of Ed Leip and Frank Trechock.

Salisbury 11, Crisfield 2   (54–37) (75–16)   September 2

	1	2	3	4	5	6	7	8	9	R	H	E
Crisfield	0	0	2	0	0	0	0	0	0	2	6	3
Salisbury	8	0	0	1	1	0	0	1	X	11	13	3

Revolinsky (winner), Barnes (loser)
Quimby, Leip, Deutsch (3), Revolinsky, Luzansky (3),
   Trechock—RBI; Luzansky—HR; Lynn, Luzansky (2)—SB

In the afternoon of September 2, the Indian sluggers let loose on the slow delivery of Crabbers pitcher Sherwood Barnes for 13 hits. In the 11-2 drubbing, the Indians scored eight runs on seven hits in the first inning. "Little Bill" Luzansky lifted a three-run bomb over the right field barrier, the first of its kind that occurred at Gordy Park during the season. Revolinsky (with a four-hitter in five innings) and Bassler (with a two-hitter in four innings) calmed the Crabbers' bats. With the Browns' 6–1 defeat to the Cardinals, the Indians took sole possession of first place by half a game.

Salisbury 5, Easton 0   (55–37) (76–16)   September 2

	1	2	3	4	5	6	7	8	9	R	H	E
Salisbury	3	0	1	0	0	1	0	0	0	5	10	0
Easton	0	0	0	0	0	0	0	0	0	0	0	2

Kohlman (winner), Kuntashian (loser)
Quimby (2), Deutsch—RBI; Guerra—2B; Deutsch—3B

For the night game, the Salisbury Indians traveled to the Talbot County town and defeated the Easton Browns 5 to 0 behind Kohlman's no-hit, no-run masterpiece for his 24th consecutive victory. He displayed the best control, fastest speed and a biggest bite on his curve than he had shown at any time during the season. He struck out nine and only two Easton hitters reached the basepaths. In the fourth inning,

Miracle on the Eastern Shore

Zimmerman, the Browns' shortstop, drew a walk then stole second while catcher Red Lenzi[7] struck out. He advanced to third while Browns first baseman Vernon grounded out to Kohlman. The next batter, left fielder Mikus, had trouble with Kohlman's "sharp-breaking curves and outdrops" to end the inning.[8] In the seventh inning, Lenzi battled Kohlman, fouling off good pitches, and worked a walk. The next batter, Vernon, drove a hot shot that stayed no higher than three feet above the ground right into Deutsch's glove. Deutsch then stepped on first base to complete an unassisted double play.

Browns pitcher Kuntashian did not fare well against the Indian bats. They had 10 hits, which led to five runs. In the first inning, Luzansky and Lynn singled. They scored on third baseman Eck's throwing error to first base on Garliss' grounder. Quimby's base hit scored Quimby and he advanced to second on center fielder Stiles's throwing error. The Indians scored another run in the third inning on two base hits and a sacrifice. In the sixth inning, the Indians scored one run on Leip's single and Deutsch's triple.

Kohlman's parents were sitting in the officials' box behind home plate. In the ninth inning with two out, his father was sitting with his legs crossed and fingers on both hands crossed while yelling out "come on, Joe, strike him out—I'm getting cramped."[9] His father at the beginning of the season promised his son a new automobile if he pitched a no-hit, no-run game. After the last out was registered, Mr. Kohlman exclaimed, "He earned the car."[10]

Leip and Garliss each made spectacular plays to save Kohlman's game. Browns second baseman Pultz hit a slow roller between third and short, for which Leip came sprinting in, scooped the ball barehanded and rifled it to first with an underhand throw in one continuous motion. Pultz was out by half a step. In the second inning, Mikus lifted a looping fly ball down the first base foul line. Garliss, in right center, ran a full 60 yards and made a leaping, one-handed catch against the fence, two feet across the foul line.

Salisbury 6, Crisfield 1 (56–37) (77–16) September 3

Crisfield	0	0	0	1	0	0	0	0	0	1	1	2
Salisbury	1	3	0	0	1	0	0	1	X	6	10	5

Comellas (winner), Boyce (loser)
Trechock, Leip, Comellas, Quimby—RBI; Comellas—2B; Lynn—3B; Garliss, Guerra, Leip—SB

Six—The Final Stretch (September 1–6)

The next day, George Comellas took the mound and looked like he was going to duplicate Kohlman's effort until the eighth inning, when Crabbers third baseman Marnie lined a single to right center. He finished with a one-hit, one-run victory, his 22nd win of the season. The Crabbers' only run came in the fourth inning when Leip dropped Crisfield shortstop Reha's fly behind third base. Leip then threw the ball into the bleachers behind first base, which allowed Reha to advance to third. Adams, the Crabbers' first baseman, drew a walk and second baseman Urban lifted a high fly to left field. Reha scored after the catch. Adams was thrown out on an attempted steal.

The Indians collected 10 hits and scored six runs against Crisfield tosser William Boyce.[11] They started in the first inning when Luzansky walked and advanced to third base on Lynn's single. Luzansky scored when Trechock hit into a double play. In the second inning, Quimby singled and advanced to third base on a wild pitch and scored on a fielder's choice. Deutsch drew a walk and scored on Comellas's two-base hit to center field. Luzansky laid down a bunt and Comellas scored when Marnie erred while fielding Lynn's grounder. In the fifth inning, Guerra started with a base hit, stole second base and scored on a single by Quimby. In the eighth inning, a run was tallied when Deutsch singled and moved to second base on a fielder's choice. He scored on a passed ball and a throwing error by catcher Myers.

Lynn snapped out of his hitting slump by going three for five with a triple. In the past 12 games, he had lost 13 points on his batting average, from .352 to .339. Quimby went two for three and Luzansky two for four. The game was a little sloppy. Marnie and Myers committed errors for the Crabbers and Leip committed three errors and Trechock had two for the Indians.

Riggin, the Crabber left fielder, made three beautiful running catches in deep left field. Luzansky made an impressive catch when he ran 55 yards almost to the center field warehouse while chasing down a long drive.

On the injury side, Guerra received a badly sprained right hand from a foul tip. Dr. Philip A. Insley, the attending physician for the Salisbury Indians, reported that there was no evidence of a fracture but that the fingers were bent backward, spraining the back of the hand. The team was unsure how long Guerra would be out of the lineup.

In 1953, Ernie Foskey, the team's bus driver, recalled one night when Comellas was pitching a game during the last week of the season.

Miracle on the Eastern Shore

"I used nine buckets of hot water on Comellas' arm that night. Hot towels were necessary to keep circulation flowing especially in his forearm which was cold as ice."[12]

Salisbury 4, Pocomoke 1   (57–37) (78–16)   September 4

Salisbury	0	0	0	0	0	2	0	1	1	4	15	5
Pocomoke	0	1	0	0	0	0	0	0	0	1	8	0

Bassler (winner), Gray (loser)
Trechock (2), Garliss, Quimby—RBI; Lynn—2B; Trechock—HR; Luzansky, Thomas—SB

The Salisbury Indians traveled to Worcester County and defeated the Red Sox 4 to 1. Bassler scattered eight hits while striking out one and walking one. Red Sox pitcher Zulu Gray gave up 15 hits to the Indian batters while also striking out five and walking one.

In the second inning, the Red Sox struck first. Daddino reached first base on an error by Deutsch and came in to score on a fielding error by Trechock on Hall's hit. Salisbury took the lead in the sixth inning when Lynn singled and Trechock homered. In the eighth, Gray hit Trechock with a pitch. Garliss sacrificed Trechock over to second, and he scored on Leip's single. Salisbury sealed the game in the last inning. Bassler singled and was sacrificed over by Luzansky. Lynn walked and Trechock popped out to the catcher, Dousha. Garliss' base hit brought in Bassler.

The Centreville Colts-Salisbury Indians game scheduled for September 5 was rained out. With only a day left in the season that already had a doubleheader scheduled, this game was never rescheduled.

Salisbury 1, Easton 0   (58–37) (79–16)   September 6

Salisbury	0	0	1	0	0	0	0	0	0	1	6	2
Easton	0	0	0	0	0	0	0	0	0	0	5	2

Kohlman (winner), Zarowsky (loser)
Kohlman—2B

On Labor Day, the Eastern Shore's regular season came to a close. Salisbury traveled up to the Talbot County town of Easton to finish the season with an unusual doubleheader. In the afternoon, the Indians played in Easton and then traveled down to Gordy Park for a nightcap with the Browns.

Six—The Final Stretch (September 1–6)

Understanding the importance of the afternoon game, Flowers sent his number one pitcher, Kohlman, to the mound. William Zarowsky started for the Browns. The attendees, nearly as many Salisburians as Easton residents, witnessed a great pitching duel with Kohlman coming out the victor. Chalking up his 25th consecutive win with a 1–0 score, he broke New York Giants' southpaw Carl Hubbell's[13] record of 24 games in a row, which was accomplished over parts of two years, 1936 and 1937. It was also his sixth shutout of the year. Kohlman limited the opponents to five hits and he scored the only run of the game. The tally came in the third inning when Kohlman doubled and advanced to third on a flyout to center field by Luzansky. Next, Lynn worked a base on balls. With two outs and runners on first and third, Trechock hit a hard grounder to Easton shortstop Ed Zimmerman, who had difficulty holding on to the ball and allowed Kohlman to score.

Zarowsky surrendered only six hits to the Indians sluggers. Pitching his best game of the season, Zarowsky kept the Indians confused, having them popping up harmless infield flies and catchable foul balls. Easton did have men in scoring positions but could not bring the runner in. During the seventh inning, Easton had two men on but catcher Lenzi hit a long fly to deep left field that ended the rally. Both teams displayed near flawless fielding despite the wet field.

Salisbury 5, Easton 4   (59–37) (80–16)   September 6

Easton	1	1	0	0	2	0	0	0	0	4	5	0
Salisbury	1	0	0	4	0	0	0	0	X	5	12	3

Revolinsky (winner), Feeley (loser)
Lynn, Luzansky (2), Trechock (2)—RBI; Luzansky (2), Trechock—2B; Garliss, Leip—SB

In the final game, the Indians slugged out a dozen hits off Easton pitcher John Feeley[14] under the lights at Gordy Park, which led to five runs. The Indians ended the season with a 10-game winning streak. Frank Trechock, who was dealing with a lengthy batting slump, went three for four with a double. Bill Luzansky went three for five with two doubles and Charles Quimby batted two for three. In the fourth inning, the Indians did the most damage, scoring four runs on two singles, a walk and two doubles. Leon Revolinsky got the win in the 5–4 contest, allowing only five hits. On the basepaths for Easton, Mikus, Pultz and Eck were credited with stolen bases. Sweeping both ends of a twin bill increased the differential between them and the second-place Easton Browns to three and a half games. The first step to the Indians' comeback story was complete. They finished in first place and won the seasonal pennant.

Some have speculated that if the Salisbury Indians continued with this impressive pace, the ball club would have accumulated a 135–27 record in a 162-game season. This could have happened. The Indians finished the season with a 10-game winning streak and were 18–2 in their last 20 games. In comparison, the 1934 Los Angeles Angels, chosen by the Minor League Baseball Association as the greatest minor league team of all time, had a record of 137–50 or a winning percentage of .732.

Group photograph of the 1937 Salisbury Indians players and members of the team's administration. Back row, from left: Jorge Comellas, Juan Montero, Frank Trechock and Frank Deutsch; middle row, from left: team treasurer John Milton, Fred Thomas, manager Jake Flowers, John Bassler, Leon Revolinsky, Joe Garliss, Joe Kohlman and business manager Melvin Murphy; front row, from left: batboy Maurice Fields, Bill Luzansky, Jose Salazar, Mike Guerra, Charles Quimby, Jerry Lynn and Edgar Leip (courtesy Judy Bowen and Jane Musser).

Six—The Final Stretch (September 1–6)

After the doubleheader, Clark C. Griffith, owner and president of the Washington Senators, sent a telegram to the *Salisbury Daily Times*: "I join the citizens of Salisbury in paying tribute to the wonder team which has performed the outstanding feat in the annals of baseball. Salisbury will ever remain renowned in memory of this great club. Congratulations."[15]

Among the news around the league came the season's greatest pitching accomplishment from the lowly Dover Orioles. Eddie Tantillo, an 18-year-old Rochester, New York, native, threw a perfect game against the Centreville Colts.

After the season ended, "Papa" Joe Cambria, seeing an opportunity for a linen and laundry business endeavor on the Eastern Shore,

Surrounded by his players, Jake Flowers received *The Sporting News* 1937 Minor League Manager of the Year scroll from Salisbury mayor Arthur W. Boyce on July 15, 1938. From left: possibly Charles Jutkiewicz (pitcher); Melvin Murphy (business manager); Robert Smithson (pitcher); Boyce; Leon Revolinsky (pitcher); possibly Robert Maier (right fielder); Charles Quimby (left fielder); Lewis Haneles (catcher); unidentified; possibly George LaPointe (shortstop); and James Conlan (center fielder) (Eastern Shore League Salisbury Baseball, Edward H. Nabb Research Center for Delmarva History and Culture, Salisbury University).

Miracle on the Eastern Shore

established the Eastern Shore Supply Company in the town of Salisbury. Designed to supply barbershops, restaurants and similar hospitality businesses with freshly laundered linens, jackets and towels for rental, the temporary headquarters was set up at Gordy Park, which he purchased in the fall, while they located a proper store somewhere in the town's business section. Cambria proudly reported that the season was very successful financially with over 80,000 paid admissions at the park.

Robert M. Clarke, the franchise holder of the Crisfield Crabbers, announced the plans for the New York Giants to purchase the club with the intention of the club becoming part of the Giants' extensive minor league farm system.

In December, baseball's national weekly publication, *The Sporting News*, announced that Jake Flowers was voted the 1937 Minor League Manager of the Year and Joe Kohlman one of the Most Outstanding Minor League Player of the Year.

Final Standings

Salisbury	59–37
Easton	56–41
Cambridge	53–43
Centreville	52–43
Federalsburg	52–45
Pocomoke City	42–55
Crisfield	40–57
Dover	32–65

The tabulation of the Indians' hurlers' earned run averages follows.

Pitcher	IP	ER	ERA
Kohlman	227	30	1.188
Pucci	7.1	1	1.267
Comellas	206	30	1.308
Bassler	172	47	2.459
Montero	88	25	2.557
Revolinsky	135	49	3.267
Kowal	10.1	5	4.455
Shelton	4.1	5	10.975
Shafnacker	1	4	36.000

Seven

Playoff Series

On September 3, representatives of the league's five leading ball clubs (Cambridge, Centreville, Easton, Federalsburg and Salisbury) met in Easton to finalize the structure of the upcoming playoffs. During the discussion, the group agreed upon a change in the format of the championship series. Instead of playing a three-game series, the final pairing would meet for a five-game series. In addition, during the first round, the first- and third-place clubs would play each other and the second and fourth place clubs would clash.

The first game of each series would be played on the grounds of the club having the highest winning percentage. The second game would be played on the opposite team's grounds. If a third game was necessary, the plate umpire at the second game would flip a coin to determine the location for the deciding game. The umpires selected for the playoffs were Henry Carrington, Albert Clark, James O'Conor and James Boyer.

In the initial series, each team received 45 percent of the gate receipts and the remaining 10 percent would go into the league treasury. In the final series, each team would receive 42½ percent and the league treasury 15 percent.

As the season moved into the playoffs, the Salisbury Indians management adjusted admission prices. For general admission, the price was 55 cents, for box seats 75 cents and children's admission was 25 cents. Five percent of Salisbury's share of the gate receipts during the playoffs played in Gordy Park would be given to the Lions Club for the purchase of a new ambulance for the local fire department.

In the first round, the Salisbury team faced the Cambridge Cardinals. Under the leadership of Fred Lucas, the Dorchester County baseball team compiled an official record of 53 wins, 43 losses. The Cambridge Cardinals finished third in the standings and averaged 4.8

Miracle on the Eastern Shore

runs per game with a team batting average of .257. The Cardinals' pitching staff was led by future major leaguer Ken Raffensberger, who had an 18–6 record and struck out 183 batters while walking only 47, and John Rodgers,[1] with a 10–1 record. During the season, Frank Jackson led the Cardinals' batters in all but two offensive categories (.328, 114 hits, 21 2B, 12 HR, 11 SB). Danny Murtaugh had the most triples for the team (4) and Iwanicki had the most RBI (75).

Salisbury 3, Cambridge 0   September 8   (1–0)

Cambridge	0	0	0	0	0	0	0	0	0	0	2	3
Salisbury	1	1	0	1	0	0	0	0	X	3	9	0

Comellas (winner), Rodgers (loser)
Trechock 2, Leip—RBI; Trechock, Quimby—2B; Guerra—SB; Lynn—Sac

For the first game of the playoff series against the Cambridge Cardinals, manager Jake Flowers sent his number two pitcher, George Comellas, to the mound. The lanky Cuban did not disappoint as he threw a two-hit shutout. It was his first shutout of the season. In the cool Delmarva weather, Comellas started the game a bit wild and for the first two innings pitched himself in and out of trouble. He walked three of the first six batters in the first two innings. In the second inning, with two Cardinals on base, he steadied himself and from then on cruised to a 3-0 victory. He struck out 12 Cardinal batters.

The Indians started the scoring in the first inning when Lynn singled and Trechock doubled him in. In the second inning, Quimby doubled and scored on Leip's single. In the fifth inning, the Indians scored their final run when Luzansky placed down a base-hit bunt and advanced to second on an error. He went to third on a sacrifice by Lynn and scored on Trechock's fielder's choice.

Cambridge pitcher John Rodgers was serviceable, allowing only three runs on seven hits. In the sixth inning, he exited the game when a ball hit by Garliss struck him in his pitching arm, which extremely affected his control. Koons relieved him in the seventh inning and quieted the Indian bats to a pair of hits through three innings.

Seven—Playoff Series

Cambridge 6, Salisbury 4   September 9   (1–1)

Salisbury	0	2	0	0	0	0	2	0	0	4	11	3
Cambridge	2	1	1	0	0	0	2	0	0	6	6	1

Revolinsky (loser), Humphries (winner)
Montero, Luzansky, Leip, Deutsch—RBI; Guerra—2B;
   Leip—SB; Montero—Sac

In front of 2,666 Delmarvans, the largest crowd of the season, the Cambridge Cardinals evened up the series with a 6-4 victory over the Salisbury Indians. The Cardinals' ace hurler, Raffensberger, began the game for Cambridge but lasted only 1⅔ innings, allowing four hits, walking one and striking out one. His replacement, Clyde Humphrey,[2] solved the Indians' bats and scattered seven hits in 7⅓ innings.

At the onset of the game, the Cardinals were in control when they scored a pair of runs in the first inning. Second baseman Murtaugh singled and center fielder Jackson followed by earning a walk. Montero, Salisbury's starting pitcher, hit the next batter, first baseman Iwanicki, to load the bases. Right fielder Healy walked in Murtaugh from third and Jackson scored on third baseman Gunkel's fielder's choice.

Just like Comellas in the game before, the cool Delmarva weather affected Montero's control. For six innings, he allowed four hits, fanned four, five walks and threw two wild pitches. He also committed one fielding error.

The Indians added two tallies in the second inning. With two outs, Leip and Deutsch hit consecutive singles. Next up was Montero, who hit a single that brought in Leip. Following the merry-go-round, Luzansky singled to bring in Deutsch. This drove Raffensberger to the showers and manager Fred Lucas sent in Humphrey, another portsider, to replace him.

Cambridge regained the two-run lead by adding a run in the second and third innings. Catcher Short singled and advanced to second on Humphrey's sacrifice. Murtaugh followed with a base hit and left fielder Henry Franz[3] reached first base on an error by Trechock. Short scored on Jackson's flyout to center field. The next inning, after Healy grounded out to third base, Gunkel walked. Shortstop Hoffner brought him in with a base hit.

The game settled down until the seventh inning, when the Indians again hit four consecutive singles from Garliss, Quimby, Leip and Deutsch to score two runs that locked up the game four apiece. Seizing

Miracle on the Eastern Shore

the opportunity to take advantage of the pendulum's swinging in Salisbury's favor, manager Jake Flowers sent in Revolinsky to face the first two batters while Comellas was warming up in the bullpen. Revolinsky walked the first batter, Jackson, and Iwanicki sacrificed Jackson over to second base. Flowers then sent Comellas, who offered his first pitch, a fastball straight down the pike, to William Johnson,[4] the Cardinals' right fielder, who drove it over the left field fence for a two-run home run and ultimately the win. A sports reporter speculated that if Comellas had a redo when facing Johnson, he would have seen only curveballs.

Though they collected 11 hits, the bottom half of the lineup carrying most of the load, the Indians stranded 13 base runners. Leip collected three hits on four at-bats with an RBI and scored one run.

For the Cardinals, Danny Murtaugh went two for five and scored a run.

Salisbury 8, Cambridge 0   September 10   (2–1)

Cambridge	0	0	0	0	0	0	0	0	0	0	1	4
Salisbury	0	0	2	0	0	0	6	0	X	8	8	1

Kohlman (winner), Raffensberger (loser)
Trechock 2, Lynn, Guerra—RBI; Luzansky—3B; Trechock—SB

With the series tied up one apiece, Cambridge Cardinals fans were heard "raising Cain," yelling "Where's that Kohlman? We beat him once and can do it again."[5] In the second game of the season, the Cardinals beat Kohlman 3 to 2 for his first and only loss. Their wish was granted but they did not like the result. Flowers did send Joe Kohlman to the mound to end the series and he responded. The Salisbury Indians eliminated the Cambridge Cardinals 8 to 0 behind Kohlman's superb one-hit pitching effort. The only Cardinal hit was a bunt by Dan Murtaugh. Kohlman struck out 10 hitters and issued zero walks.

The Cardinals sent out southpaw Kenneth Raffensberger on short rest and he surrendered eight hits, struck out 11 Salisbury batsmen and walked two. The third inning was Raffensberger's downfall when, after striking out Deutsch and Kohlman, he gave up three consecutive singles that led to two runs crossing the plate. Luzansky singled to left, then Lynn singled to center. Luzansky advanced to third and Lynn took second on the throw to the plate. Trechock drove both runners in with a scorching single off the shins of Cardinals shortstop Hoffner.

SEVEN—Playoff Series

In the seventh inning, the Indians scored six runs on three Cardinal errors and four hits, including a double. One particularly amusing play occurred when the Cardinals' fielding skills failed them. Guerra hit a would-be single in the right field and stretched it into a double. The fleet-footed Salisbury catcher slid ahead of the throw at second. Healy, who retrieved the ball, threw wildly and the ball bounced across the infield and settled near the bleachers. As Guerra headed toward third base, Short ran over to the bleachers and threw off balance to Iwanicki, who had positioned himself at home plate. The ball got away and Guerra, with a broad grin on his face, crossed home plate.

Statistics for the Salisbury-Cambridge Series

	G	AB	R	H	O	A	
Luzansky	3	11	3	4	5	0	3B, 1 RBI, .363 AVG
Lynn	3	12	3	5	7	5	1 RBI, SAC, .416 AVG
Trechock	3	10	0	2	1	11	2 E, 4 RBI, 2B, SB, .200 AVG
Guerra	3	13	0	3	27	0	SB, 2B, 1 RBI, .230 AVG
Garliss	3	13	2	2	5	0	.153 AVG
Quimby	3	11	2	2	2	0	2B, .181 AVG
Leip	3	12	2	6	1	5	2 RBI, SAC, .500 AVG
Deutsch	3	12	2	2	27	3	1 RBI, .166 AVG
Kruk	1	1	0	0	0	0	.000 AVG
Comellas	2	3	0	0	0	6	.000 AVG
Montero	1	2	0	1	1	2	E, 1 RBI, SAC, .500 AVG
Revolinsky	1	0	0	0	0	1	.000 AVG
Kohlman	1	4	1	1	2	3	.250 AVG

Trechock	3 DP
Lynn	4 DP
Deutsch	3 DP
Leip	1 DP

	G	IP	R	H	SO	BB	
Comellas	2	11	1	4	12	6	W
Montero	1	6	4	4	4	5	WP
Revolinsky	1	0.1	1	0	0	1	L
Kohlman	1	9	0	1	10	0	W, HBP

For the final series of the 1937 season, the Salisbury Indians' next opponent was the Centreville Colts. The fourth-seed Colts caught the second-seed Easton Browns dealing with a batting slump and took two out of three from them, blanking the Browns 5 to 0 in the first game, losing 4 to 1 in the second game and wrapping up the series with a 7-2 victory.

During the season, Eddie Feinberg led the team in hitting with a .334 batting average and 80 runs batted in. Alex Pitko added the power with 22 doubles, eight triples and a league-leading 20 home runs. Walter Carroll stole 18 bases to lead the team. Tom Ogden led the pitching staff with wins (14) and Lloyd Gross with strikeouts (132).

Centreville 9, Salisbury 1   September 12   (0–1)

Salisbury	0	0	0	0	0	0	1	0	0	1	5	0
Centreville	1	0	0	1	0	1	2	4	X	9	15	1

Comellas (loser), Ogden (winner)
Trechock—RBI; Thomas—3B

Continuing on their high in getting past the Easton Browns, the underdog Centreville Colts took the first game from the Salisbury Indians by a score of 9 to 1. A paid crowd of 2,735 mobbed the Centreville ballpark's grandstand, bleachers and sidelines in a town of 1,292 residents. For the first six innings, the Colts' young right hander, Tom "Whitey" Ogden of Clifton Heights, Pennsylvania, and George Comellas had a pitchers' duel with the hometown hurler faring better. Ogden held Salisbury to four hits while the Colts' bats lit up Comellas for nine hits and two walks during that stretch. Ogden was the winning pitcher when Centreville snapped Comellas's consecutive-win streak at 20 on August 20.

The Indians throughout the game failed to take advantage when runners reached third base. In the first inning, two Indians were in scoring position after a walk, a hit batsman and a wild pitch. Trechock flied out to Wurst and Feinberg made a sensational stop to retire Garliss. In the third inning, Salisbury threatened when Thomas tripled with two outs. After Lynn walked, Trechock was awarded first base on catcher interference when Knapp's glove nipped his bat. Unfortunately, the rally failed when Ogden struck out Garliss. The Indians' only run came in the seventh when, with two outs, Luzansky singled. Thomas and Lynn walked, which loaded the bases. Ogden pitched two balls to the next batter, Trechock, and manager O'Rourke yanked him for Douglas Voth.[6] Trechock singled to right field, scoring Luzansky. Rist stopped the scoring with a perfect throw from right field to nail

SEVEN—*Playoff Series*

Thomas at home plate. Voth retired the next six straight Indian batters to end the game.

The Colts started their scoring in the first inning. Troy hit a comebacker right through the pitcher's mound. After Carroll struck out, Pitko hit a looper over shortstop. The two runners advanced when Feinberg was called safe on a fielder's choice. Rist hit into a fielder's choice, forcing Feinberg out at second while allowing Troy to score. Pitko was caught stealing third to end the inning. They loaded the bases in the second but did not score. In the third, they wasted two consecutive hits. In the fourth, Wurst lifted Comellas's first pitch over the right field fence, and in the sixth, they added another run on a single by Wurst and a double by Troy. Revolinsky relieved Comellas in the seventh inning but did not fare any better. Rist hit a two-run blast beyond the right field fence following Pitko's double. In the eighth, the Colts completed the rout with four runs. Wurst singled and Voth walked. After Troy struck out, both scored on Carroll's long two-bagger. Pitko fouled out near the right field fence. Feinberg doubled, bringing in Carroll, and scored on Rist's triple to the scoreboard.

Rist led the Colts with a single, a triple and a home run, followed by Wurst with a home run and two singles. Troy, Carroll and Pitko each hit a single and a double. In total, the Colts exploded with a 15-hit game. Of the five Indian hits, only Thomas's triple went for extra bases.

Defensively for the Indians, right fielder Garliss made a spectacular catch into the crowd while chasing down a foul ball along the right field fence. Leip as usual was solid at the hot corner. For the Colts, Norman Wurst was superb at first base.

Centreville 3, Salisbury 2 September 14 (0–2)

Centreville	1	0	0	1	0	0	0	0	1	3	6	2
Salisbury	1	1	0	0	0	0	0	0	0	2	5	4

Kohlman (loser), Gross (winner)
Guerra, Luzansky—RBI; Garliss (2), Quimby, Leip—SB

On September 13, the grounds at Gordy Park were heavily saturated by an early morning rainstorm, and the weather was cold. As a result, the second game was delayed until the next day, affecting the original schedule. The schedule that was agreed upon had Salisbury playing game one in Centreville, traveling home to play games two and three and, if necessary, going to Centreville for game four and Salisbury

Miracle on the Eastern Shore

for game five. President Kibler made a ruling to adjust the schedule owing to the postponement. Salisbury would be traveling to Centreville (Wednesday afternoon) for game three, returning home for game four on Thursday and heading to Centreville for the final game.

In game two, the Centreville Colts knocked down another "Goliath" from Salisbury's stellar pitching staff. Joe Kohlman and Lloyd Gross battled in another pitchers' duel that resulted in Kohlman losing 3 to 2, snapping his consecutive winning streak at 26. Kohlman allowed six hits and struck out 10 batsmen and walked one. His teammates, unfortunately, committed four costly errors.

In front of 3,000 crazed fans, Centreville scored first in the opening frame when Trechock threw wildly after gathering up Carroll's grounder, which allowed him to reach first base safely. Carroll scored on Pitko's double. Salisbury tied it up in the bottom half of the inning when Lynn walked. He advanced to third on Trechock's seeing-eye single up the middle. Lynn scored when Troy had trouble getting the ball out of his glove while fielding Guerra's grounder.

The deadlock was broken in the second inning by successive singles by Deutsch, Kohlman, and Luzansky, with the third hit allowing Deutsch to score. The Colts evened the score in the fourth inning. Pitko singled and scored on an error by Trechock trying to throw Pitko out at second on Knapp's fielder's choice. The game tightened up until the ninth inning. Kohlman struck out the first two batters but then gave up a scratch hit to right field by Rist. Knapp was safe at first when Leip fielded his grounder and short-hopped his throw to first base. On the play, Rist advanced to third. Knapp and Rist engineered a double steal. Guerra rifled the ball to Lynn, who was covering second base, who immediately whipped the ball back at Guerra to catch Rist at home plate. Unfortunately, the throw was wide and Rist scored the winning run.

Lloyd Gross equaled Kohlman's effort by holding the Indians to five hits, striking out nine and walking one. After the game, Kohlman reflectively philosophized the game. "Well, you have to lose sometimes, and somebody has to be the loser. I guess the gang was just trying too hard in here."[7]

The Indians were originally scheduled to play an exhibition game against the House of David traveling team at Baltimore's Bugle Field but had to withdraw because they were still in the playoffs. The House of David ball club instead played against the Baltimore Police, who agreed to step in and serve as Salisbury's replacement for the game.

Seven—Playoff Series

Salisbury 6, Centreville 3   September   15 (1–2)

Centreville	0	0	0	0	1	1	1	0	0	3	9	2
Salisbury	1	0	2	1	0	1	1	0	0	6	7	1

Bassler (winner), List (loser)
Quimby (3), Bassler, Luzansky—RBI; Quimby—2B; Deutsch—3B; Luzansky—HR

In front of 1,500 Centreville fans, the Salisbury Indians rebounded after dropping two straight games to the Centreville Colts with a 6-3 victory. Before the game, E. Olin Willis,[8] on behalf of the Queen Anne's County fans, presented a purse of $100 to Centreville manager Joe O'Rourke. Salisbury manager Jake Flowers tapped southpaw John Bassler to take the mound. He was quite effective, allowing six hits, striking out one batter and walking none through 5⅓ innings. In the sixth inning, Comellas relieved him and allowed only three hits, struck out one batter and walked two.

For the Centreville Colts, List started the game giving up two hits and two walks with one strikeout in the first inning. In the second inning, Voth relieved him after List walked the first batter. Voth pitched a five-hitter for the last eight innings while striking out three batters and walking two. The game was played under protest after an incident in the sixth inning.

The play in question involved how many bases a runner may take after an errant throw lands in the bleachers. Leip was on first when Deutsch singled to center field. Colts outfielder Carroll relayed the ball to the shortstop, Feinberg, who rifled it to first base in an attempt to catch Deutsch, who had strayed from the base. The throw rolled into the crowd along the baseline. The four umpires got together and decided that both runners were awarded two bases. Leip scored and Deutsch advanced to third. O'Rourke adamantly argued that the runners should have been awarded only one base. Later that night, Kibler overruled the protest. According to the Official Baseball Rule 5.06(b)(4)(G) regarding throws into the crowd, runners are awarded the next base, plus an extra one.

Salisbury 7, Centreville 2   September 16   (2–2)

Centreville	0	2	0	0	0	0	0	0	0	2	5	2
Salisbury	1	0	4	0	1	1	0	0	X	7	7	1

Bassler (winner), Ogden (loser)
Trechock (5), Quimby—RBI; Bassler—2B; Trechock—HR; Luzansky (2)—SB; Garliss, Lynn—Sac

Miracle on the Eastern Shore

More than 3,500 wild and enthusiastic fans, the largest crowd to attend a ball game on the Eastern Shore, saw the Salisbury Indians even the series up with timely hits and major league–level base running. Flowers sent Montero to face the Colts. From the outset, he did not possess his best stuff, allowing three hits in the first inning, but his teammates saved him with sharp fielding. His control declined further in the second inning. After he walked Troy, Carroll grounded to Lynn, who tossed it to Trechock covering second, forcing out Troy. Montero then walked Pitko and Feinberg flied out to Garliss in right field. Carroll advanced to third on the catch. Carroll and Pitko executed a successful double steal, scoring Carroll. Rist worked a walk and Knapp singled to center to score Pitko. Flowers saw enough and pulled Montero for Bassler, who made Miller fly out to Quimby to end the rally.

Utilizing perfect control, a fine curve and a good fastball, Bassler shut the Colts down by pitching a one-hitter for 6⅓ innings. He also struck out six and walked one. In the eighth, Rist became the first Colt to reach first base since the third inning. He squeaked a single just past Lynn. The game ended with a spectacular one-handed running catch by Quimby on pinch hitter Shillingford's long fly to left. A reporter labeled Quimby as the "Pepper Martin"[9] of the series.

After scoring one run in the first, the Indians put a four-spot on the scoreboard in the third inning. Luzansky walked and advanced to second when Thomas skillfully laid a bunt down and reached first base safely. Lynn laid down another bunt and Luzansky scored when Colts hurler Ogden overthrew the ball to third. Ogden gave up six of the Indians' seven hits. Trechock connected with Ogden's delivery and sent it out of Gordy Park and onto the roof of a nearby factory. That shot sent Ogden to the showers, bringing in List, who quieted the Indians' bats.

In the fifth inning, Quimby hit a solo home run. In the sixth, Luzansky walked, stole second and scored on an infield grounder. In the seventh, both teams were retired in order.

Known during the season as Hard Luck Lefty, Bassler had been the Indians' saving grace, winning both games he appeared in to even the series. Luzansky gave the Colts an exhibition of how to run the bases by stealing everything but manager Joe O'Rourke's cud of tobacco. Trechock was the offense that night, batting in five runs with a single and a home run. Trechock and Quimby were outstanding in the field.

SEVEN—*Playoff Series*

Salisbury 7, Centreville 0   September 17   (3–2)

Centreville	0	0	0	0	0	0	0	0	0	0	0	1
Salisbury	0	0	2	0	1	1	1	0	2	7	10	1

Kohlman (winner), Gross (loser)
Trechock (2), Lynn, Leip (2), Luzansky—RBI; Trechock, Leip—2B; Leip, Luzansky—HR; Lynn, Deutsch—SB; Thomas—Sac

After the rain postponed the final game, the Centreville Colts and the Salisbury Indians met on Friday, September 17, to finish the series. Over 2,000 fans sardined around the little Centreville ballpark, overflowing down both foul lines and crowding both dugout roofs, to witness the Indians clinch the championship behind 22-year-old right hander Joe Kohlman's no-hit, no-run pitching performance, his second of the season. Kohlman struck out six Colts and walked one.

The Centreville Colts used two pitchers. Gross gave up six hits in four innings. He struck out one batter and walked two. Voth, who relieved Gross with no outs in the fifth inning, allowed four hits in five innings, fanning one batter and walking two.

In the third inning, Salisbury scored two runs when Thomas and Lynn singled and Trechock doubled them in. In the fifth inning, they scored a run on two hits, a walk and an error. In the sixth, Deutsch singled and scored on Leip's double. In the seventh inning, Thomas walked, stole second, advanced to third when Knapp threw wildly to peg him out at second and scored on a wild pitch. In the ninth, Leip hit a tremendous shot over the right center field fence. Luzansky added a solo home run of his own.

After the game, Kibler was congratulated for his success as president of the league. In the eighth inning, Kohlman's mother called the *Daily Times* for an update. After receiving the news that her son was pitching a no-hit, no-run ball game, she dropped the phone. His teammates behind him helped him along. Leip and Trechock had a busy afternoon, throwing out runners at first with beautiful pickups. For the outfielders, it was an easy day with only two chances leaving the infield. Luzansky and Quimby gloved a putout apiece.

Miracle on the Eastern Shore

Statistics for the Salisbury-Centreville Series

	G	AB	R	H	O	A	
Luzansky	5	24	8	7	5	1	1 RBI, 2B, HR, 2 SB, .291 AVG
Thomas	4	9	5	3	23	2	3B, SAC, .333 AVG
Lynn	5	15	3	4	7	9	1 RBI, SB, SAC, HBP, E, .266 AVG
Trechock	5	19	2	6	10	25	8 RBI, 2B, HR, 3E, .315 AVG
Garliss	5	18	0	1	6	0	2 SB, SAC, .055 AVG
Quimby	5	19	1	3	8	1	4 RBI, 2B, HR, SB, .157 AVG
Leip	5	19	2	2	4	11	2 RBI, 2B, HR, SB, 2E, .105 AVG
Deutsch	5	16	3	5	43	2	3B, SB, .312 AVG
Comellas	2	3	0	0	0	5	.000 AVG
Guerra	2	5	0	0	11	2	.000 AVG
Revolinsky	1	0	0	0	2	1	.000 AVG
Kruk	1	1	0	0	0	0	.000 AVG
Kohlman	2	6	0	2	2	2	.333 AVG
Bassler	2	6	0	1	0	1	1 RBI, 2B, .166 AVG
Montero	1	1	0	0	0	0	.000 AVG

Leip	1 DP
Lynn	2 DP
Deutsch	2 DP
Trechock	1 DP

	G	IP	R	H	SO	BB	
Comellas	2	8.2	4	12	4	4	L, 2 WP
Revolinsky	1	2	6	6	1	1	
Kohlman	2	18	3	6	16	2	W, L
Bassler	2	11.2	2	7	7	1	2 W
Montero	1	2.2	2.4	1	3		

Eight

Exhibition Games

During the season, teams would schedule nonleague games to help subsidize the organization and to support community needs. The Salisbury Indians played five games, of which they won four. Their opponents ranged from semiprofessionals to Class A clubs and a major league team.

Salisbury 1, South Philadelphia 0   June 14   (6 innings)

South Philadelphia	0	0	0	0	0	0	0	3	3
Salisbury	0	1	0	0	0	0	1	4	1

Kowal (winner), Toland (loser)
Lynn—2B

On June 14, 1937, the Salisbury Indians played an exhibition game on their day off with a club from the Philadelphia League, believed to be the South Philadelphia Hebrews. Halted in the sixth inning by rain, Salisbury won the game 1–0. Frank Kowal fanned nine batters and allowed but one hit before exiting the game in the fourth with an injured arm. Days later it became clear that Kowal was done for the season. Comellas finished the fourth and Michael Depko, recently signed by the Trenton club and sent to Salisbury for seasoning, pitched the last two innings, giving up two hits and striking out three. This would be the only appearance of Depko wearing a Salisbury Indians uniform in a game. Trenton club infielder Tony Miller replaced Trechock at shortstop, which was the second and last time Miller played for the Indians in the 1937 season. His first game was on May 22 against the Crisfield Crabbers. Frank Thomas, who signed with Trenton on May 29, replaced Guerra as the catcher. During the game, Jerry Lynn had two hits, including a double, and Luzansky and Thomas had one hit each.

Miracle on the Eastern Shore

Salisbury 7, Trenton 2   September 7

Trenton	1	0	0	0	0	0	0	1	0	2	5	0
Salisbury	1	1	0	0	1	0	3	1	X	7	9	1

Flowers (winner), Holmes (loser)
Thomas, Trechock (2), Lynn (2)—RBI; Luzansky, Flowers, Lynn—2B; Thomas, Luzansky—Sac

After the regular season ended and before the playoffs started, the Salisbury Indians hosted the New York-Pennsylvania League Trenton Senators in a Lions Club hospital benefit game. The Senators, managed by Spencer Abbott,[1] ended the 1937 season with a record of 54 wins and 80 losses, eighth in the NYPL. Before the game, Montero, who appeared in 21 games with the Senators, was asked his opinion about his former team. "Trenton O.K. but semi-pro team, we fix, big score, make um mad!"[2]

The Indians trounced the Class A outfit 7 to 2. Manager Jake Flowers called his own number to be the starting pitcher. Although age had robbed his speed of any sting, it hadn't touched his curve and control. Pitching for the first time in 16 years, he allowed four hits in the first five innings. He chalked up five strikeouts and gave up a run and a base on balls. Jose Salazar, the new Cuban hurler making his Eastern Shore debut, pitched a one-hitter over the final four innings, walking three and fanning two.

Offensively, Luzansky, Flowers and Lynn hit doubles, Trechock and Lynn had two RBI each and John Kruk, the other new recruit, went two for three. Flowers leaned on one of Matty Holmes's[3] fastballs and lined it to the deep left field corner of the ballpark for a two-base hit. It would have been a triple for a younger man. After he left the game, he came up in the press box and quipped, "Well boys, how did you like that triple I stretched into a double?"[4]

The game was halted briefly in the fifth inning, when Salisbury mayor Alfred T. Truitt, on behalf of the *Baltimore News-Post*, presented the newspaper's "most valuable player" trophy to Joe Kohlman. Rodger H. Pippen,[5] sports editor of the *News-Post*, had planned to attend but was forced to cancel the trip at the last minute.

At the conclusion of the game, owner Joe Cambria reported that the total gross gate receipts were $675. After deducting park expenses of $75, Indians business manager Melvin Murphy was tasked with delivering one-third of the gate receipts ($200) to the Lions Club for their ambulance fund.

EIGHT—Exhibition Games

Salisbury 3, Philadelphia Athletics 2   September 20

Philadelphia	0	0	2	0	0	0	0	0	0	2	7	0
Salisbury	0	0	0	0	0	0	1	2	X	3	8	0

Bassler (winner), Woodend (loser)
Flowers, Quimby, Leip—RBI; Leip—SB; Lynn—Sac

On September 20, three days after winning the Eastern Shore Baseball League championship, the Salisbury Indians arranged another exhibition game outside of their class. This time they moved up to the major leagues with an invitation extended out to the Connie Mack–managed Philadelphia Athletics. Mack's team had a disappointing season, finishing in seventh place in the American League with a record of 54–97.

The wonder team had to come from behind to defeat the A's by a 3-2 score. For the Athletics, five mainstays were in the lineup, outfielders Wally Moses and Bob Johnson, first baseman Gene Hasson, second baseman Rusty Peters and utility player Lynn Nelson.[6] Also for the A's were catcher Bill Conroy and infielder Wayne Ambler, who had seen a bit of action in the last six weeks.[7] A trio of hurlers, Delaney, George Woodend and Bill Kalfass, took the hill for Philadelphia.[8] During the game, Flowers utilized Salazar, Comellas and Bassler against the A's hitters. Starting pitcher Salazar managed a six-hitter through five innings with one strikeout and three walks. Comellas pitched hitless sixth and seventh innings and struck out three. Bassler, credited with the victory, allowed one hit in two innings and struck out three and walked one.

The Athletics took an early lead in the third stanza by scoring two runs. After Warren Huston[9] singled, Peters launched a long fly that ended up as a triple when Quimby fell while tracking it down. The mishap allowed Huston to score. Peters scored when Johnson flied out to Luzansky and Thomas couldn't handle Luzansky's perfect throw. In the seventh frame, Salisbury got on the scoreboard. Quimby led off the inning with a walk and was forced out at second when Deutsch hit into a fielder's choice. Deutsch then moved to second on Garliss' hot shot that ricocheted off the glove of Peters. Leip walked to fill the bases. Manager Flowers called his own number to pitch-hit for Comellas and drove a long flyout to right, allowing Deutsch to score. Luzansky closed the inning with a groundout.

In the next inning, the Indians took the lead. Thomas opened the

Miracle on the Eastern Shore

inning with a single to center, followed by Luzansky sacrificing Thomas over to second. Thomas moved to third when Trechock grounded out to Peters. Thomas scored the tying run on Quimby's single to center. Quimby moved to second on Deutsch's liner to left. Garliss singled to fill the bases and Leip walked in the winning run. Bassler struck out to end the inning.

Salisbury 7, House of David 4   September 21

House of David	0	0	2	1	0	0	1	0	0	4	11	1
Salisbury	0	1	4	1	0	0	0	1	X	7	14	1

Comellas (winner), Swaney (loser)
Thomas, Lynn—2B; Porter—HR

The next day (September 21), Salisbury hosted the Baltimore-based House of David baseball club at Gordy Park. Known as "the men that have never shaved" in the newspapers, the visitors "put on an unusual exhibition of humorous, fancy and skillful ball juggling," much like the Harlem Globetrotters in basketball.[10] This exhibition of ball handling led to the invention of the "game of pepper." Since 1913, the House of David baseball team traveled through rural America playing competitive baseball.

Originally planned for September 14, the game was postponed owing to Salisbury's participation in the playoffs.

Using a trio of pitchers (Comellas, Bassler and Salazar, each pitching three innings), Salisbury defeated the Baltimore team 7 to 4. Comellas pitched a two-hitter, Bassler allowed five hits and Salazar four hits. Lynn, Trechock and Leip collected seven of the 14 hits during the night. Princess Anne native and Syracuse Chiefs outfielder Richard C. Porter,[11] who started the game in right field, sent a pitch over the right field fence in his first at-bat. The 35-year-old veteran was a major league baseball player from 1929 to 1934 for the Cleveland Indians and Boston Red Sox. Before and after his major league career, he played 14 seasons for three teams in the International League (Baltimore Orioles, Newark Bears and Syracuse Chiefs), compiling a .328 batting average with 123 home runs.

The proceeds from the exhibition game were divided among the players, the Peninsula General Hospital and the Wicomico Children's Home.

Eight—Exhibition Games

House of David 7, Salisbury 6   September 22

House of David	0	0	0	4	1	0	2	0	0	7	5	0
Salisbury	4	0	0	1	1	0	0	0	0	6	11	1

Revolinsky (loser), Janesko (winner)
Thomas, Leip, Trechock—2B; Luzansky—SB

The final game of the 1937 season for the Salisbury Indians ended with a loss. On September 22, the Indians traveled to Oriole Park and played against Baltimore's House of David baseball team for the second consecutive day with the local team capturing a 7-6 victory. The Indians held a 4–0 lead for three innings until ace hurler George Comellas hit a wild streak that had the "bewhiskered" hitters tying the game in the fourth frame on a hit, an error, four walks and a stolen base. House of David pitcher Mike Janesko[12] shut the door by holding the Eastern Shore champions scoreless in the last four innings, and his teammates scored the tying and winning runs in the seventh for the win. Three Salisbury pitchers (Comellas, Revolinsky and Montero) contributed to the House of David team's victory by walking 11 batters.

Comellas pitched one-hit baseball for five innings, striking out three and walking five. Revolinsky was sent in and pitched a two-hitter for three innings, striking out two and walking four. Montero came in to pitch the last inning, giving up two hits and walking two. The Indians outhit their opponents 11 to five but their pitchers' wildness was their undoing.

Ball clubs around the region expressed interest to play the "wonder team." One such team, the Glen Burnie ball club of the Baltimore Semi-Pro League, who represented the state of Maryland in the 1937 national semipro championship tournament in Wichita, Kansas, tried to arranged a series but it never panned out. The Hagerstown (Maryland) Old Export ball club of the Washington County League proclaimed "they were ready for a series with Salisbury" after sweeping the Federalsburg A's over the weekend of September 18–19 but no games were scheduled.[13]

An exciting contest occurred on September 12 when the Washington Elite Giants of the Negro National League played a doubleheader against a team made up of Eastern Shore Baseball League "stars" from five of the eight clubs (Cambridge, Crisfield, Dover, Easton and Pocomoke). Harry O'Donnell, business manager of the Dover Orioles, was in charge of the team. The Giants defeated them 15 to 4 and 3 to 0.

NINE

Indians in the Major Leagues

On September 19, Frank Trechock, Jerry Lynn and Mike Guerra made their major league debut with the Washington Senators during a doubleheader with the Chicago White Sox. Trechock appeared in the first game at shortstop and collected two singles in four trips to the plate. Afield he made two errors that were more than less costly, but he also came up with two fairly clever plays. He had two putouts and four assists, including two double plays.

In the nightcap, Lynn took his familiar position at second base and collected two hits in three at-bats, including a double. He had four putouts and three assists and was the pivot man for three double plays. He connected with two of the Senators' five hits off Vernon Kennedy.[1] In the same game, Guerra caught three pitchers—another recruit, Arnold Anderson, and Dick Lanahan and Bucky Jacobs.[2] He committed two errors and went hitless with two strikeouts in three at-bats. Guerra was replaced in the ninth inning for Jimmy Wasdell.[3]

Clark Griffith, owner of the Washington Senators, set aside 1,000 tickets for box seats in the grandstand at Griffith Stadium for any Salisburian who wanted to attend the September 19 game to root for the Salisbury stars. The tickets, priced at $1.10, were available throughout Salisbury at the following places: Bennett's Drug Store, Church Street Pharmacy, County Trust Company, Red Star Bus office and the bus office at the Wicomico Hotel, Ulman's Confectionary, Waller's Confectionary, Watson's Smokehouse and White & Leonard's Drug Store. A motorcade was planned to travel from Salisbury to Washington, D.C. The attendees driving their cars would meet at Gordy Park at eight in the morning and leave at 8:30 following the Red Star buses to the Matapeake-Annapolis ferry and onward to Washington. Each ticket holder was able to purchase a round-trip ferry ticket for 55 cents and received a "Salisbury Booster" badge. When the Indians made their bow during the games, a call was made for any Salisburians in the crowd to stand up. Almost all who were attending rose to their feet.

Joe Kohlman appeared in two games. On September 26, he pitched eight innings for a no-decision in a 7–7 tie against the Philadelphia Athletics. He pitched a nine-hitter, relying mostly on the curveball, before being benched for a pinch hitter in the bottom of the eighth inning while the Senators were leading 7 to 4. The game ended in the 11th inning on account of darkness. In the first inning, Kohlman allowed one run when, after his triple, Billy Werber[4] scored on Johnson's double. Kohlman retired the A's in order in the second. A double and two singles in the third permitted the A's to score twice. For the next three frames, Kohlman allowed only two hits. In the seventh, Newsome singled, stole second and came around on Werber's single. In the eighth, Kohlman handled the three batters. In the end, he struck out three, walked one and committed a balk. Also, he assisted on one putout. At the plate, Kohlman registered his first major league hit in the second inning when he drove a clean shot between first and second base. He finished the game going one for three.

Kohlman's second outing was the nightcap of a doubleheader against the Philadelphia Athletics on October 3. With a 4-3 victory, he was awarded his first win in his major league career. During the contest, he gave up five hits while walking two through five innings before the game was shortened on account of darkness.

After the season concluded, Bucky Harris, the Senators' manager, shared his evaluation regarding the Eastern Shore League recruits. He believed that they "simply aren't ready for this league."[5] Guerra had a disappointing outing and in Harris's mind "may never find his way to the majors."[6] Trechock was undersized and played a mixed game at shortstop. While he did field two nice plays, the two errors were quite costly. Lynn, on the other hand, played a faultless game and, in Harris's opinion, "showed signs of developing into a major league prospect."[7]

The last Indian sold to the Washington Senators was Jorge "George" Comellas, who never got the chance to take the mound for the major league team during the 1937 season. Comellas eventually entered the Big Show during the 1945 season with the Chicago Cubs.

Ed Leip was another Salisbury Indian that spent some time in the major leagues. The Washington Senators called him up in September 1939 and he appeared in nine games. The next year, Washington waived Leip to the Pittsburgh Pirates and he appeared in 21 games, mostly in September from 1940 to 1942.

Miracle on the Eastern Shore

Other ballplayers from around the league had the opportunity to spend some time in the major leagues. The 1937 Cambridge Cardinals had three future major leaguers on their roster. Ken Raffensberger played 15 years in the major leagues on several teams (St. Louis Cardinals [1939], Chicago Cubs [1940–41], Philadelphia Phillies [1943–47] and Cincinnati Reds/Redlegs [1947–54]). Dan Murtaugh played for three major league teams (Philadelphia Phillies, 1941–43, 1946; Boston Braves, 1947; and Pittsburgh Pirates, 1948–51). Charles Marchlewicz, known as "Chip Marshall," played one game with the St. Louis Cardinals in 1941.

The Dover Orioles' John Wittig spent five years with two major league teams, the New York Giants (1938–1939, 1941, 1943) and the Boston Red Sox (1949). Easton Browns first baseman James "Micky" Vernon would eventually play 14 years for the Washington Senators, three years for the Cleveland Indians, two years for the Boston Red Sox and one year each for the Pittsburgh Pirates and the Milwaukee Braves.

Player Biographical Sketches

* — data acquired from World War II Draft Registration Cards.

^ — data are incomplete, unable to locate five box scores.

WLADYSLAW A. ANDRZEJEWSKI

[1916 PHILADELPHIA, PENNSYLVANIA–1975 WILMINGTON, DELAWARE; R/R 5–10½ 165*]

Wladyslaw Andrzejewski, son of Polish immigrants Kazmierz and Augustyna (Szczepanska) Andrzejewski, played under the moniker Walter "Chick" Andrews. He attended Wilmington Trade School, winning the Delaware State scholastic baseball championship in 1932. In 1934, he spent the season with the Delaware Gypsies and the Alco Leather Company Blue Sox of the Wilmington City League. In 1935, he continued with the Alco Leather Company and split his time between the Alco Leather Company ball club of the Wilmington City League and the Wilmington Athletic Association in the New Castle County Baseball League during the 1936 season. In mid–July 1936, Poke Whalen, Joe Cambria's scout, signed Andrzejewski to a contract with the Trenton Senators (NYPL). In the first two games of the 1937 season, he played center field for the Salisbury Indians. After that, he returned to Wilmington, Delaware, and spent the rest of the 1937 season splitting his time between the Pennsylvania Railroad Athletic Association of the Atlantic Seaboard League and the Alco Leather Company ball club. For the 1938 season, he remained with the Alco Leather Company ball club. Andrzejewski played with the Diamond Ice and Coal Company ball club of the Industrial Baseball League in 1939. The next year, he was with the Elmhurst Athletic Association of the New Castle County Baseball League. During World War II, Andrzejewski was stationed at the Pusey and

Player Biographical Sketches

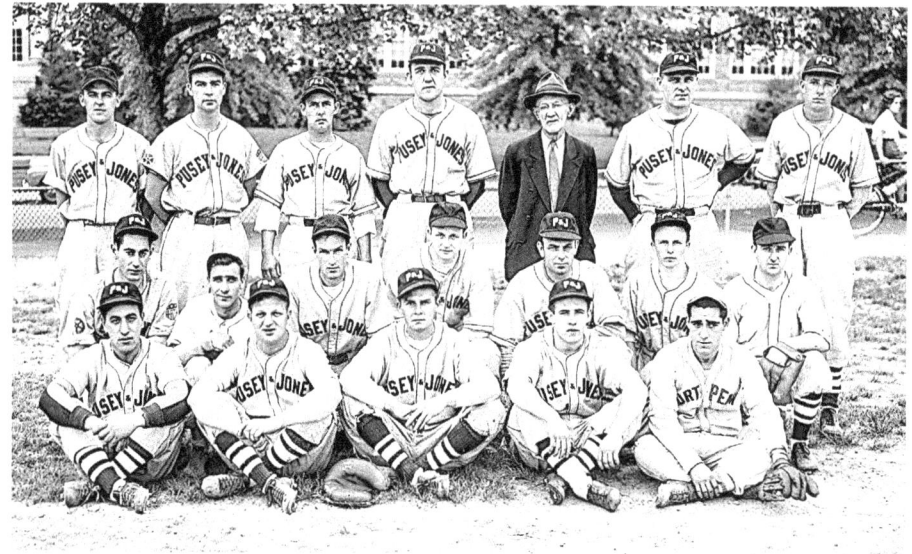

Wladyslaw Andrzejewski (back row, first on left) on the Pusey and Jones Corporation baseball team, 1944. At the beginning of the season, Wladyslaw A. Andrzejewski (1916–1975), known as Walter Andrews, appeared in the first two games for the Salisbury Indians, playing in center field (Pusey and Jones Corporation baseball team opening game, 1944, 72350_5412, Pusey and Jones Corporation photograph collection [Accession 1972.350], Hagley Museum & Library, Wilmington, DE 19807).

Jones Corporation, a major shipbuilder and industrial equipment manufacturer, where he played for the company's ball club. He joined the Pulaski Legion's ball club after the war. He was employed for 39 years as an electrician with the Penn Central Transportation Company.[1]

Regular-Season Statistics

GP	AB	R	H	RBI	2B	3B	HR	SB	SF	HBP	E	PO	A	DP	AVG	SLG
2	6	0	0	0	0	0	0	0	0	1	0	1	0	0	0.000	0.000

John Bassler

[1914 Sheboygan, Wisconsin–1980 Sheboygan County, Wisconsin; L/L 5–11 173]

Son of Russian immigrants John and Emile (Eiffert) Bassler, John Bassler attended St. Paul Lutheran School and graduated from Central High School in Sheboygan, Wisconsin, in 1932. He started his baseball career at the age of 15 playing for several semiprofessional teams in local Sheboygan leagues. In 1935, he became the property of the Washington Senators and spent a few years with several teams in the Texas leagues (the Taft Tigers of the Texas Valley League; Refugio Firemen and Corpus Christi Clippers of the South Texas League). In 1937, Bassler was sent to the Trenton Senators (NYPL) and pitched several games, accumulating a record of two wins and two losses. He was transferred to the

Nicknamed "Hard Luck Lefty," John Bassler (1914–1980) was the lone southpaw pitcher on the team, accumulating a 10–10 record during the season, striking out 111, walking 57 with two shutouts. During the playoffs, he won two important games for the Indians (courtesy Mary Jane [Revolinsky] Martinez).

Player Biographical Sketches

Salisbury Indians and, although nicknamed "Hard Luck Lefty," was a mainstay in the pitching rotation. During the playoff run, Bassler won two crucial games. He returned to the Salisbury Indians for the 1938 season, helping them win another championship. In 1939, he started the season with the Greenville Spinners (PIED). In late August, he joined the Springfield Nationals (EL). In 1940, Bassler was ordered to report to the Springfield ball club but he decided to hold out and was sold to the Trois-Riveres Renards (QUPL). During the season, he injured his pitching arm and went to several specialists for treatment but his arm failed to respond. He was released from the team in August. Bassler returned to Sheboygan and began working at the Kohler Company. In 1944, he lost sight in one eye from an accident at the plant. He was employed for 39 years, retiring in 1979. He died the next year.[2]

Regular-Season Statistics

GP	AB	R	H	RBI	2B	3B	HR	SB	SF	HBP	E	PO	A	DP	AVG	SLG
38	71	11	16	7	0	0	0	0	7^	0^	5	6	39	4	.225	.225

IP	H	BB	SO	Cpgs	Sho	W	L	Pct.
172	162	57	111	14	2	10	10	.500

Playoff Statistics

GP	AB	R	H	RBI	2B	3B	HR	SB	SF	HBP	E	PO	A	DP	AVG	SLG
2	6	0	1	1	1	0	0	0	0	0	0	0	0	0	.166	.333

IP	H	BB	SO	Cpgs	Sho	W	L	Pct.
11.2	7	1	7	0	0	2	0	1.000

Exhibition Statistics

GP	AB	R	H	RBI	2B	3B	HR	SB	SF	HBP	E	PO	A	DP	AVG	SLG
2	3	1	1	0	0	0	0	0	0	0	0	0	0	0	.333	.333

IP	H	BB^	SO^	Cpgs	Sho	W	L	Pct.
5	6	1	3	0	0	1	0	1.000

JAMES BERGEN

[POSSIBLY 1917 TRENTON, NEW JERSEY–1985 BRISTOL, PENNSYLVANIA; 6–1 165]

James Bergen's first game with the Salisbury Indians was a doubleheader against the Dover Orioles on July 7. Before that, it was reported

Player Biographical Sketches

that he was playing for a semipro team in North Carolina. After playing 10 games for the Indians, he "jumped" his contract on July 15. Although he was placed on the suspended list in the Eastern Shore League, he played for the Trenton Senators (NYPL) for the rest of the season. He was released from Trenton in March 1938.[3]

Regular-Season Statistics

GP	AB	R	H	RBI	2B	3B	HR	SB	SF	HBP	E	PO	A	DP	AVG	SLG
10	48	7	19	1	1	1	0	0	1^	0^	0	19	0	0	.404	.458

ROBERT SMITH BRADY

[1914 HANOVER, PENNSYLVANIA–1985 PHOENIX, ARIZONA; L/L 5-11 165]

Before playing with the Salisbury Indians, Bob Brady, son of William and Ella (Smith) Brady, was the batboy for the 1928 champion Hanover Raiders (BLRI). He appeared on the suspended list for the Harrisburg Senators (NYPL) from June to September 1934. In 1935, he was on the roster of the Hanover Athletic Club of the York-Adams County League. For the next season, he split his time with the Taneytown ball club of the Frederick County League and the Hanover Athletic Club. He was the starting first baseman for the 1937 Salisbury

Robert Brady, ca. 1939. Robert S. Brady (1914–1985), the Indians' starting first baseman when the season started, batted .246 with seven RBI in 15 games before he was released from the team concerning his eligibility (courtesy Carole Krout).

Player Biographical Sketches

Indians before being released on June 19 due to his apparent ineligibility. In early August, he tried out for the Zanesville Bees (MATL) but did not make the roster. In 1938, Brady played for the Taneytown and Reistertown ball clubs of the Baltimore-Carroll County League. In 1941, Brady signed to play first base with the Hanover Athletic Club of the York-Adams County League, a ball club he played with back in 1935 and 1936. His obituary stated that he had been under contract with the St. Louis Browns. During World War II, he served in the U.S. Army, rising to the rank of sergeant. In 1950, he was working as a welder for a steel plant in Baltimore, Maryland. By 1974, he resided in Phoenix, Arizona.[4]

Regular-Season Statistics

GP	AB	R	H	RBI	2B	3B	HR	SB	SF	HBP	E	PO	A	DP	AVG	SLG
15	61	11	15	7	0	0	0	2	1^	4^	3	141	8	13	.246	.246

THADDEUS GENTRY CASH

[1916 CANTON, OHIO–1995 JOHNSON CITY, TENNESSEE; L/? 5–11 174]

Thad "Doc" Cash, son of Charles and Allie (Durham) Cash, was a 1935 graduate of Boones Creek High School (Johnson City, Tennessee), where he was the nation's second-leading scorer in basketball. He attended East Tennessee State Teachers College, Johnson City (now East Tennessee State University) for one year and in 1936 joined the Hunter Pioneers of the Watauga Valley loop. He also signed a contract with the Pulaski (Virginia) semipro baseball team. At the end of the year, Cash was being pursued by scouts from Detroit, Birmingham and New Orleans; however, he decided to sign for the 1937 season with the Albany Senators (IL), who assigned him to the Trenton Senators (NYPL). His contract was assigned to the Salisbury Indians on April 28, 1937. Cash played the first eight games for the Salisbury Indians until his outright release on May 28. In July, he joined the Huntington Booster Bees (MTNS) and spent the rest of the 1937 season and all of the 1938 season with them. In 1939, Cash was released to the Yakima Pippins (WINT), spending two months with the club before he was released to the Welch Miners (MTNS). In June 1939, he joined the Bluefield Blue-Grays (MTNS). In May 1940, he was sold to the Jackson Senators (SEAL). From June 1940 to August 1940, he was optioned to the Salem-Roanoke Friends (VIRL). He finished his career with the Elizabethton Betsy Red Sox (APPY) from 1941 to June 1942. He was a lifelong Washington

Player Biographical Sketches

Thaddeus Cash (right) with the Bluefield Blue Grays, 1939. Thaddeus "Doc" Cash (1916–1995) tried out for the Salisbury Indians' third baseman position. He appeared in eight games, batting .310 with five RBI and two doubles. After his release from the team, he joined the Huntington Booster Bees of the Mountain State League. The man with him here may be Orville Barr (courtesy Kevin Ellis).

County (Tennessee) resident and farmer and retired as owner and operator of Cash's Grocery store. He was a World War II Army veteran.[5]

Regular-Season Statistics

GP	AB	R	H	RBI	2B	3B	HR	SB	SF	HBP	E	PO	A	DP	AVG	SLG
8	29	5	9	5	2	0	0	1	0	0	0	9	9	1	.310	.379

Jorge Vivino Comellas y Pono

[1916 Havana, Cuba–2001 Miami, Florida; R/R 6–0 185]

From the Luyano neighborhood of Havana, Cuba, Jorge Vivino Comellas y Pono made his professional debut on the Marinao team of

Player Biographical Sketches

the Cuba League's 1935–1936 winter season after a revolution closed the University of Havana and ended his collegiate career. On March 10, 1936, "George" arrived in the United States via Tampa, Florida. One of the first nine Cuban players to be signed to a contract by Joe Cambria, he was assigned to the York White Roses (NYPL). During the season, York relocated to Trenton, New Jersey, and became the Trenton Senators. After the season, he returned to Cuba and spent the winter playing for the Santa Clara team. On April 12, 1937, he made another trip to the United States to join the Salisbury Indians. To help him acclimate to the English-speaking nation, Cambria gave him pocket cards that included essential information like sample menus written in English so he could order meals. On August 28, 1937, the Washington Senators purchased Comellas's contract but he did not see any game action. During the 1937–1938 winter break, Comellas returned for a second season with the Santa Clara team, which won the pennant. In January 1938, the Charlotte Hornets (PIED) purchased his contract, and by March, it was reported that Comellas was being sent to the Greenville Spinners (SALL). During the 1938–1939 winter season, Comellas joined the Almendares team. For the majority of the 1939 season, Comellas was on the Greenville ball club's roster. By August, he was transferred to the Salisbury Indians and stayed with the team through the 1940 season. In the next season, the Springfield Nationals (EL) purchased Comellas outright from Salisbury. In August, the Pittsfield Electrics (CAML) secured his contract. In 1942, he played for the Utica Braves (CAML) and in 1943 for the Portsmouth Cubs (PIED). In September 1943, Portsmouth released Comellas to the Los Angeles Angels (PCL), where he stayed through the 1944 season. While in Los Angeles, he picked up two more nicknames, "Pancho" and "El Curveador del Pacifico." On May 7, 1944, Comellas pitched a no-hit, no-run seven-inning game against San Francisco. He started the 1945 season with the Chicago Cubs and appeared in his first major league game on April 19. On May 31, he was optioned back to Los Angeles. He was recalled back to Chicago on August 23. On December 10, the Chicago Cubs announced the outright sale of Comellas to Los Angeles. For the 1945–1946 winter season, he returned to the Almendares of the Cuban League. During the 1946 season, he joined the Tuneros de San Luis Potosi (MEX). By early May, it was reported that Comellas was taking over the team's managerial position. During the winter, he returned to the Almendares. Before the 1947 season began, the Tuneros de San Luis Potosi folded and there were no reports that

Player Biographical Sketches

Comellas played anywhere else in 1947. In the 1947–1948 winter season, he played for the Alacranes Blue Sox. Before Christmas, he rejoined the Almendares club. In January 1948, Los Angeles sold his contract to the Portsmouth Cubs (PIED). In December, the Havana Cubans (FINL) purchased his contract and he spent the next two years with the club. He tried to make the rosters of the Fort Lauderdale Braves (FINL) and the Montgomery Rebels (SALL) for the next two years. In 1973, he petitioned for U.S. naturalization. Around 1974, Comellas was involved

Jorge "George" Comellas (1916–2001), a Cuban signed by Cambria, started the season with 20 consecutive wins, breaking the record of 19 consecutive wins in a season set by Rube Marquard in 1912. He finished the season with a 22–1 record, striking out 204 batters in 206 innings while issuing just 66 walks. On June 29, he struck out 21 batters (courtesy Eastern Shore Baseball Hall of Fame Museum).

Player Biographical Sketches

with the Mambises Baseball Academy in Miami and he coached at the Caribes Baseball Academy from 1980 to 1982.[6]

Regular-Season Statistics

GP	AB	R	H	RBI	2B	3B	HR	SB	SF	HBP	E	PO	A	DP	AVG	SLG
29	88	9	17	15	3	0	0	1	1^	1^	6	6	60	2	.193	.227

IP	H	BB	SO	Cpgs	Sho	W	L	Pct.
206	143	66	204	18	0	22	1	.957

Playoff Statistics

GP	AB	R	H	RBI	2B	3B	HR	SB	SF	HBP	E	PO	A	DP	AVG	SLG
4	6	0	0	0	0	0	0	0	0	0	0	0	11	0	.000	.000

IP	H	BB	SO	Cpgs	Sho	W	L	Pct.
19.2	16	10	16	0	0	1	1	.500

Exhibition Statistics

GP	AB	R	H	RBI	2B	3B	HR	SB	SF	HBP	E	PO	A	DP	AVG	SLG
4	3	0	0	0	0	0	0	0	0	0	0	0	1	0	.000	.000

IP	H	BB^	SO^	Cpgs	Sho	W	L	Pct.
10.1	5	5	6	0	0	1	0	1.000

MICHAEL FRANCIS DEPKO

[1918 PLYMOUTH, PENNSYLVANIA–1951 NANTICOKE, PENNSYLVANIA; R/R 6–4½ 225]

Michael "Tiny" Depko, son of Joseph (a Polish immigrant) and Lillian (Zcolkowskie), split his time between the Nanticoke Nationals of the Wyoming League and the Wilkes-Barre Barons during the 1936 season. In 1937, Depko started the season by pitching one game for the Nanticoke Nationals before reporting to the Barons' farm team, the Leaksville-Draper-Spray Triplets (BIST). He also appeared with two semiprofessional ball clubs, the Slatington ball club and the Tri-City team. In mid–June, Depko was traded to the Trenton Senators (NYPL), who then optioned him to the Salisbury Indians for "further seasoning." He appeared in one game with the Indians in a relief effort (the June 14 exhibition game against South Philadelphia). By June 26, he was pitching for the Rome Colonels (CAML). In early August, he was recalled back to Trenton and spent the remainder of the season with them. In 1938, he was on the roster of the Greenville Spinners (EL) and the Rome Colonels (CAML). In 1939, he played for the Springfield Nationals (EL) and in 1940 was optioned to the Wilmington Blue Rocks (ISLG) for a month before returning back to Springfield in July 1940 to be released. During the 1940s, he was employed at the Rome Cable Corporation. On September 22, 1951, he was struck by an automobile and died while walking along Route 11 in West Nanticoke, Pennsylvania, a short distance south of Nanticoke Bridge.[7]

Exhibition Statistics

GP	AB	R	H	RBI	2B	3B	HR	SB	SF	HBP	E	PO	A	DP	AVG	SLG
1	1	0	0	0	0	0	0	0	0	0	0	0	0	0	.000	.000

IP	H	BB	SO	Cpgs	Sho	W	L	Pct.
2	2	0	3	0	0	0	0	.000

FRANK ALFRED DEUTSCH

[1915 ALLENTOWN, PENNSYLVANIA–1995 ALLENTOWN, PENNSYLVANIA; 6–2 198)

Frank Deutsch, son of Joseph and Rose (Pummer) Deutsch, was an Allentown First Ward youth who played basketball and baseball with the St. Peter's Cubs. In early 1936, he tried out for the Harrisburg Senators (EL) but did not make the team. The Easton Fleas of the Eastern Pennsylvania League signed him for the 1937 season. While Easton was playing against the East Greenville Tigers on July 17, scouts for the Washington Senators were there to look over several East Greenville players. Deutsch impressed them so much that they offered him a contract, which he signed. They sent him to the Baltimore Orioles (IL), where he played two games before he was sent to the Salisbury Indians with a 24-hour recall option. Deutsch played his first game with Salisbury on July 21 and remained with the team for the rest of the season. Deutsch, it was reported in mid–August 1937, was a guest of the Salisbury Fire Department at the smoke-eaters' annual crab feast and for two solid hours, he ate crabs and drank orange soda. For the 1938 season, the local newspaper reported in the month of March that Deutsch signed his contract with the Salisbury Indians; however, in the month of May, he did not make the team and he decided to return to the

Player Biographical Sketches

Frank A. Deutsch (1915–1995) joined the Indians in mid–July to become the permanent replacement at first base. He appeared in 43 games, batting .287 with 25 RBI, five doubles, a triple and two home runs (courtesy Judy Bowen and Jane Musser).

Easton Fleas. On June 1, Easton released him and he signed with Salisbury again. Deutsch split the 1939 season with the Gordon Garage of the Class A League and the East Greenville team of Bux-Mont County League. In 1940, he split the season with the East Greenville team and the Class A League's Queen City. In 1941, he split the season with the Class A League's Phoenix A.C. and the East Greenville team, and in 1942, he played for the Phoenix team. A semipro basketball player with the Tri-State League, he was inducted into the 1st and 6th Ward Athlete's Hall of Fame in Allentown. He was a brakeman for the Philadelphia Bethlehem and New England Railroad at Bethlehem Steel Corporation for 37 years before retiring in 1974.[8]

Player Biographical Sketches

Regular-Season Statistics

GP	AB	R	H	RBI	2B	3B	HR	SB	SF	HBP	E	PO	A	DP	AVG	SLG
43	157	26	45	25	5	1	2	3	4^	3^	6	417	45	25	.287	.369

Playoff Statistics

GP	AB	R	H	RBI	2B	3B	HR	SB	SF	HBP	E	PO	A	DP	AVG	SLG
8	28	5	7	1	0	1	0	1	0	0	0	60	5	5	.250	.321

Exhibition Statistics

GP	AB	R	H	RBI	2B	3B	HR	SB	SF	HBP	E	PO	A	DP	AVG	SLG
3	10	2	3	0	0	0	0	0	0	0	1	17	2	0	.300	.300

ALBERT WINSLOW ELLIOTT, JR.

[1919 LEWISBURG, PENNSYLVANIA–1995 TACOMA, WASHINGTON; L/R 6–0 170]

Albert "Young Buck" Elliott, Jr., son of former minor leaguer and Bucknell University standout Albert "Buck," Sr., and Margaret (Collins) Elliott, was with the Glen Rock team of the Southern York County League in 1936. In 1937, he graduated from Glen Rock High School, where he captained the basketball team, winning the York County championship, and before signing a contract with the Washington Senators, he was a member of the New Freedom baseball club of the York-Adams County League. He arrived on July 1 to join the Salisbury Indians in time to play two games against the Cambridge Cardinals. On July 7, he was transferred to the Trenton Senators (NYPL). He returned to Salisbury on July 18 to play his third and fourth games with the Indians. In the month of August, he was on the roster of the Zanesville Bees (MATL). Per the contract he signed, which included a $5,000 signing bonus, his father negotiated that the Washington Senators support his future college expenses as he was turning down numerous college basketball scholarships. He attended West Chester State Teachers College (now West Chester University) in 1937 and 1938. In 1938, he was sent to Florida, playing for the Orlando Senators (1938–1939) and the Daytona Beach Islanders (1939) (both FLOR). After that, he played for clubs in various leagues, such as the Reading Chicks (ISLG) (1940), Utica Braves (CAML) (1942), Durham Bulls (PIED) (1942) and Springfield Rifles (EL) (1942). Elliott served as a fighter pilot in World War II

Player Biographical Sketches

and when he returned to the United States, he enrolled in Arizona State College at Tempe (now Arizona State University) and earned a bachelor of arts degree in physical education in 1949. Also in 1945, he was the athletic director at Luke Air Force Base in Maricopa County, Arizona, and served as the player-manager for the Luke Field Dukes. The next year he led the Mesa Realtors to the *Denver Post* and state semi-pro championships. In 1947, he was the player-manager for the Phoenix Senators (AZTX), which had future New York Yankees legend Billy

"Buck" Elliott, Jr., with the Phoenix Senators, 1947. Albert "Young Buck" Elliott, Jr. (1919–1995), appeared in four games with the Indians in July filling in at first base. He collected two hits in 14 at-bats, one hit being a double. In August, he was on the roster of the Zanesville Bees of the Middle Atlantic League (courtesy Terry Elliott).

Player Biographical Sketches

Martin on its roster. During this time, Elliott became associated with an influential promoter, race car owner and owner of the Bisbee-Douglas franchise, J.C. Agajanian, which led to his involvement with Agajanian's auto racing program. In 1948, Elliott took assignments with two Pittsburgh Pirates farm clubs, the New Orleans Pelicans (SOUA) and the Fort Wayne Generals (CENL), as well as a Cleveland Indians farm club, the Dayton Indians (CENL). On May 28, 1949, he agreed to be the player-manager and business manager for the Bisbee-Douglass Copper Kings (AZTX) and won the Arizona-Texas League's manager of the year. In 1951, while scouting for the Pittsburgh organization in Mexico and Southern California, he accepted the position of player-manager of the Great Falls Electrics (PION) and led them to the league championship. The next year, he became player-manager of the Modesto Reds (CALL). In July, he was released by Modesto and quickly picked up by the Billings Mustangs (PION). In 1953, he became player-manager for the Phoenix Senators and accepted the position of a business manager with the Phoenix ball club, then known as the Phoenix Stars, for the next season. In 1955, he signed a contract with the Salinas Packers (CALL), a Pittsburgh Pirates farm club, and by late July was promoted to be the skipper of the Billings Mustangs. He retired at the end of the season to become a field supervisor of the General Tire Company. From 1959 to 1985, he was a scout for various major league teams: Philadelphia (1959–1960), San Diego (1969), Kansas City (1970), New York Mets (1970–1976), Baltimore (1976–1978), New York Yankees (1979–1980) and Oakland (1980–1985).[9]

Regular-Season Statistics

GP	AB	R	H	RBI	2B	3B	HR	SB	SF	HBP	E	PO	A	DP	AVG	SLG
4	14	2	2	0	1	0	0	0	1	0	1	30	2	1	.143	.214

D'ARBY RAYMOND FLOWERS

[1902 CAMBRIDGE, MARYLAND–1962 CLEARWATER, FLORIDA; R/R 5–11 170]

"Jake" Flowers, son of William and Lyda (Ford) Flowers, attended Washington College as a three-sport athlete. He began his professional baseball career with the Cambridge Canners (ESHL) and the Jersey City Skeeters (IL) in 1922. Returning to Cambridge for the 1923 season, he played there until the month of July, when the St. Louis Cardinals

Player Biographical Sketches

purchased him for $1,500. In early 1924, Flowers was farmed out to the Fort Smith Twins (WA). At the end of August, Flowers was sold to the Oakland Oaks (PCL) for $7,500. He would play the last six weeks of the 1924 season and almost the entirety of the next season with Oakland until he broke his ankle while sliding into a base in late September. He injured his thumb earlier in the season and needed it operated on.

D'Arby "Jake" Flowers (1902–1962), a native son of Cambridge, Maryland, and skipper of the Salisbury Indians, led the team to two consecutive league championships in 1937 and 1938 (courtesy Mary Jane [Revolinsky] Martinez).

Player Biographical Sketches

He joined St. Louis in 1926. During the 1927 St. Louis training camp, Flowers ruptured a small artery in his left leg when a batted ball struck him at the close of the pregame fielding practice. In April 1927, he was traded to the Brooklyn Robins and stayed with the team until 1931, when he went back to the Cardinals midseason. In early 1932, Flowers was released outright by the Cardinals to the Minneapolis Millers (AA). In June, St. Louis purchased his contract and in early 1933 traded him to the Brooklyn Dodgers. His big league career came to an abrupt halt in 1934, when, while with the Cincinnati Reds, he sustained several injuries—pulled leg muscle and a broken right wrist from a fastball thrown by Paul Dean. After recovery, he was sent to the Toronto Maple Leafs (IL). At the beginning of the 1935 season, Toronto traded Flowers to the Memphis Chicks (SOUA), who then sold him to the Rochester Red Wings (IL). After being let go by the Buffalo Bisons (IL), he ended his career with the Indianapolis Indians (AA). After his playing career ended, Flowers managed the Salisbury Indians from 1937 to 1938 and the Pocomoke City Red Sox (ESHL) in 1939. He won two pennants with Salisbury and was named Minor League Manager of the Year in 1937 by *The Sporting News*. He even appeared in two games in 1937, both exhibitions games. He pitched five innings against the Trenton Senators on September 7 and pinch-hit against the Philadelphia A's on September 20. Flowers served as a Pittsburgh Pirates coach from 1940 to 1945 and a member of the Boston Braves staff in 1946. He was president and general manager of the Milwaukee Brewers (AA) from 1947 to 1950, resigning to become the first base coach for the Cleveland Indians in 1951 and 1952. Afterward, Flowers scouted for the New York Yankees (1953–1955), the Kansas City Athletics (1956) and the Orioles (1960). He moved to Clearwater, Florida, around 1952, becoming a real estate broker in the late 1950s. He moved back to Cambridge, Maryland, in 1962. From 1958 to 1960, a sandlot league in Wicomico County (Maryland) on the Eastern Shore was named after him (the Jake Flowers Sandlot Baseball League).[10]

Exhibition Statistics

GP	AB	R	H	RBI	2B	3B	HR	SB	SF	HBP	E	PO	A	DP	AVG	SLG
2	4	0	1	1	1	0	0	0	0	0	0	0	0	0	.250	.500

IP	H	BB	SO	Cpgs	Sho	W	L	Pct.
5	4	1	5	0	0	1	0	1.000

Player Biographical Sketches

JOSEPH ALLEN GARLISS

[1916 NEWARK, NEW JERSEY–1989 BALTIMORE, MARYLAND; R/R 5–11 185]

A native of Newark, New Jersey, Joseph Garliss, son of Lithuanian parents Frank and Bronislawa (Lav) Gareliss (Garliss), attended the Georgia Military Junior College. At the start of the 1937 season, the Chattanooga Outlooks (SOUA) optioned Garliss to the Charlotte Hornets (PIED) in April. By May, he was playing for the semipro St. Mary's Celtics of Alexandra (Virginia). He joined the Salisbury Indians on August 19, as a replacement for right fielder Joe Reznichak, who was forced out of the lineup with a broken ankle. In the 1938 season, he remained with Salisbury until mid–June, when he was forced out of the lineup with an injured leg. The Savannah Indians (SALL) picked him up and kept him on their roster until March 1939. In the fall of 1938, he was a fullback for the Dixie Football League's Washington Presidents and Richmond Arrows. For the 1939 season, he split his time between the Richmond Colts (PIED) and Newport News Builders of the Southside semipro league. In 1940, Garliss signed with the Chattanooga Outlooks (SOUA). In April, he was released and signed with the Deland Red Hats (FLOR). He played under the monikers of Lee Raiford and Lee Garliss at Deland, possibly to preserve his intercollegiate eligibility. It was also rumored that Garliss "jumped" his contract with the Sanford Seminoles (FLOR). In mid–July 1940, the Chattanooga Lookouts (SOUA) optioned him to DeLand. After the season, he played for the Washington Presidents of the Dixie Football League. In 1941, he returned to the Chattanooga ball club. On May 3, the local newspaper reported that Garliss quit the team after a dispute with the front office over whether he owed the club $85 that he borrowed. He became so angry that he tossed his baseball uniform out the window and left the park before the game. He quit not because of the money he owed but the disappointment that $100 more would not be lent to him. His baseball career was interrupted by World War II, where he served as a navigator-bombardier in the 8th Army Air Force. He served for 45 months and flew 33 missions over France and Germany. In 1946, he signed a contract with the Baltimore Orioles (IL). By June, Garliss was released unconditionally and was picked up by the Montgomery Rebels (SEAL). At the end of 1946, he was released to the Pensacola Fliers (SEAL) and put on the suspended list on April 1947. He was released to

Player Biographical Sketches

Joseph A. Garliss (1916–1989) joined the Salisbury Indians on August 19 and became the permanent replacement for right fielder Joe Reznichak, who was forced out of the lineup with a broken ankle. Garliss appeared in 19 games, batting .314 with 11 RBI and a double (courtesy Mary Jane [Revolinsky] Martinez).

the Burlington Bees (CARL) in September 1947 and was placed again on the suspended list. After failing to receive a contract in 1948, he started working as a salesman for McCarthy Hicks Inc., a wholesale liquor distributor. When he retired, he was employed as a vending machine manufacturer's representative.[11]

Player Biographical Sketches

Regular-Season Statistics

GP	AB	R	H	RBI	2B	3B	HR	SB	SF	HBP	E	PO	A	DP	AVG	SLG
19	70	12	22	11	1	0	0	3	1^	0^	2	23	3	0	.314	.328

Playoff Statistics

GP	AB	R	H	RBI	2B	3B	HR	SB	SF	HBP	E	PO	A	DP	AVG	SLG
8	31	2	3	0	0	0	0	2	1	0	0	11	0	0	.096	.096

Exhibition Statistics

GP	AB	R	H	RBI	2B	3B	HR	SB	SF	HBP	E	PO	A	DP	AVG	SLG
2	7	0	3	0	0	0	0	0	0	0	0	2	1	0	.428	.428

FERMIN ROMERO GUERRA

[1912 LA HABANA, CUBA–1992 MIAMI, FLORIDA; R/R 5–10 155]

Born in Havana, Cuba, Fermin "Mike" Guerra, son of Canary Island parents Fermin and Cesilia (Romero) Guerra, never received a proper education but instead sold fruit at the Plaza del Vapor, the old Havana market, and went to Almendanes Park to work as a batboy. Guerra was one of the first Cubans signed by Cambria and arrived on March 10, 1936, in the United States via Tampa, Florida, along with future fellow Salisbury teammate Jorge Comellas. Guerra was sent to the Albany Senators (IL) for spring training in 1936. Cambria commented, "I don't know how Guerra will hit Double-A pitching but he's a good receiver and has a strong arm." In June, Albany optioned Guerra to the York White Roses (NYPL). While playing the season, the team moved to New Jersey and was christened the Trenton Senators on July 2. In 1937, Guerra played for the Salisbury Indians. Because he could not speak English, he, along with Comellas, would carry pocket cards that included essential information like sample menus written in English so he could order meals. On August 28, the Washington Senators purchased Guerra's contract. On September 19, he appeared in his first major league game and went hitless in three at-bats. Senators manager Harris declared after the game that Guerra might never make it to the majors. In 1938, Guerra started with the Charlotte Hornets (PIED) and by April 12, was slated to go to the Greenville Spinners (SALL) but instead was sent back to Salisbury. On June 2, he quit the team and, along with Jose Salazar, left on an early bus for Cuba. His reason: he would be the only Cuban on the

Player Biographical Sketches

team during a period of discrimination toward Cuban baseball players in the Eastern Shore League. Between 1939 and 1942, he bounced around the Washington Senators' farms, Charlotte, Greenville and Chattanooga. He also spent time with the Springfield Nationals (EL) (1940–41) and Mexican League's Pericos de Puebla [Puebla Parrots] (1943). In 1952 and 1954, he played for the Havana club (FINL) and finished his career

One of four Cuban players on the team, Fermin "Mike" Guerra (1912–1992) was the Indians' starting backstop, hitting .296 while belting 77 RBI with 16 doubles, two triples and 14 home runs while stealing 19 bases. After the season ended, he was sold to the Washington Senators and appeared in one game (courtesy Eastern Shore Baseball Hall of Fame Museum).

Player Biographical Sketches

with the Mexican League's Leones de Yucatán [Yucatan Lions]. Guerra also played Cuban Winter League baseball for two decades, 1934–55. In November 1959, the Detroit Tigers signed Guerra to be a scout in Cuba, which he did until 1961. Guerra played a combined nine major league seasons for the Washington Senators (1937, 1944–46, 1951), Philadelphia Athletics (1947–50) and Boston Red Sox (1951). In 1937, Washington Senators manager Bucky Harris commented to a reporter about his evaluation of Guerra to a reporter: "Guerra, the catcher from Salisbury, was not impressive and may never find his way to the majors." One time Guerra sent a contract back to legendary Philadelphia A's manager Connie Mack unsigned with a note saying: "If you will pay my income tax, I'll sign this." On May 18, 1951, the Red Sox traded Guerra to the Nationals. The reason for the trade: with so many Cubans on the roster, Washington needed a catcher who could communicate with them. Guerra managed the Havana Cubans (FINL) in 1952 and Leones de Yucatan (MEX) in 1955. In 1953, while managing the Marianao Tigers in the Cuban League, he was stabbed in front of his hotel by one of his "fans" in the Dominican Republic's summer baseball league. In 1958, he was the manager of the Rojos del Águila de Veracruz [Veracruz Eagle Reds] (MEX).[12]

Regular-Season Statistics

GP	AB	R	H	RBI	2B	3B	HR	SB	SF	HBP	E	PO	A	DP	AVG	SLG
79	314	71	93	77	16	2	14	19	5^	2^	11	589	59	12	.296	.493

Playoff Statistics

GP	AB	R	H	RBI	2B	3B	HR	SB	SF	HBP	E	PO	A	DP	AVG	SLG
5	18	0	3	1	1	0	0	1	0	0	0	38	2	1	.166	.222

Exhibition Statistics

GP	AB	R	H	RBI	2B	3B	HR	SB	SF	HBP	E	PO	A	DP	AVG	SLG
1	0	0	0	0	0	0	0	0	0	0	0	0	0	0	.000	.000

EDWIN JOSEPH HULLINGS

[1912 BEVERLY, NEW JERSEY–1993 MT. HOLLY, NEW JERSEY; 6–0 200]

A Burlington Township (New Jersey) High School graduate, "Jap" Hullings, son of Edwin and Agnes (Ziegler) Hullings, played baseball for Beverly (New Jersey) teams for many years before he got the call to

Player Biographical Sketches

travel to the Delmarva Peninsula. Because of the injury to Reznichak's ankle, Salisbury needed a replacement in right field and quickly signaled to the Trenton Senators of this need for a "reliable and sturdy flychaser." A Trenton representative phoned El Robbins, a well-known Florence (New Jersey) baseball leader, who then contacted Frank Bertino, the Beverly Reelers' manager, who spoke with Hullings, who was on vacation. Hullings agreed and made a quick bus trip to Maryland. He played in seven games with the Salisbury club from August 13–18. In 1940, he was working for the Comet Wall Papers.[13]

Regular-Season Statistics

GP	AB	R	H	RBI	2B	3B	HR	SB	SF	HBP	E	PO	A	DP	AVG	SLG
7	26	5	5	3	2	1	0	0	0	0	2	2	0	0	.192	.346

High school image of Edwin Hullings, 1930. Needing a quick replacement in right field, Edwin J. Hullings (1912–1993) answered the call and drove down from Burlington, New Jersey, to appear in seven games. He collected five hits in 26 at-bats, three for extra bases, while bringing in three base runners ("U.S., School Yearbooks, 1880–2012"; School Name: Burlington Township High School; Year: 1930. Ancestry.com. U.S., School Yearbooks, 1900–2016 [database online]. Lehi, UT, USA: Ancestry.com Operations, Inc., 2010).

JOSEPH JAMES KOHLMAN

[1913 PHILADELPHIA, PENNSYLVANIA–1974 PHILADELPHIA, PENNSYLVANIA; R/R 6–0 190]

Son of Raymond and Katherine (Stute) Kohlman, Joseph "Blackie" "Joe Boy" Kohlman attended Pleasantville (New Jersey) High School.

Player Biographical Sketches

After graduation, he pitched for the Pleasantville Athletic Club, where he threw two no-hitters. In 1934, Kohlman received an invitation to try out for the Philadelphia Athletics. By April, he was sent to the Reading Red Sox (NYPL). Unable to secure a spot on the roster, he joined the semiprofessional Kearney Lumbers. In 1935, Kohlman

After losing his first game of the 1937 season, Joseph J. Kohlman (1913–1974) chalked up 25 consecutive victories (26, if you include the playoffs), breaking Carl Hubbell's record of 24 games won in a row. He struck out 257 and walked 55 in 227 innings with six shutouts. He pitched two no-hit, no-run games (one in the regular season and one in the playoffs). After the Indians won the championship, he was sold to the Washington Senators and appeared in two games (courtesy Mary Jane [Revolinsky] Martinez).

Player Biographical Sketches

tried out for the Philadelphia A's again. In March, the Williamsport Grays (NYPL) took over the rights of Kohlman, and in two months, he was sent to the Beckley Miners (MATL). In 1936, Kohlman tried out for the Wilkes-Barre Barons (NYPL), and by May the club released him. He returned home and played with the Vineland ball club of the South Jersey League. In August, Kohlman was picked up by the Baltimore Orioles (IL). During the 1936–1937 winter season, he was touring with a baseball team in Puerto Rico, and by April 1937, Kohlman received a four-day tryout with the Trenton Senators (NYPL). He was optioned to the Salisbury Indians and spent the entire season with the team. He was voted the Most Outstanding Minor League Player of the Year by *The Sporting News*. On August 28, the Washington Senators purchased Kohlman's contract. His first game with the Senators occurred on September 26. In June 1938, Washington optioned him to the Greenville Spinners (SALL). Washington recalled Kohlman in September. After the season, he was optioned to the Charlotte Hornets (PIED) and in October he was drafted to the Jersey City Giants (IL). By July 1939, he was shipped to the Knoxville Smokies (SOUA). In October, the Memphis Chickasaws (SOUA) acquired Kohlman from Jersey City. In September 1940, the Cleveland Indians purchased his contract from Memphis. In March 1941, Memphis tried to option him to the Williamsport Grays but the minor league officials refused the arrangement. Instead, in April, Memphis agreed to sell him to the Greenville Buckshots (CSTL). Two months later, he joined the Anniston Rams (SEAL) and stayed with the team until early May 1942, when he was sold on a 30-day tryout with Jacksonville Tars (SALL). By late May, Kohlman was released to the Meridian Eagles (SEAL). In 1943, he signed up for a tryout with the Montgomery Rebels (SOUA), who in turn released him to the Richmond Colts (PIED). In July, he entered the armed services and served in the U.S. Army until 1946. In the 1950s, it was reported that Kohlman owned a service station in Plainfield, New Jersey.[14]

Regular-Season Statistics

GP	AB	R	H	RBI	2B	3B	HR	SB	SF	HBP	E	PO	A	DP	AVG	SLG
36	105	12	19	14	7	0	0	0	7^	0^	1	15	55	2	.181	.247

IP	H	BB	SO	Cpgs	Sho	W	L	Pct.
227	126	55	257	23	6	25	1	.962

Player Biographical Sketches

Playoff Statistics

GP	AB	R	H	RBI	2B	3B	HR	SB	SF	HBP	E	PO	A	DP	AVG	SLG
3	10	1	3	0	0	0	0	0	0	0	0	4	5	0	.300	.300

IP	H	BB	SO	Cpgs	Sho	W	L	Pct.
27	7	2	26	3	2	2	1	.666

FRANCIS JOHN KOWAL

[1910 MIDDLETOWN, CONNECTICUT–1981 LOS ANGELES, CALIFORNIA; R/R 6–1 193*]

Frank "Cookie" Kowal, son of Polish immigrants Jakob and Agnieszka (Jakia) Kowal, pitched for several semipro Middletown (Connecticut) outfits (the Middletown Giants, the Middletown State Asylum ball club and the Middletown Polish National Alliance) from 1930 to 1936. He pitched four regular-season games for the Salisbury Indians as well as an exhibition game against South Philadelphia. During the exhibition game on June 14, Kowal had to exit the game in the fourth inning with an injured arm. Days later it became clear that Kowal was done for the season. In 1938, he voluntarily retired after failing to win a spot on the Indians' roster. He joined the DC ball club of the Baltimore Amateur League and retired at the end of the year. From 1930 to 1943, he was employed with the Russell Manufacturing Company in Middletown, Connecticut. Before 1950, he moved to Los Angeles, California.[15]

Regular-Season Statistics

GP	AB	R	H	RBI	2B	3B	HR	SB	SF	HBP	E	PO	A	DP	AVG	SLG
4	4	1	1	0	0	0	0	0	0	0	1	0	3	0	.250	.250

IP	H	BB	SO	Cpgs	Sho	W	L	Pct.
11.1	16	8	8	0	0	2	0	1.000

Exhibition Statistics

GP	AB	R	H	RBI	2B	3B	HR	SB	SF	HBP	E	PO	A	DP	AVG	SLG
1	1	0	0	0	0	0	0	0	0	0	0	0	0	0	.000	.000

IP	H	BB	SO	Cpgs	Sho	W	L	Pct.
3.2	1	0	9	0	0	1	0	1.000

Player Biographical Sketches

JOHN KRUK

[1912 ARLINGTON, NEW JERSEY–1993 KEARNY, NEW JERSEY; R/R 6–3 185)

Born in Arlington, a neighborhood in Kearny, New Jersey, John Kruk, son of Ukrainian immigrants John and Dora (Kushner) Kruk, attended Kearny High School and played for the Arlington Athletics Association and the Glen Ridge club of the Essex County League in the 1930s and early 1940s. Cambria personally signed Kruk, who negotiated a $1,000 signing bonus, after seeing him playing for the DuPont Mechanical during the championship series of the New Jersey

John Kruk (1912–1993) of Arlington, New Jersey, appeared in the last game of the regular season at first base (courtesy Buddy Kruk).

Player Biographical Sketches

Industrial League. Story has it that he promptly bought a cream-colored Chrysler convertible. Kruk arrived on September 1 and saw action in the last game of the season, two playoff games as a pinch hitter and one exhibition game against Trenton. In 1938, he was invited to try out for the Greenville Spinners (PIED). By May, he was released to the St. Augustine Saints (FLOR), where he stayed for two months before being released. Around 1937, he began working at DuPont. He served in World War II as a sergeant in the military police at the McCook Army Air Force Base in Nebraska. While there, he received the nickname "Long John" while playing for the McCook Air Base Bombers from 1944 and 1945. After the war, he was appointed to the Kearny Police Department, retiring around 1974.[16]

Regular-Season Statistics

GP	AB	R	H	RBI	2B	3B	HR	SB	SF	HBP	E	PO	A	DP	AVG	SLG
1	4	0	0	0	0	0	0	0	0	0	0	12	2	0	.000	.000

Playoff Statistics

GP	AB	R	H	RBI	2B	3B	HR	SB	SF	HBP	E	PO	A	DP	AVG	SLG
2	2	0	0	0	0	0	0	0	0	0	0	0	0	0	.000	.000

Exhibition Statistics

GP	AB	R	H	RBI	2B	3B	HR	SB	SF	HBP	E	PO	A	DP	AVG	SLG
1	3	1	2	0	0	0	0	0	0	0	0	0	0	0	.666	.666

EDGAR ELLSWORTH LEIP

[1910 TRENTON, NEW JERSEY–1983 ZEPHYRHILLS, FLORIDA; R/R 5–9 160]

Edgar Leip, son of Edgar and Nellie (Wigglesworth) Leip, attended Trenton Senior High School. He began his professional baseball career when he joined the Trenton Senators in August 1936. From 1937 to 1938, he played for the Salisbury Indians. On July 16, 1938, the team celebrated Leip's accomplishments on "Eddie Leip Night." In 1939, Leip joined the Greenville Spinners (PIED) and played the entire season with them until mid–September, when he was called up to the Washington Senators. He appeared in his first major league game on September 16. In April 1940, the Washington Senators waived Leip to the Pittsburgh

Player Biographical Sketches

Pirates, who then assigned him to the Syracuse Chiefs (IL). In mid-September, Leip was called up to the Pirates. At the end of April 1941, Leip was farmed out to the Albany Senators (EL) by the Pirates. In September, he was called up to the Pirates. He started the 1942 season on the Pirates' roster as a pinch runner. On May 3, the Pirates optioned Leip to the Toronto Maple Leafs (IL) under a 24-hour recall privilege. In late September, he served in the U.S. Army and rose to the rank of

Edgar E. Leip (1910–1983) was the Indians' third baseman. He played in 95 games, batting .284 with 42 RBI, 17 doubles, two triples and a homer while stealing 25 bases (courtesy Mary Jane [Revolinsky] Martinez).

Player Biographical Sketches

lieutenant. He fought overseas in the African and Italian campaigns. In April 1946, the Pirates released Leip to Albany. For the next two seasons, he served as player-manager for the Salisbury Pirates (NCSL) and the Leesburg Pirates (FLOR). From 1949 to 1950, he played for the Danville Leafs (CARL).[17]

Regular-Season Statistics

GP	AB	R	H	RBI	2B	3B	HR	SB	SF	HBP	E	PO	A	DP	AVG	SLG
95	334	61	95	42	17	2	1	25	0^	1^	38	99	166	16	.284	.356

Playoff Statistics

GP	AB	R	H	RBI	2B	3B	HR	SB	SF	HBP	E	PO	A	DP	AVG	SLG
8	31	4	8	4	1	0	1	1	1	0	2	5	16	2	.258	.387

Exhibition Statistics

GP	AB	R	H	RBI	2B	3B	HR	SB	SF	HBP	E	PO	A	DP	AVG	SLG
5	15	3	5	1	1	0	0	1	0	0	0	5	2	0	.333	.400

WILLIAM MICHAEL LUZANSKY

[1916 TRENTON, NEW JERSEY–1997 TRENTON, NEW JERSEY; L/L 5–7 150]

Son of Hungarian immigrants Stephen and Elizabeth (Zsitnyar) Luzansky, William "Hunk" Luzansky played for the American Legion Trenton Post 93 Schroths in 1932 and 1933, winning the New Jersey Legion Championship both years. He was awarded the Schumann-Heink Sportsmanship Trophy during the 1933 National Junior American Legion Baseball Championship. Nicknamed "Gabby" in his teens, he attended Trenton High School. In 1936, he played for the Plattsburg Majors of the Northern League. He spent the 1937 season with the Salisbury Indians. In 1938, he was optioned to the Greenville Spinners (SALL). In 1939, Luzansky refused to report to Greenville and was placed on the voluntary retired list. On June 3, 1940, Minor League president William G. Bramham reinstated Luzansky, who then joined Greenville. On June 20, Greenville optioned Luzansky to the Hollywood Chiefs (FECL) but he declined to report to his new team; instead, he returned home to Pennsylvania. He spent the 1941 season with the Harrisburg Senators (ISLG). At the end of the 1941 season, Luzansky was

Player Biographical Sketches

sold to the Albany Senators (EL). From 1942 to 1943, he served in the U.S. Army, reaching the rank of sergeant. While there, he played baseball. From 1944 to 1946, he was on the Albany ball club's roster. On February 24, 1947, Luzansky was released by Albany and joined the semipro Quakertown Athletic Association of the Eastern Pennsylvania League. During his career, he worked as a supply clerk for the Trenton city engineer's office and as an automobile mechanic.[18]

William M. Luzansky (1916–1997) played in all 96 games in 1937, hitting .331 with 69 RBI, 25 doubles, seven triples and eight home runs while stealing 28 bases (courtesy Mary Jane [Revolinsky] Martinez).

Player Biographical Sketches

Regular-Season Statistics

GP	AB	R	H	RBI	2B	3B	HR	SB	SF	HBP	E	PO	A	DP	AVG	SLG
96	387	100	128	69	25	7	8	28	3^	5^	3	173	10	2	.331	.493

Playoff Statistics

GP	AB	R	H	RBI	2B	3B	HR	SB	SF	HBP	E	PO	A	DP	AVG	SLG
8	35	11	11	2	1	1	1	2	0	0	0	10	1	0	.314	.485

Exhibition Statistics

GP	AB	R	H	RBI	2B	3B	HR	SB	SF	HBP	E	PO	A	DP	AVG	SLG
5	20	3	6	0	1	0	0	1	1	1	1	3	0	0	.300	.350

JEROME EDWARD LYNN

[1916 SCRANTON, PENNSYLVANIA–1972 SCRANTON, PENNSYLVANIA; R/R 5–10 164]

"Freckled-faced" Jerry Lynn, son of Thomas and Alice (Mangan) Lynn, attended North Scranton Junior High School. In 1933, he played for the Potomac A.C. of the Scranton Association. The next year, he began the season with the D Class Jeanette Reds (PASA), transferred to the Beckley Black Knights (MATL) and finished the season with the Mount Airy Graniteers (BIST). In 1935, Lynn tried out for the Scranton Miners (NYPL) and was released in May, refusing to accept an offer to play in the Class D Bi-State League. The Stroudsburg Poconos (ISLG) picked him up for the rest of the season. In 1936, after being released by the Williamsport Grays (NYPL), he was picked up by the Class A Wilkes-Barre Barons (NYPL) as a replacement player. By mid–May, he was released and picked up by the Carbondale Pioneers (NYPL). In February 1937, Lynn signed with the Trenton Senators and joined the Salisbury Indians in May. During the 1937 season, a newspaper op-ed noted that "Jerry Lynn has been covering second like Charley Gehringer and hitting like Joe DiMaggio. In addition, he has been covering the sector of right field that Reznichak's bad ankle prevents him from reaching." On August 28, the Washington Senators purchased Lynn's contract. On September 19, he appeared in his only major league game and went two for three with a double. He made three outs and assisted on three with no errors—this included three double plays. In late October, Washington optioned Lynn to its farm outfit, the Charlotte Hornets (PIED). In the offseason, he worked at his father's gasoline service station in Daleville, Pennsylvania. In 1938, Lynn spent the entire season with Charlotte Hornets (PIED). On April 10, Lynn served as the acting manager during an exhibition game against the Washington Nationals. In 1939, he was traded to the Class A Springfield Nationals (EL). The next year, Lynn was traded to the Williamsport Grays (EL). From 1941 to 1946, he served in the 268th Quartermaster Bakery Company of the U.S. Army with a rank of private first class during World War II. In 1943, while in service, the Elmira Pioneers acquired Lynn in a player purchase. After

Indians starting second baseman Jerome E. Lynn (1916–1972) hit a league-leading .342 with 60 RBI, 23 doubles, two triples and seven home runs. After the season, he was sold to the Washington Senators and appeared in one game (courtesy Mary Jane [Revolinsky] Martinez).

Player Biographical Sketches

the war, he was operating a tavern in Scranton and was ready to quit baseball until he received a contract from Elmira. After not making the roster, he was transferred to the Class B Spartanburg Peaches (TRIS). In 1947, he started the year with the Mathews club of the Central Carolina Textile League, and on July 3 he joined the Rock Hill Chiefs (TRIS). He returned to Rock Hill for the 1948 season. In 1949, after being released by Spartanburg, Lynn stayed in the town of Spartanburg working as a beer distributor. In 1950, he returned to Scranton and worked as a bartender.[19]

Regular-Season Statistics

GP	AB	R	H	RBI	2B	3B	HR	SB	SF	HBP	E	PO	A	DP	AVG	SLG
93	360	96	123	60	23	2	7	8	0^	16^	32	192	240	34	.342	.411

Playoff Statistics

GP	AB	R	H	RBI	2B	3B	HR	SB	SF	HBP	E	PO	A	DP	AVG	SLG
8	27	6	9	2	0	0	0	1	2	1	1	14	14	6	.333	.333

Exhibition Statistics

GP	AB	R	H	RBI	2B	3B	HR	SB	SF	HBP	E	PO	A	DP	AVG	SLG
5	19	3	6	5	3	0	0	0	1	0	0	4	4	0	.315	.473

ANTHONY JOSEPH MILLER

[1916 BALTIMORE, MARYLAND–1992 BALTIMORE, MARYLAND; R/R 6–1 161]

Tony Miller, son of Anthony Phillip and Catherine (Dieter) Miller, played for the Apache Indians in the Baltimore Amateur League in 1936. In 1937, he played in two games with the Salisbury Indians, the May 22 game against the Crisfield Crabbers and the June 14 exhibition game against South Philadelphia. He signed a contract with the Rome Colonels (CAML) in mid–June. He also played several games for the Trenton Senators (NYPL) at the end of the season. In 1938, he started the season with the St. Augustine Saints (FLOR). By July 28, he was with the Salisbury Indians. In 1940, he was working for the Glenn L. Martin Company, an aircraft and aerospace manufacturing company in Baltimore, Maryland. He served in the U.S. Navy during World War II.[20]

Player Biographical Sketches

Regular-Season Statistics

GP	AB	R	H	RBI	2B	3B	HR	SB	SF	HBP	E	PO	A	DP	AVG	SLG
1	1	1	0	0	0	0	0	0	0	0	0	0	0	0	.000	.000

Exhibition Statistics

GP	AB	R	H	RBI	2B	3B	HR	SB	SF	HBP	E	PO	A	DP	AVG	SLG
1	2	0	0	0	0	0	0	0	0	0	1	0	0	0	.000	.000

JUAN Fernando MONTERO

[B. 1913 SURGIDERO DE BATABANO, CUBA; R/R 5-11 165]

Juan Montero won a gold medal with the Cuban national team in the 1930 Central American Games. He pitched for the Almendares Alacranes in the 1931–33 winter season. From 1936 to 1938, he played for the Marianao Games. The story has it that Joe Cambria sneaked Montero at the young age of 14 into the United States to play in a New York state league. Montero's father, believing he was too young to play, returned him home. For the 1937 season, Cambria sent Montero to the Trenton Senators (NYPL). After the July 7 game against the Hazleton Mountaineers, Montero was sent down to the Salisbury Indians and pitched his first game on July 11 against the Dover Orioles. Flowers stated that Montero "should be a great pitcher [and] has plenty of stuff." He remained with Salisbury for the rest of the season. For the 1938 season, he was with the Greenville Spinners (PIED) and St. Augustine Saints (FLOR). In 1941, he split his time with the Springfield Nationals (EL) and the Pittsfield Electrics (CAML). For the next two seasons, he was with the Springfield Rifles (EL). In 1944, he split his time between the Jersey City Giants (IL) and the Chattanooga Lookouts (SOUA). From 1941 to 1943, he was with the Habana Leones of the Cuban League during the winter season. For the 1943–44 winter season, he split his time between Habana and Cienfuegos in Cuba. In 1945, Montero pitched for the Tecolotes de Nuevo Laredo in the Mexican League. In the 1945–46 winter season, he bounced around Cuba, appearing with Cienfuegos, Almendares, Marianao and Habana. He was with Algodoneros de Torren in 1946 and 1947, split between the Alijadores de Tampico and the Tuneros de San Luis. In the 1947–1948 winter league, his last, Montero played for the Alacranes. He returned to the United States to join the Miami Beach Flamingos (FINL) from

Player Biographical Sketches

1948 to 1949. In 1950, he split his time between Miami Beach and the Augusta Tigers (SALL). Montero stayed with Augusta in 1951 and finished his career in 1952 with the Pampa Oilers (WTNM) and Lubbock Hubbers (WTNM).[21]

Regular-Season Statistics

GP	AB	R	H	RBI	2B	3B	HR	SB	SF	HBP	E	PO	A	DP	AVG	SLG
12	34	5	6	5	1	1	0	0	1^	1^	2	5	26	2	.176	.264

IP	H	BB	SO	Cpgs	Sho	W	L	Pct.
88	77	45	43	7	2	7	2	.778

Juan F. Montero (b. 1913) started the 1937 season with the Trenton Senators. In July, he was sent to Salisbury, becoming the third Cuban on the team, and put together a 7–2 record with two shutouts (courtesy Eastern Shore Baseball Hall of Fame Museum).

Player Biographical Sketches

Playoff Statistics

GP	AB	R	H	RBI	2B	3B	HR	SB	SF	HBP	E	PO	A	DP	AVG	SLG
2	3	0	1	1	0	0	0	0	1	0	1	1	2	0	.333	.333

IP	H	BB	SO	Cpgs	Sho	W	L	Pct.
8.2	8	8	5	0	0	0	0	.000

Exhibition Statistics

GP	AB	R	H	RBI	2B	3B	HR	SB	SF	HBP	E	PO	A	DP	AVG	SLG
2	1	0	0	0	0	0	0	0	0	0	0	0	0	0	.000	.000

IP	H	BB	SO	Cpgs	Sho	W	L	Pct.
2	1	2	0	0	0	0	0	.000

RICHARD TWILLEY PORTER

[1901 PRINCESS ANNE, MARYLAND–1974 PHILADELPHIA, PENNSYLVANIA; L/R 5–10 170]

Dick Porter, son of Caleb and Sally (Long) Porter, was nicknamed "Twitchy" and "Wiggles" for his spastic batting stance. He played two exhibition games (both against the House of David baseball club) for the 1937 Salisbury Indians. He attended Allen Elementary School, Wicomico High School and St. John College of Annapolis. He was a professional baseball player from 1921 to 1952, playing

Dick Porter, while with the Syracuse Chiefs, 1940. Veteran baseball player Richard Twilley Porter (1901–1974) appeared in two exhibition games. He collected one hit, a home run, in seven at-bats (James Trader Papers, Edward H. Nabb Research Center for Delmarva History and Culture, Salisbury University).

Player Biographical Sketches

six major league seasons (Cleveland Indians [1929–1934] and Boston Red Sox [1934]), and before and after his major league career, played 14 seasons for three teams in the International League (Baltimore Orioles, Newark Bears and Syracuse Chiefs). He also managed several clubs from 1938 to 1952 (Syracuse Chiefs, Anniston Rams, Wilkes-Barre Barons, Birmingham Barons, Toronto Maple Leafs, Utica Blue Sox, Fall River Indians, St. Petersburg Saints and Salisbury Reds). After retiring, he worked as a sports director for Scott & Graver and Ballantine beer distributor. During World War II, he served in the U.S. Coast Guard.[22]

Exhibition Statistics

GP	AB	R	H	RBI	2B	3B	HR	SB	SF	HBP	E	PO	A	DP	AVG	SLG
2	7	1	1	1	0	0	1	0	0	0	0	1	0	0	.142	.571

Mario Rudolph Pucci

[1912 Perth Amboy, New Jersey–1980 Edison, New Jersey; R/R 6–0 195*)

"Moe" Pucci, son of Ferruccio and Mary (Solari) Pucci, played semiprofessional baseball in the 1930s with the Clover and Meadowbrook baseball teams in Perth Amboy. Academically, he attended Rutgers College. He once pitched against Satchel Page in 1932. On May 30, Pucci pitched a Sunday game in his hometown then, with only one hour of sleep, he traveled to Easton (Maryland) to make his pitching debut for the Salisbury Indians in the first game of the doubleheader. He won the game and returned to Perth Amboy. He continued to play local semipro ball throughout the 1940s. He worked for 35 years as a potter with the Rheem's Manufacturing Company of Metuchen, retiring in 1958. When he died, he was a 41-year resident of Woodbridge, New Jersey.[23]

Regular-Season Statistics

GP	AB	R	H	RBI	2B	3B	HR	SB	SF	HBP	E	PO	A	DP	AVG	SLG
1	2	1	1	0	0	0	0	0	2	0	0	0	2	0	.500	.500

IP	H	BB	SO	Cpgs	Sho	W	L	Pct.
7.1	12	3	0	0	0	1	0	1.000

Performing on one hour of sleep, Mario "Moe" Pucci (1912–1980) traveled down from Perth Amboy, New Jersey, to appear in one game for the Salisbury Indians, pitching a 7–2 gem against the Easton Browns (courtesy Gary Pucci).

CHARLES MARION QUIMBY

[1917 CENTREVILLE, MARYLAND–2013 INDIAN LAKE ESTATES, FLORIDA; R/R 6–0 180]

A native son of the Eastern Shore, Charles Quimby, son of Carroll and Carrie (Dean) Quimby, received an invitation to try out for the 1937 Salisbury Indians. He would make the team and stay with them through the 1938 season. On July 19, 1938, Salisbury hosted a "Charlie Quimby Night" to honor him. In September 1938, he was sold to the Washington Senators. In February 1939, he was optioned to the

Player Biographical Sketches

Charlotte Hornets (PIED), and by June the Senators canceled his option as he had been with the Orlando Senators (FLOR) since May, where he received the nickname "Mule." In December, Charlotte bought his contract, and by May 1940, he was with the Springfield Nationals (EL). He was released to the Greenville Spinners (PIED) in June and

The Indians' starting left fielder, Charles M. Quimby (1917–2013), batted .262 with 64 RBI, 16 doubles, a triple and five home runs in 93 games (courtesy Mary Jane [Revolinsky] Martinez).

Player Biographical Sketches

stayed with them until March 1941, when he was released and joined the Anniston Rams (SEAL). From May to July, Quimby was on the roster of the Gadsden Pilots (SEAL) and at the end of July, he was optioned to the Montgomery Rebels (SEAL). On August 4, 1942, the Birmingham Barons (SOUA) purchased Quimby's contract. In 1943, he was transferred to the Syracuse Chiefs (IL) but instead of joining the team, he was inducted into the U.S. Marines. Before entering the service, Quimby had to undergo treatment for his bad legs as the draft board classified him as a 4-F (unfit for military service). After being discharged, he joined Montgomery in June 1946. He started the 1947 season playing with the Lancaster Red Roses (ISLG) but on June 11, he was with the Poughkeepsie Giants (COLL) and stayed with them throughout the 1948 season. In March 1949, he received a conditional release to join the Miami Beach Flamingos (FINL). By April, he was playing with the West Palm Beach Indians (FINL). In May 1950, the Bangor Bangors (NATL) acquired Quimby from the Class C St. Jean Braves (PROV). One month later, "Chuck" Quimby was recalled to St. Jean. For the next two seasons, he accepted the position of player-manager for the Tallahassee Citizens (ALFL) and the Statesboro Pilots (GASL). In the 1953 season, he was hired as the player-manager of the Fort Walton Beach Jets (ALFL) but resigned on May 8 when he found it difficult to work with the front office and general manager. For the rest of the 1953 season, he played for the Graceville Oilers (ALFL). For his career, Quimby won seven pennants (Salisbury 2x, Montgomery 2x, Springfield and St. Jean, along with a pennant won by the Cristobal club in the Isthmus of Panama 1947–48 winter loop).[24]

Regular-Season Statistics

GP	AB	R	H	RBI	2B	3B	HR	SB	SF	HBP	E	PO	A	DP	AVG	SLG
93	347	47	91	64	16	1	5	8	10^	3^	5	101	13	1	.262	.357

Playoff Statistics

GP	AB	R	H	RBI	2B	3B	HR	SB	SF	HBP	E	PO	A	DP	AVG	SLG
8	30	3	5	4	1	0	1	1	0	0	0	10	1	0	.166	.300

Exhibition Statistics

GP	AB	R	H	RBI	2B	3B	HR	SB	SF	HBP	E	PO	A	DP	AVG	SLG
5	17	2	5	1	0	0	0	0	0	0	0	3	0	0	.294	.294

Player Biographical Sketches

LEON JOHN REVOLINSKY

[1912 NEW BRUNSWICK, NEW JERSEY–2008 TAMPA, FLORIDA; S/R 5–11 186]

Leon Revolinsky, son of John and Catherine (Pensak) Revolinsky, attended Perth Amboy (New Jersey) High School and in 1936 was playing for the local semiprofessional ball clubs (Highland Park Athletic Association, Empires ball club of the WPA City League and Fords Field Club).

Leon J. Revolinsky (1912–2008) compiled a 13–2 record with two shutouts, one being a no-hit, no-run contest. He struck out 102 batters and walked 96 in 135 innings (courtesy Mary Jane [Revolinsky] Martinez).

Player Biographical Sketches

Nicknamed "Bobo" later in life owing to his similarity to another "Bobo," Louis Newsom, he was a hefty right-handed wise-cracking pitcher with a great fastball. Revolinsky received a contract from the Trenton Senators in 1937 and was sent to play the entire season with the Salisbury Indians. On August 22, Revolinsky entered baseball's mythical hall of fame when he pitched a no-hit, no-run 1–0 game against the Dover Orioles. In 1938, he split his time with Salisbury, the Greenville Spinners (SALL) and the St. Augustine Saints (FLOR). On August 2, 1938, Salisbury hosted a "Leon Revolinsky Night" to honor him, the club clown and the Indians' steadiest ball game winner for the past two years. In 1939, he pitched briefly for the Oswego Netherlands (CAML) and returned home to New Brunswick, New Jersey. From 1939 to 1949, he played for several local semipro ball clubs (Schwartz Athletic Association, St. Mary's, Hercules Powder, Gas House Gang and Somerville Towners). In 1940, he was working for the National Lead Company in Perth Amboy and by 1957 he was selling automobiles for the Rutgers Chevrolet Company of New Brunswick, New Jersey, as well as scouting for the Cleveland Indians. He would later become a successful salesman for Laffin Chevrolet in South River, New Jersey, working for the dealership for over 25 years.[25]

Regular-Season Statistics

GP	AB	R	H	RBI	2B	3B	HR	SB	SF	HBP	E	PO	A	DP	AVG	SLG
25	57	10	10	7	2	0	1	0	2^	0^	2	9	38	3	.175	.245

IP	H	BB	SO	Cpgs	Sho	W	L	Pct.
135	89	96	102	9	2	13	2	.867

Playoff Statistics

GP	AB	R	H	RBI	2B	3B	HR	SB	SF	HBP	E	PO	A	DP	AVG	SLG
2	0	0	0	0	0	0	0	0	0	0	0	2	2	0	.000	.000

IP	H	BB	SO	Cpgs	Sho	W	L	Pct.
2.1	6	2	1	0	0	0	1	.000

Exhibition Statistics

GP	AB	R	H	RBI	2B	3B	HR	SB	SF	HBP	E	PO	A	DP	AVG	SLG
2	2	0	0	0	0	0	0	0	0	0	0	0	2	0	.000	.000

IP	H	BB	SO	Cpgs	Sho	W	L	Pct.
2	1	4	2	0	0	0	1	.000

Player Biographical Sketches

JOSEPH THEODORE REZNICHAK, JR.

[1911 PERTH AMBOY, NEW JERSEY–1991 RED BANK, NEW JERSEY; R/R 5–11 190]

Joseph "Little Joe" Reznichak, son of Joseph Reznichak (a Polish immigrant) and Victoria (Dregier) Reznichak (New Jersey-born Polish

A rare photograph taken of Joe Reznichak, the Indians' right fielder, with his foot in a cast as he settles in to watch a game from the grandstands. Joseph T. Reznichak, Jr. (1911–1991), started the 1937 season with the Trenton Senators. He was released in May when the team reduced its roster and became the Indians' starting right fielder. He appeared in 61 games, batting .294 with 46 RBI, nine doubles, a triple and eight home runs. He was put on the injury list in August when it was found out that Reznichak had been playing with a broken ankle since June 24 (Walter Thurston Photograph Collection, Edward H. Nabb Research Center for Delmarva History and Culture, Salisbury University).

Player Biographical Sketches

American), attended Perth Amboy High School and Perkiomen School of Pennsburg, Pennsylvania. He received a bachelor of science in education from Bucknell University, where he was an all-round athlete lettering in baseball, basketball and football. In 1935, he played in the first Orange Bowl game, where Bucknell defeated the University of Miami 26–0. Joe Reznichak played halfback for the 1935–1936 Orange Tornadoes of the American Football Association. His obituary mentioned that he also played for the Pittsburgh Pirates (now Pittsburgh Steelers) that year. In April 1937, Reznichak signed a contract to play the outfield for the Trenton Senators (NYPL). On May 4, he was released to Trenton when the club was forced to reduce its roster to the league limit of 16 players. On May 26, he appeared in his first game for the Salisbury Indians. On June 24, he supposedly sprained his ankle during the game. After being out of the lineup for three games, he returned on June 29. On July 21, the *Daily Times* reported that Joseph Reznichak and his wife were planning to housesit for Salisbury mayor Truitt while the mayor and his wife embarked on a European tour for the remaining month of July and would return in late August. On August 9, Salisbury manager Flowers reported that for the past six weeks Reznichak was playing on a fractured ankle. He would be out of the lineup for the next three weeks with his ankle in a cast. Unfortunately, Reznichak was out for the season. On August 18, Reznichak accepted a position to coach football at Panzer College of Physical Education and Hygiene for one year. On June 2, 1938, it was reported that Reznichak was planning to return to Salisbury in a couple of days but it never came to fruition. Reznichak was a World War II U.S. Navy veteran. He taught world history and citizenship at Perth Amboy High School for 40 years before retiring in 1976. He was also the head coach for football, baseball and basketball at the high school.[26]

Regular-Season Statistics

GP	AB	R	H	RBI	2B	3B	HR	SB	SF	HBP	E	PO	A	DP	AVG	SLG
61	235	49	69	46	9	1	8	5	2^	3^	5	68	8	1	.294	.442

Exhibition Statistics

GP	AB	R	H	RBI	2B	3B	HR	SB	SF	HBP	E	PO	A	DP	AVG	SLG
1	2	0	0	0	0	0	0	0	0	0	1	0	0	0	.000	.000

Player Biographical Sketches

JOSE FRANCISCO TOMAS SALAZAR

[1917 CATALINA DE GUINES, HAVANA, CUBA–1997 HIALEAH GARDENS, FLORIDA; R/R]

Son of Luis and Paula (Perez) Salazar, Jose Salazar became the third Cuban pitcher signed by Joe Cambria to play for the Salisbury Indians.

Jose F. Salazar (1917–1997), the fourth Cuban player for the Salisbury Indians, joined the team in September and appeared in three exhibition games (courtesy Eastern Shore Baseball Hall of Fame Museum).

Player Biographical Sketches

In early August, Salazar reported to Salisbury. He was officially added to the roster on September 1 when the team could carry a roster of 18 men according to the league bylaws. His Eastern Shore debut was in relief during an exhibition game against the Trenton Senators on September 7. He would appear in two other exhibition games (Philadelphia A's and the House of David team). In spring 1938, Salazar split his time between the Greenville Spinners (PIED) and the Trenton Senators (EL), thanks to the Eastern Shore League passing the "alien rule," which labeled non–American-born players as "class men." In May 1938, he returned to Salisbury when the regulation was voided. However, in June 1938, the decision was reversed and Salazar voluntarily retired. In 1977, he filed a petition to become a U.S. citizen.[27]

Exhibition Statistics

GP	AB	R	H	RBI	2B	3B	HR	SB	SF	HBP	E	PO	A	DP	AVG	SLG
3	1	1	1	0	0	0	0	0	0	0	0	0	0	0	1.000	1.000

IP	H	BB^	SO^	Cpgs	Sho	W	L	Pct.
12	11	6	4	0	0	0	0	.000

Joseph Robert Shafnacker

[1915 Sayreville, New Jersey—1981 Sayreville, New Jersey; 6–1 185*]

Joseph Shafnacker, son of Frederick and Barbara (Griffin) Shafnacker, attended St. Mary's High School of South Amboy, New Jersey. In 1935, he played for the Sayreville Athletic Association and in 1936 with the Parlin Athletic Club. In 1937, he was playing for the Sayreville Victorian Catholic Club when around July 3, he was invited to join the Salisbury Indians. He started two games for Salisbury, the first game of a doubleheader on July 7 and on July 8. Unfortunately, he lasted less than an inning in both games. In 1938, he appeared on the rosters of the Parlin ball club of the Interborough League and the Sayreville Rangers. Shafnacker served in the 2nd Battalion of the 321st Infantry Regiment in the U.S. Army as a first lieutenant during World War II. His career after the war involved electrical and industrial supervision, including a code enforcement officer for Sayreville, New Jersey.[28]

Player Biographical Sketches

Joseph R. Shafnacker (1915–1981) posing in front of the barracks, ca. 1944. The St. Mary's High School of South Amboy graduate started two games for the Salisbury Indians in early July 1937 (courtesy George Shafnacker).

Regular-Season Statistics

GP	AB	R	H	RBI	2B	3B	HR	SB	SF	HBP	E	PO	A	DP	AVG	SLG
2	0	0	0	0	0	0	0	0	0	0	0	0	0	0	.000	.000

IP	H	BB	SO	Cpgs	Sho	W	L	Pct.
1	5	1	0	0	0	0	0	.000

VERNON WATSON SHELTON

[1917 AQUIA, VIRGINIA–1988 FREDERICKSBURG, VIRGINIA; R/R 6–0 175*]

Son of Elliott and Nellie (Watson) Shelton, Vernon Shelton resided in Aquia, Virginia, and played for several semiprofessional teams in

Player Biographical Sketches

Stafford County, Virginia, including the Brooke Station and White Oak baseball teams in the 1930s. In 1936, he was on the roster of the semi-professional Quantico Indians. During the 1937 season, Vernon Shelton pitched one game for the Salisbury Indians on May 22 against the Crisfield Crabbers. He returned to the Quantico ball club and played through

Vernon Shelton, in his U.S. Navy uniform, shown in the yard of the family home in Brooke, Virginia, ca. 1942–1943. After trying out for the Salisbury Indians, Vernon W. Shelton (1917–1988) appeared in one game in May, where he pitched 4.1 innings, giving up seven hits, walking three and striking out one (courtesy Aubrey Shelton).

Player Biographical Sketches

the 1938 season. He was employed as a civil engineer at Quantico Marine Corps Base and served in the U.S. Navy during World War II.[29]

Regular-Season Statistics

GP	AB	R	H	RBI	2B	3B	HR	SB	SF	HBP	E	PO	A	DP	AVG	SLG
1	1	0	0	0	0	0	0	0	0	0	0	0	1	0	.000	.000

IP	H	BB	SO	Cpgs	Sho	W	L	Pct.
4.1	7	3	1	0	0	0	0	.000

ARTHUR ALBERT STEINFADT

[1915 MONTREAL, CANADA–1995 BELLEVIEW, WASHINGTON; L/L 6–1 178]

Son of Lithuanian immigrants William and Martha (Eisenhart) Steinfadt [Preikschatt], Arthur Steinfadt emigrated from Montreal, Canada, to the United States when he was three and half months old. His family settled down in the Cleveland suburban town of Maple Heights, Ohio, where he attended the local high school. When he graduated in 1933, he became the first student-athlete from Maple Heights High School to be drafted by a major league baseball team,

Photograph of Arthur Steinfadt, taken while with the Army Corps of Engineers in World War II, ca. 1943. Arthur A. Steinfadt (1915–1995) appeared in six games for the Salisbury Indians at the beginning of the 1937 season, batting .250 with three RBI, two doubles and one home run. After losing out to Bob Brady to be the starting first baseman, he was released and joined the Charlotte Hornets of the Piedmont League in late June. He played several games until his release in the first week of July (courtesy Eric Steinfadt).

the Washington Senators. In December 1934, he was offered a contract by the Zanesville Grays (MATL). He was optioned to the Butler Indians (PASA) in May 1935 and returned to Zanesville in September. From June to August 1936, he was on the roster of the Monessen Indians (PASA). He appeared in six games for the Salisbury Indians at the beginning of the 1937 season. After losing out to Bob Brady as the team's first baseman, he was released and joined the Charlotte Hornets (PIED) in late June. He played several games until his release in the first week of July. In April 1938, he worked out with the Ottawa Braves (CAML) and secured a roster spot as the club's first sacker. Steinfadt played very well until late June when he was released after getting into bad graces with the club's management. He returned to Cleveland, Ohio. In 1940, he was working for the Red Steel Corporation in Cleveland. In 1942, he became a U.S. citizen. He served in the U.S. Army Corps of Engineers during World War II. By 1950, he was a manager of an insurance company. Family lore has it that Steinfadt was called up by the Washington Senators. During this short stint with the Senators, he was going to have his first at-bat in the ninth inning of a game but the Senators took the lead in the eighth inning. As the home team, they did not bat in the ninth. He never got another chance to be in a game and was sent down to the minor leagues.[30]

Regular-Season Statistics

GP	AB	R	H	RBI	2B	3B	HR	SB	SF	HBP	E	PO	A	DP	AVG	SLG
6	20	3	5	3	2	0	1	0	1	1	1	33	1	2	.250	.500

FREDERICK BENDELL THOMAS

[1914 WASHINGTON, D.C.–2007 COLONIAL BEACH, VIRGINIA; L/R 6–0 168]

Fred "Little Knocky" Thomas, son of Lewis and Lillith (Madison) Thomas, attended McKinley Tech High School and the University of Maryland, playing baseball and basketball. He decided to turn professional in his junior year, and on May 27 he signed with the Trenton Senators (NYPL). Trenton sent him to the Salisbury Indians and he first appeared in a game on June 4 against the Easton Browns. He remained with the team through the 1938 season. In 1940, he was employed at the Washington Gas Light Company. In 1942, he played for the Stanleigh Inn ball club of the Washington Industrial League. In

Player Biographical Sketches

Frederick B. Thomas (1914–2007) decided to turn pro after his junior year at the University of Maryland. In June, he joined the Salisbury Indians as the backup catcher and utility player and appeared in 49 games, batting .287 with 22 RBI, four doubles and a triple (courtesy Mary Jane [Revolinsky] Martinez).

1943, Thomas tried out for the Utica Braves (EL). In 1944, he was with the Colesville Cardinals. In 1947, he was with the Washington Industrial League's Heurich Brewers. Thomas worked for more than 20 years with the U.S. Postal Service, retiring from the motor vehicle department in 1974. He was inducted into the Washington Home Plate Club's Sandlot Hall of Fame in 1971 and into the Jocks Reunion Hall of Fame in 1992.[31]

Player Biographical Sketches

Regular-Season Statistics

GP	AB	R	H	RBI	2B	3B	HR	SB	SF	HBP	E	PO	A	DP	AVG	SLG
49	153	34	44	22	4	1	0	8	4^	2^	5	295	23	6	.287	.326

Playoff Statistics

GP	AB	R	H	RBI	2B	3B	HR	SB	SF	HBP	E	PO	A	DP	AVG	SLG
4	9	5	3	0	0	1	0	0	1	0	0	23	2	0	.333	.555

Exhibition Statistics

GP	AB	R	H	RBI	2B	3B	HR	SB	SF	HBP	E	PO	A	DP	AVG	SLG
5	16	4	6	1	2	0	0	0	1	0	0	29	0	1	.375	.500

FRANK ADAM TRECHOCK

[1915 WINDBER, PENNSYLVANIA–1989 MINNEAPOLIS, MINNESOTA; R/R 5–10 175]

Frank Trechock, son of Polish immigrants Stanley and Mary (Jaworski) Trechock, attended New Brunswick High School. The newspapers consistently misspelled his last name (Treschock). After graduation, he played several years of local semiprofessional ball (Plainfield Athletic Club of the Union County Baseball League, Bound Brook Bakelites of the Middlesex County Industrial League and New Brunswick Athletic Association). One day in the summer of 1936, Alex Sabo, New Brunswick native and catcher for the Trenton Senators, extended Trechock an invitation to accompany him to see a Trenton Senators game. Before the game, Trechock participated while the players went through their practice drills. His "playing around" impressed the club officials so much that he was offered a contract on the spot to play with the Senators in 1937. The 1937 season started with Trechock playing with the Bakelites. In early May, he joined the Salisbury Indians. On August 28, the Washington Senators purchased Trechock's contract. On September 19, he appeared in his only major league game and went two for four. He made two outs and assisted four with two errors—this included two double plays. In late October, Washington optioned Trechock to their North Carolina farm, the Charlotte Hornets (PIED), where he played through the 1939 season. On September 11, 1939, Trechock was traded to the Minneapolis Millers (AA). Trechock would stay with the Millers

Player Biographical Sketches

until 1948. Remembered for his great fielding technique, one newspaper reported, "Trechock was a master of the half hop." His baseball career would be interrupted by World War II with him serving with the 81st Infantry Division from August 1943 to February 1946. In May 1948, the Millers released Trechock to the Jersey City Giants (IL). After he

Frank A. Trechock (1915–1989) was the Indians' starting shortstop. He appeared in all 96 games, batting .338 with a league-leading 84 RBI, 20 doubles, two triples, 19 home runs and 15 stolen bases. After the season, he was sold to the Washington Senators and appeared in one game (courtesy Mary Jane [Revolinsky] Martinez).

Player Biographical Sketches

played a few games, Jersey City released him to the Louisville Colonels (AA). In July, Trechock was traded to the Milwaukee Brewers (AA). In February 1949, Trechock was given a conditional release to the Buffalo Bisons (IL). He would remain with the team until June 1951, when he was released. He worked as a construction worker when he left the Millers in 1948. Later, he was an employee of the Metropolitan Waste Control Commission from 1967 to 1982.[32]

Regular-Season Statistics

GP	AB	R	H	RBI	2B	3B	HR	SB	SF	HBP	E	PO	A	DP	AVG	SLG
96	388	93	131	84	20	2	19	15	1^	4^	44	165	250	37	.338	.546

Playoff Statistics

GP	AB	R	H	RBI	2B	3B	HR	SB	SF	HBP	E	PO	A	DP	AVG	SLG
8	29	2	8	12	2	0	1	1	0	0	5	11	36	4	.275	.448

Exhibition Statistics

GP	AB	R	H	RBI	2B	3B	HR	SB	SF	HBP	E	PO	A	DP	AVG	SLG
4	17	2	6	2	2	0	0	0	0	0	0	3	2	1	.352	.470

Chapter Notes

Preface

1. Bill James, *The New Bill James Historical Abstract* (New York: Free Press, 2001), 163.

Chapter One

1. Walter Brooks Miller (1860–1927), born in Baltimore, MD, was the owner of a wood bundling mill and president of the John B. Parsons Home for Aged in Salisbury, MD. A baseball enthusiast, he assisted in the formation of the first Eastern Shore League. *Salisbury Daily Times*, 20 Aug. 1927, pp. 1, 4.

Mager Brevoort Thawley (1884–1958), born in Caroline County, MD, was the owner of the A.B. Cochrane Lumber Company and the vice president and director of the Bank of Crisfield. *Salisbury Daily Times*, 5 Apr. 1958, p. 16.

James Harry Rew (1877–1933), born in Accomack, VA, practiced law in Parksley, VA. From 1911 to 1927, he was a member of the Virginia House of Delegates. *Richard Times-Dispatch*, 4 Aug. 1933, p. 5.

2. William Gibbons Bramham (1874–1947) was president of the National Association of Professional Baseball Leagues from 1933 through 1946. Before that, he was president of four leagues at the same time (the Piedmont League, the South Atlantic League, the Virginia League and the Eastern Carolina League). *Salisbury Daily Times*, 9 July 1947, p. 13.

3. *St. Louis Globe-Democrat*, 1 Feb. 1933, p. 15.

4. *Ibid.*

5. *Ibid.*

6. Daniel H. Pasquella (1900–1970; R/R 5-11 169), born in Philadelphia, PA, whose real name was Dante Pasquariello, had a 12-year career from 1920 to 1937. He was a manager for the Crisfield Crabbers from 1926 to 1928 and 1937, the Greenville Spinners in 1929 and the Jeannette Reds in 1930. The Sporting News Player Contract Cards, ScanID: 1099018034 Dan'l. H. Pasquella, https://digital.la84.org/digital/collection/p17103coll3/id/167832/rec/1.

7. Joseph Francis Carr (1879–1939), best known as the Father of Professional Football when he served as president of the NFL from 1921 to 1939, was appointed in 1930 as the promotional director for the minor leagues and was instrumental in reviving baseball in smaller towns during the Depression years. *Pittsburgh Press*, 21 May 1939, p. 17.

8. Ralph Edward Clas (1908–1988), born in Maple Groves, MD, was a retired painter and a U.S. Army veteran of WWII. *Hanover Evening Sun*, 18 Apr. 1988, p. 9; Ancestry.com. U.S., World War II Draft Cards Young Men, 1940–1947 [database online]. Lehi, UT, USA: Ancestry.com Operations, Inc., 2011.

Alfred Thomas Truitt (1897–1971), born in Pittsville, MD, was mayor of Salisbury from 1935 to 1937. With his cousin Charles J. Truitt, he purchased the *Salisbury Times*. He ran a real estate business and had an insurance and travel agency. During World War II, he joined the Army Air Force and served in the China-Burma-India theater with the

Notes—Chapter One

rank of lieutenant colonel. *Salisbury Daily Times*, 15 Sept. 1971, pp. 1, 14.

Dr. William Kenneth Knotts (1901–1970), born in Sudlersville, MD, was an ophthalmologist and general practitioner for 40 years. *Wilmington Morning News*, 15 Jan. 1970, p. 60; World War II Draft Cards.

Harry Covington Butler (1888–1966), born in Bryantown, MD, served in World War I as a captain in the U.S. Army. He helped organize Company K of the Maryland National Guard. He served one term in the Maryland House of Delegates from 1924 to 1926 and served as the state's attorney for Queen Anne's County. *Wilmington Morning News*, 19 Sept. 1966, p. 4.

Hanson Horsey (1889–1949), born in Elkton, MD, was a minor league pitcher from 1910 to 1918. He played one game for the Cincinnati Reds in 1912. He was a minor league umpire between 1924 and 1948. In 1947, he served as an instructor at Bill McGowan's umpire school. *Hagerstown Morning Herald*, 2 Dec. 1949, p. 29; The Sporting News Player Contract Cards, ScanID: 1025018679 Hanson Horsey, https://digital.la84.org/digital/collection/p17103coll3/id/96845/rec/1.

Olen Hoyt Bloodsworth (1903–1958), born in Mt. Vernon, MD, operated an insurance business in Princess Anne for 26 years. *Salisbury Daily Times*, 20 Oct. 1958; World War II Draft Cards.

James Cornelius Wesley Tawes (1882–1965), born in Crisfield, MD, was a retired seafood packer and past director of the Bank of Crisfield. *Salisbury Daily Times*, 6 Aug. 1965, p. 14.

John Millard Tawes (1894–1979), born in Crisfield, MD, was the 54th governor of Maryland. He was also elected state treasurer and comptroller. Lawrence Kestenbaum, *PoliticalGraveyard.com: The Internet's Most Comprehensive Source of U.S. Political Biography*. https://politicalgraveyard.com.

John Franklin Baker (1886–1963; L/R 6–0 178), born in Trappe, MD, played for the Philadelphia Athletics from 1908 to 1914 and the New York Yankees from 1916 to 1919 and 1921 to 1922. Nicknamed "Home Run Baker," he hit only 96 home runs in his career. The Sporting News Player Contract Cards, ScanID: 1025008081 Home Run Baker, https://digital.la84.org/digital/collection/p17103coll3/id/18485/rec/1.

Harrison Merrill Walters (1891–1951), born in Pocomoke City, MD, was the owner of the H. Merrill Walters Insurance Agency. World War II Draft Cards.

Allen Polk Schoolfield (1892–1969), born in Pocomoke City, MD, was a partner in the firm of Schoolfield and Ham, a clothing business since 1911. *Salisbury Daily Times*, 10 Mar. 1969, p. 8; World War II Draft Cards.

Edward Wilfred Ross (1889–1963), born in Pocomoke City, MD, served as a town clerk in Pocomoke City and postmaster from 1919 to 1922 and served as mayor from 1936 to 1942. *Salisbury Daily Times*, 6 July 1963, p. 1; World War II Draft Cards.

9. *Hanover Evening Sun*, 15 Jan. 1937, p. 8.

10. *Ibid.*

11. *Ibid.*

12. *Cumberland Evening Times*, 14 Jan. 1937, p. 12.

13. John Thomas Kibler (1886–1971; R/R 5–7 1/2 160), a Chestertown, MD, native, had a seven-year minor league baseball career from 1909 to 1916. He began a college coaching career in 1908 at Lehigh University (1908–1909) and continued at Ohio State University (1909–1912). He became the athletic director at Washington College in 1913, serving until 1947. He was the president of the ESL in 1937 and again in 1946 and 1947. He later was employed as a scout for the Boston Braves (1949–1950) and the Philadelphia Phillies (1951–1959). During World War I, he was wounded twice and gassed in France. Serving in World War II, he ended up with the rank of lieutenant colonel. The Sporting News Player Contract Cards, ScanID: 1025020362 J. Thos Kibler, https://digital.la84.org/digital/collection/p17103coll3/id/110529/rec/2; *Star-Democrat*, 18 Apr. 1952, p. 10; *Baltimore Sun*, 20 Oct. 1971, p. 25.

14. The Shaughnessy playoff system was implemented in 1933 by Francis

Notes—Chapter One

Joseph "Shag" Shaughnessy (1884–1969), the general manager of the Montreal Royals (IL).

15. *Salisbury Daily Times*, 17 Feb. 1937, p. 8.

16. James Murry Boyer (1909–1959), a Templeville, MD, native and graduate of Western Maryland College, played with the Martinsburg Blue Sox and Waynesboro Red Birds from 1928 to 1929 and was an umpire in the Eastern Shore League (1937–1939), International League (1940), American Association (1941–1943) and American League (1944–1950). The Sporting News Player Contract Cards, ScanID: 1099035549 Jim Boyer, https://digital.la84.org/digital/collection/p17103coll3/id/34374/rec/24.

James J.H. O'Connor, born in Baltimore, MD, in 1915, served as an umpire in the Eastern Shore League (1937–1938), Eastern League (1938–1939, 1947–1948), Bi-State League (1940), Mountain State League (1940), Virginia League (1940–1941), Middle Atlantic League (1941–1946), International League (1949–1950) and American Association (1951–1953). The Sporting News Player Contract Cards, ScanID: 1099036099 James O'Connor, https://digital.la84.org/digital/collection/p17103coll3/id/35739/rec/57.

Albert "Buddy" Clark served as an umpire in the Eastern Shore League in 1937. The Sporting News Player Contract Cards, ScanID: 1055001661 Albert Clark, https://digital.la84.org/digital/collection/p17103coll3/id/34002/rec/2.

Thomas Crane served as an umpire in the Eastern Shore League from 1937 to 1938. The Sporting News Player Contract Cards, ScanID: 1055002049 Thomas Crane, https://digital.la84.org/digital/collection/p17103coll3/id/36763/rec/1.

James Ross Gilbert (1892–1964), born in Lambertville, NJ, served as an umpire in the Eastern Shore League (1937–1938) and the Interstate League (1940–1941). The Sporting News Player Contract Cards, ScanID: 1055003639 James Ross Gilbert, https://digital.la84.org/digital/collection/p17103coll3/id/38318/rec/4.

John Joseph Toach (1893–1966), born in Trenton, New Jersey, served as an umpire in the Eastern Shore League (1937–1939), the Virginia League (1941) and the South Atlantic League (1942). The Sporting News Player Contract Cards, ScanID: 1056005025 John Toach, https://digital.la84.org/digital/collection/p17103coll3/id/40977/rec/2.

Henry William Carrington (1901–1980), born in Waterbury, CT, attended Washington College and served as an umpire in the Eastern Shore League (1937–1940, 1946), the Interstate League (1940–1941) and the Pony League (1945–1946). He was a basketball and soccer coach at Washington College from 1942 to 1946. The Sporting News Player Contract Cards, ScanID: 1099035597 Henry Carrington, https://digital.la84.org/digital/collection/p17103coll3/id/34824/rec/2.

George Leo Ekaitis (1906–1950), born in Donora, PA, served as an umpire in the Eastern Shore League (1937–1938, 1940–1941, 1946) and the Interstate League (1941). The Sporting News Player Contract Cards, ScanID: 1055002871 George Ekaitis, https://digital.la84.org/digital/collection/p17103coll3/id/35628/rec/1.

17. Pittsville, MD, native Charles Jones Truitt (1900–1990) was managing editor and co-owner of the *Salisbury Times* and founded the Eastern Shore's first radio station. In 1940, he became the vice president and general manager of Peninsula Broadcasting Company. *Baltimore Sun*, 29 May 1990, p. 14.

18. Joseph Carl Cambria (1890–1962) played in the minor leagues from 1909 to 1912. From 1930 to 1947, he owned several minor league teams, such as the Hagerstown Hubs/Parkersburg Parkers/Youngstown Tubers/Youngstown Buckeyes (1930–1932), the Baltimore Black Sox (1932–1933), the Harrisburg Senators/York White Roses/Trenton Senators/Springfield Nationals (1935–1940), the Albany Senators (1933–1936), the Salisbury Indians (1937–1940), the Greenville Spinners (1940) and Havana, Cuba (1946–1947). He served as a scout for the Washington Senators from 1934 to 1960 and the Minnesota Twins from 1960 to 1962. The Sporting News Player Contract Cards, ScanID: 1025010031 Joe

Notes—Chapter One

Cambria, https://digital.la84.org/digital/collection/p17103coll3/id/11916/rec/4.

19. See biography on page 19.

20. A native of Baltimore, Melvin E. Murphy (1902–1941) had several tryouts with professional teams before he moved to the business side of the game. He served as the business manager for the Salisbury Indians from 1937 to 1940. During the 1937 season, he would travel back and forth from Baltimore to Salisbury. In 1938, he established a permanent residence in Salisbury. Later, he took over Cambria's linen supply company. *Salisbury Daily Times*, 6 Feb. 1941, p. 1.

John Milton started with Cambria as a batboy at Baltimore's Bugle Field. In 1936, he served as the secretary of the York White Roses of the New York-Penn League. He became the secretary and treasurer of the Salisbury Indians in 1937. From 1938 to 1940, he served as the secretary/treasurer and acting business manager of the Greenville Spinners. *Baltimore Sun*, 23 May 1937, p. 22; *Greenville News*, 13 Jan. 1938, p. 11.

Born in Whitesville, DE, Ernest Thomas Foskey (1898–1997) was the groundskeeper of Gordy Park from 1937 to 1939. He worked for the city of Salisbury for 25 years on the police force and later as an electrician and meter attendant. He served in Company I, 29th Division, 115th Infantry in the U.S. Army during World War I. He was gassed severely in the Argonne Forest and had to spend nine years in a sanitorium when he returned home. *Salisbury Daily Times*, 6 July 1997, p. 8; *Salisbury Daily Times*, 23 July 1953, p. 14.

A native of Crisfield, Elijah Cleveland "Ligie" Johnson Disharoon (1908–1975), son of Julius and Virginia (Adams) Johnson and adopted son of William and Effie Disharoon, started as a batboy for the Salisbury Indians of the early 1920s when only 15 years old. He took over the groundskeeping duties at Gordy Park after Foskey resigned in 1939 and, starting in 1946, the Wicomico County War Memorial Field. In 1949, he took over the groundskeeping duties for the Goldsboro (NC) Cardinals of the Coastal Plain League. He resigned in 1951 for a job with a local hatchery. He also was a self-employed hauler. *Salisbury Daily Times*, 12 Aug. 1957, p. 8; *Salisbury Daily Times*, 12 Jan. 1952, p. 8; *Salisbury Daily Times*, 7 Apr. 1951, p. 10; *Salisbury Daily Times*, 11 Jan. 1950, p. 1; *Salisbury Daily Times*, 6 Apr. 1948, p. 9; *Salisbury Daily Times*, 21 Feb. 1975, p. 9.

21. Born in Sparrows Point, MD, John Joseph "Poke" Whalen (1893–1979) played baseball for Springfield College (1914–1917). After graduating, he played with the Frederick Hustlers of the Blue Ridge League (1915–1921). From 1922 to 1928, he managed several Class D teams in the Old Eastern Shore League (Parksley Spuds, Laurel Blue Hens, Cambridge Canners and Salisbury Indians). From 1940 to 1942, he managed several minor league ball clubs (Pocomoke City Chicks of the Eastern Shore League, Tarboro Orioles of the Coastal Plains League and the Hornell Maples of the Pennsylvania-Ontario-New York League). From 1945 to 1963, he served as a scout for the Pittsburgh Pirates (1945–1952), Philadelphia Athletics (1953–1954), Baltimore Orioles (1954–1956) and Cleveland Indians (1958–1963). *Baltimore Sun*, 8 July 1941, p, 11; The Sporting News Player Contract Cards, ScanID: 1099027385 John J. (Poke) Whalen, https://www.baseball-reference.com/register/player.fcgi?id=whalen002joh.

Born in Crisfield, Maurice Littleton Fields (1921–2003) left high school at 16 years old to become the batboy for the Salisbury Indians in 1937. He returned to school and graduated from Wicomico High School. He pitched for the Willards Wildcats of the Central Shore League from 1945 to 1952, managing 1952–1953. He made a career in the oil distribution business working for D&L Sharrar for 29 years and Cato Oil, Inc., for 10, retiring in 1977. Fields enlisted in the U.S. Navy during World War II. *Salisbury Daily Times*, 19 Jan. 2003, p, 26; *Salisbury Daily Times*, 27 Mar. 2003, p. 4.

22. Felix Leonard "Len" Shires (1908–1987; R/R 5–10 174), born in Italy, TX, had a professional baseball career from 1928 to 1936, when he played for 15

Notes—Chapter One

teams in nine leagues. He served in the U.S. Army from 1942 to 1945 as a member of the athletic staff at O'Reilly General Hospital. *Springfield Leader and Press*, 21 Oct. 1944, p. 5; *Decatur Daily Review*, 6 May 1935, p. 6.

23. Frank Stewart Spring (1917–1973; R/R 5–11 1/2 203), born in Cumberland, MD, attended St. Mary's Industrial School in Baltimore, MD. He played with the Cloverland Dairy Club of the Baltimore Semi-Pro League. He did not make it to the Salisbury trial. *Baltimore Sun*, 19 Aug. 1935, p. 1; *Salisbury Daily Times*, 6 Feb. 1937, p. 8; World War II Draft Cards; The Sporting News Player Contract Cards, ScanID: 1042004715 Frank Spring, https://digital.la84.org/digital/collection/p17103coll3/id/131001/rec/973.

Possessing "a fastball and deceptive curve," John Woodrow Bates (1917–1996; 6–2 185) tried out for the York ball club of the New York-Penn League in 1936. In 1937, he was with the Eastern League's Sixth District Democrats. *Baltimore Sun*, 2 Aug. 1937, p. 11; *Baltimore Evening Sun*, 28 Apr. 1936, p. 30; The Sporting News Player Contract Cards, ScanID: 1003002344 J. Woodrow Bates, https://digital.la84.org/digital/collection/p17103coll3/id/10673/rec/1.

With "a fine assortment of stuff," James Archie Ralph (1918–1998; 6–0 165) pitched for the Laurel (DE) High School. He did not play for any team in the 1937 season. In World War II, he served in the field artillery battalion of the U.S. Army with the rank of corporal. *Wilmington Morning News*, 8 Feb. 1937, p. 14.

See page 195 for Charles Quimby's biography.

24. See page 177 for Fermin Guerra's biography.

Claude Martin Larned (1912–1998; 5–10 1/2 190) played the 1937 season with the Trenton Senators. Baseball-Reference.com; World War II Draft Cards.

William Stephen Lyman (1913–1988; 6–0 192) was educated in the Scranton school system. He was on the roster of the northeast Pennsylvania semipro league's Honesdale ball club and the Scranton Miners (NYPL) during the 1937 season. He served in the Pennsylvania National Guard. Beginning in 1938, he operated the Lyman-Feldman Service Station and managed Lenn's Service Station. *The Morning Times*, 15 Dec. 1988, p. 20; *Scranton Times*, 10 June 1937, p. 26; World War II Draft Cards.

Clifton Bell Keyser (1914–1997; 6–1 183) played in 1938 on the Lander ball club of the Tri-County League. *Frederick News*, 8 Aug. 1938, p. 12.

25. Leslie Waters Butcher (1914–1996; R/R 6–2 175) played with the semipro Chevy Chase Greys from 1934 to 1935. He tried out for the Philadelphia Athletics in 1936 and spent the season with the Pulaski ball club of the Valley League. He spent the 1937 season with the Trenton Senators, the Winston-Salem ball club (PION) and the Ayden Aces (CPL). In 1938, he played for the Greenville Spinners (SALL) and BIST's Mayodan Millers and the Reidsville Luckies. From 1939 to 1940, he played for the Tallassee Indians (ALFL). Other teams he played for in 1940 were the Hickory Rebels (THL) and the Lexington Indians, the Landis Dodgers and the Thomasville Tommies (all from NCSL). *Standard-Speaker*, 27 Apr. 1937, p. 13; *Greenville News*, 17 Apr. 1938, p. 25; Baseball-Reference.com; The Sporting News Player Contract Cards, ScanID: 1025009837 Leslie Butcher, https://digital.la84.org/digital/collection/p17103coll3/id/20546/rec/20.

Russell William Gurth (1914–1997; L/L 5–10 175) spent the 1937 and 1938 seasons with the Ayden Aces (CPL). *The News and Observer*, 3 July 1937, p. 9; Baseball-Reference.com; The Sporting News Player Contract Cards, ScanID: 1018002777 Russell Gurth, https://digital.la84.org/digital/collection/p17103coll3/id/69660/rec/1.

Herbert Fletcher Pierson (1914–1995; 6–0 178) spent the 1937 season with a Trenton semipro ball club. He also received notice by being the leader of the Kansas City Philharmonic orchestra's horn section—his instrument: the French horn. *Reading Times*, 7 Mar. 1938, p. 12.

Notes—Chapter One

See page 158 for John Bassler's biography.

See page 198 for Leon Revolinsky's biography.

In 1936, Alexander Trippe played for the Wilmington Athletic Association of the New Castle County League. In the 1937 season, he played for the Edge Moor ball club of the same league. *Wilmington Morning News*, 20 Sept. 1937, p. 13; *Wilmington Morning News*, 16 July 1936, p. 13.

26. See page 161 for Robert Brady's biography.

See page 206 for Arthur Steinfadt's biography.

27. See page 209 for Frank Trechock's biography.

See page 190 for Tony Miller's biography.

Lambertville, NJ, native Paul Benjamin Jarrett (1918–1993; R/R 6–0 170) signed a contract with the Trenton Senators on October 1936 and was released on May 1941. The Sporting News Player Contract Cards, ScanID: 1022003939 Paul Jarrett, https://digital.la84.org/digital/collection/p17103coll3/id/88522/rec/18.

After trying out for the Trenton Senators, Samuel Kravitz (1914–1965; R/R 5–9 164) received letters from the officials of the Salisbury club on May 15 to report to the team at Baltimore. After not getting on the team, he played for the Belmar Braves for the 1937 season. From May to July 1938, he was with the Ayden Aces (CPL). *Asbury Park Press*, 16 May 1937, p. 13; *Asbury Park Press*, 25 June 1937, p. 23; The Sporting News Player Contract Cards, ScanID: 1025000967 Sam Kravitz, https://digital.la84.org/digital/collection/p17103coll3/id/121306/rec/2.

In 1939, Regino Armando Paytuvi Perez (1910–1994) appeared on the roster of the Wilson Tobs (CPL). A former University of Havana star, he was the starting left fielder for the Cuban National Team that won gold in the 1930 Central American Games. *Richmond Times-Dispatch*, 16 Jan. 1939, p. 13; Baseball-Reference.com.

Carmen Stephen Soltis (1916–2003; R/R 5–8 145) spent the 1937 season on the roster of the Ozark Cardinals/Evergreen Greenies ball club (ALFL). On April 1938, he was released to the Andalusia Bulldogs (ALFL). In March 1939, he was optioned to the Macon ball club and returned to the Henderson ball club in May 1939. He returned to the Andalusia ball club in September 1939. In January 1940, Soltis was released to the Monroe ball club. Baseball-Reference.com; The Sporting News Player Contract Cards, ScanID: 1042002589 Carmen Soltis, https://digital.la84.org/digital/collection/p17103coll3/id/153530/rec/2.

See page 184 for Edgar Leip's biography.

See page 162 for Thaddeus Cash's biography.

28. See page 157 for the biography of Wladyslaw Andrzejewski, aka Walter Andrews.

Samuel George Britton (1913–1996; L/L 5–10 182), along with Sam Kravitz, traveled to Baltimore on May 15, 1937. After failing to win a spot on the Salisbury roster, he played for the Belmar Braves for the 1937 season. *Asbury Park Press*, 16 May 1937, p. 13; *Asbury Park Press*, 25 June 1937, p. 23; The Sporting News Player Contract Cards, ScanID: 1005005586 Sam Geo. Britton, https://digital.la84.org/digital/collection/p17103coll3/id/3410/rec/12.

See page 186 for William Luzansky's biography.

During the 1937 season, Lewis Franklin James (1915–2006; 5–11 168) was on the roster of the Frederick Hustlers. In 1938, he tried out for several teams in the Eastern Shore League. *Frederick News*, 20 Oct. 1937, p. 6; *Frederick News*, 29 Apr. 1938, p. 7; World War II Draft Cards; "Frank James, Jr." *YMCA of Frederick County's Alvin G. Quinn Sports Hall of Fame.* https://frederick-hof.org/inductee/lewis-frank-james-jr/.

29. *Asbury Park Press*, 16 May 1937, p. 13.

30. George Edward Short (1906–2002; R/R 5–11 185), born in Harrington, DE, and a graduate of Washington & Lee University, was player-manager for the Federalsburg Athletics in 1937 until released in August and picked up by

Notes—Chapter Two

the Cambridge Cardinals. He spent the 1938 season with the Pocomoke City Red Sox. The Sporting News Player Contract Cards, ScanID: 1041001359 George Short, https://digital.la84.org/digital/collection/p17103coll3/id/148267/rec/67.

Howard Victor "Vic" Keen (1899–1976; R/R 5–9 165), born in Bel Air, MD, was a former Snow Hall High School pitcher who played for the Philadelphia Athletics (1918), Chicago Cubs (1921–1925) and St. Louis Cardinals (1926–1926). His career spanned from 1918 to 1934. In 1937, he was manager of the Pocomoke City Red Sox and in 1939 manager of the Salisbury Indians. The Sporting News Player Contract Cards, ScanID: 1025020127 Vic Keen, https://digital.la84.org/digital/collection/p17103coll3/id/120494/rec/10.

Frederick Warrington Lucas (1903–1987; R/R 5–10 165), born in Vineland, NJ, had an 18-year career (1922–1939) including a stint with the Philadelphia Phillies (1935–1936). He later worked for the New York Mets as a scout. The Sporting News Player Contract Cards, ScanID: 1099009301 Fred Lucas, https://digital.la84.org/digital/collection/p17103coll3/id/143416/rec/1.

31. *Baltimore Evening Sun*, 12 May 1937, p. 26.

Chapter Two

1. Ernest Sheldon Jones (1895–1983), born in Vienna, MD, served 22 years in various public offices: a member of the House of Delegates (1930–1934), Salisbury mayor (1934–1936), People's Court judge (1939–1947), secretary to the Wicomico County Commissioners (1947–1951) and justice of the peace and trial magistrate (1962–1963). He was a World War I U.S. Army veteran. *Daily Times*, 2 May 1983, p. 2.

2. Wicomico County native Larry Anthony Brown (1913–1994; ?/L 5–11 175) tried out but did not make the season roster of the Cambridge Cardinals in 1937 and 1938. The Sporting News Player Contract Cards, ScanID: 1006001022 L.G. Brown, https://digital.la84.org/digital/collection/p17103coll3/id/8910/rec/594; World War II Draft Cards.

3. Charles Herbert Mast (1915–2000; 6–0 177), born in Coatesville, PA, played just one season with the Cambridge Cardinals. The Sporting News Player Contract Cards, ScanID: 1028004623 Charles Mast, https://digital.la84.org/digital/collection/p17103coll3/id/162177/rec/3; World War II Draft Cards.

4. Frank Elwell Jackson (1913–1996; R/R 5–11 180), born in Pompton Lakes, NJ, had a six-year minor league career from 1937 to 1942 before enlisting to serve during World War II. The Sporting News Player Contract Cards, ScanID: 1022002201 Frank Jackson, https://digital.la84.org/digital/collection/p17103coll3/id/86800/rec/28.

Charles Anthony Marchlewicz (1919–2007; R/R 5–10 178), born in Wilmington, DE, under the moniker "Chip Marshall" had a 13-year baseball career (1937–1952) that included a small stint in the major leagues (one game with the St. Louis Cardinals in 1941). During World War II, he served in the U.S. Army. *Canadian Attic*. http://canadianattic.blogspot.com/2019/08/august-28-2019.html; The Sporting News Player Contract Cards, ScanID: 1099014274 Charles A. Marchlewicz, https://digital.la84.org/digital/collection/p17103coll3/id/176728/rec/2.

5. *Salisbury Daily Times*, 20 May 1937, p. 7.

6. Edward J. Hayden played for the Cambridge Cardinals in June 1937 and with the Dover Orioles in July 1937. The Sporting News Player Contract Cards, ScanID: 1019005065 Edward J. Hayden, https://digital.la84.org/digital/collection/p17103coll3/id/69068/rec/1.

7. Daniel Edward Murtaugh (1917–1976; R/R 5–9 160), born in Chester, PA, started his baseball career with the Cambridge Cardinals, playing two seasons with them (1937–1938). He played for three major league teams (Philadelphia Phillies, 1941–1943, 1946; Boston Braves, 1947 and Pittsburgh Pirates, 1948–1951). He had a 29-year association with the Pittsburgh organization as a player, manager, front-office executive and coach. He won two World Series (1960 and 1971) as

Notes—Chapter Two

manager. From 1943 to 1945, he served in the U.S. Army during World War II. The Sporting News Player Contract Cards, ScanID: 1099016736 Danny Murtaugh, https://digital.la84.org/digital/collection/p17103coll3/id/161021/rec/1.

8. Samuel Ronchetti, Jr. (1915–2006; 5–7 145), born in Vineland, NJ, played for the Cambridge Cardinals in 1937. From 1941 to 1945, he served with the U.S. Army, first as a physical therapist and then as a medic. *Vineland Daily Journal*, 13 Apr. 2006, p. 4; World War II Draft Cards.

9. Thomas Semple (b. 1915; R/R 5–8 1/2 200), born in Philadelphia, PA, tried out with the Cambridge Cardinals but was released in June 1937. He served in the U.S. Army from 1942 to 1945. The Sporting News Player Contract Cards, ScanID: 1040004137 Thomas Semple, https://digital.la84.org/digital/collection/p17103coll3/id/118150/rec/1; World War II Draft Cards.

10. Robert Joseph Iwanicki (1915–2011; L/L 6–0 177), born in Passaic, NJ, played for the Charleroi Tigers in 1936 before spending two seasons with the Cambridge Cardinals. He served with the Army Air Corps during World War II. The Sporting News Player Contract Cards, ScanID: 1022001999 Robert Jos Iwanicki, https://digital.la84.org/digital/collection/p17103coll3/id/90299/rec/1.

11. Anthony Joseph "Tony" O'Buzz (1916–2005; 5–10 178), Plymouth, PA, played one season with the Crisfield Crabbers. After World War II, he tried out for the Sioux Falls Canaries in 1946. The Sporting News Player Contract Cards, ScanID: 1099007000 Anthony J. O'Buzz, https://digital.la84.org/digital/collection/p17103coll3/id/163815/rec/26; World War II Draft Cards.

12. Anthony Levan played for the Crisfield Crabbers in June 1937. The Sporting News Player Contract Cards, ScanID: 1026003137 Anthony Levan, https://digital.la84.org/digital/collection/p17103coll3/id/141556/rec/1.

13. See page 204 for Vernon Shelton's biography.

14. Cape Charles, VA, native Ryland Benjamin Ward (1895–1984) was the brother-in-law of William Fletcher Harrison (1889–1969) and James Oliver Harrison (1906–1938) of Crisfield, MD. *Daily Times*, 26 Aug. 1984, p. 3; *Crisfield Times*, 21 Oct. 1938, p. 6; Find a Grave. http://www.findagrave.com.

15. Harold Stanley Cullen (1890–1956), a native of Crisfield, MD, and a former Somerset County road engineer, was associated with the Railway Express Company. *Crisfield Times*, 23 Nov. 1956, p. 8.

Hezekiah "Hezzy" Brittingham (1882–1943), an African American native of Pocomoke City, MD, was the groundskeeper for the Crisfield Crabbers in the old ESL. He organized and managed a Negro baseball team, the Crisfield Giants. *Crisfield Times*, 10 Dec. 1943, p. 3; *Morning News*, 7 Dec. 1943, p. 19.

16. Elwood "Freeston" Sterling (1880–1960), a native of Crisfield, MD, was engaged in the plumbing and tinsmith contracting business. *Crisfield Times*, 10 Nov. 1978, p. 4.

17. Wallace Edward Dize (1902–1981), born in Crisfield, MD, worked 34 years with the Baltimore Department of Transit and Traffic. *Daily Times*, 13 Feb. 1981, p. 3.

Preston Ervin Thomas (1900–1995), a native of Onancock, VA, was the founder of the National Neon Sign Service in Salisbury, MD. *Daily Times*, 9 June 1995, p. 14.

18. Columbus Warren Sterling (1887–1958), a native of Crisfield, MD, was a seafood and produce dealer. In the 1930s, he was an ice cream manufacturer. *Daily Times*, 25 Mar. 1958, p. 12.

19. *Wilmington Morning News*, 24 Apr. 1937, p. 13.

20. See page 182 for Frank Kowal's biography.

21. William Wess Ratterree (1911–1949; R/R 6–1 190), born in Warren, AZ, had a five-year minor league career (1937–1941). He was a lieutenant in the U.S. Naval Reserve during World War II. The Sporting News Player Contract Cards, ScanID: 1036006449 Wess. Ratterree, https://digital.la84.org/digital/collection/p17103coll3/id/104330/rec/2.

Thomas A. Waldron spent June 1937

Notes—Chapter Two

with the Federalsburg Athletics. The Sporting News Player Contract Cards, ScanID: 1046003829 Thomas A. Waldron, https://digital.la84.org/digital/collection/p17103coll3/id/174204/rec/18.

Maynard Owen Schoen (1915–1996; 6-4 180), born in Elizabeth, IN, played for the Federalsburg Athletics in 1937 and tried out for the Toledo Mud Hens (AA) in 1939. The Sporting News Player Contract Cards, ScanID: 1040000693 Maynard O. Schoen, https://digital.la84.org/digital/collection/p17103coll3/id/116564/rec/3; World War II Draft Cards.

Kendall Arthur Moran (1916–2002; R/R 6-1 195), born in Burlington, NC, played two seasons with the Federalsburg Athletics from 1937 to 1938. He served in the U.S. Army from 1944 to 1946 and was stationed in Osaka, Japan. *St. Louis Star-Democrat*, 16 May 2002, p. 7; The Sporting News Player Contract Cards, ScanID: 1099016296 Kendall Moran, https://digital.la84.org/digital/collection/p17103coll3/id/142030/rec/58.

James Paul Toland (1917–1988 5-11 175), born in Philadelphia, PA, started the 1937 season with the Federalsburg Athletics. After being released in July, he played for the Dover Orioles. The Sporting News Player Contract Cards, ScanID: 1045000133 James P. Toland, https://digital.la84.org/digital/collection/p17103coll3/id/122611/rec/2; World War II Draft Cards.

22. Robert Eugene Stant (1912–1978; L/L 5-8 155), born in Crisfield, MD, spent two seasons with the Federalsburg Athletics (1937–1938) and two seasons with the Sunbury Senators/Indians (ISLG) (1939–1940). The Sporting News Player Contract Cards, ScanID: 1042005843 R. Eugene Stant, https://digital.la84.org/digital/collection/p17103coll3/id/141111/rec/3.

George Harvey "Zip" LeGates (1906–1989; L/R 5-7 185), born in Harrington, DE, played three seasons in the Eastern Shore League from 1937 to 1939. He tried out for the Frederick Warriors in 1929 and the Allentown Buffalos in 1932.

He served in the U.S. Army from 1941 to 1945. The Sporting News Player Contract Cards, ScanID: 1026001687 Harvey Legates, https://digital.la84.org/digital/collection/p17103coll3/id/147421/rec/2; World War II Draft Cards.

23. Possibly Charles Leonard Miller (1914–1991; 5-10 156), born in Ironton, NJ, tried out with the Federalsburg A's in 1937. World War II Draft Cards; The Sporting News Player Contract Cards, ScanID: 1030005355 Charles L. Miller, https://digital.la84.org/digital/collection/p17103coll3/id/140195/rec/1.

Charles Sharp Morris (1913–1995; R/R 5-11 160), born in Farmington, DE, had a three-year minor league career from 1937 to 1939. He served in the U.S. Army from 1942 to 1946. The Sporting News Player Contract Cards, ScanID: 1031005465 Charley Morris, https://digital.la84.org/digital/collection/p17103coll3/id/174197/rec/270.

24. Harry Johnson "Dink" Boyce (1910–1968; R/? 5-11 165), born in Parksley, VA, was with the Federalsburg Athletics from April 1937 to June 1938. He served in the U.S. Army Air Corps from 1942 to 1945. The Sporting News Player Contract Cards, ScanID: 1005001902 Harry Boyce, https://digital.la84.org/digital/collection/p17103coll3/id/17834/rec/15.

25. Michael S. Mosher (1913–2002; 5-11 1/2 172), born in Mayfield, PA, spent four years in the minor leagues from 1937 to 1941. He served in the U.S. Army during World War II. *The News Leader*, 12 May 1939, p. 10; The Sporting News Player Contract Cards, ScanID: 1031006559 Michael Mosher, https://digital.la84.org/digital/collection/p17103coll3/id/160669/rec/5.

26. Stephen John Finta, Jr. (1916–1964; ?/R 6-2 210), born in Bath, PA, played for the Dover Orioles until he was released in May 1938. The Sporting News Player Contract Cards, ScanID: 1014005127 Stephen J. Finta Jr., https://digital.la84.org/digital/collection/p17103coll3/id/76535/rec/1.

27. Joseph Archer (b. 1917; R/? 5-9 158) spent the 1937 season with the Dover Orioles. The Sporting News Player

Notes—Chapter Two

Contract Cards, ScanID: 1002000631 Joe Archer, https://digital.la84.org/digital/collection/p17103coll3/id/10106/rec/14.

28. Edward Bernard Roetz (1905–1965; R/R 5-10 160), born in Philadelphia, PA, served as player-manager for the Dover Orioles in 1937. He played 16 games in 1929 for the St. Louis Browns. He played 11 seasons in the minor leagues (1926–1928, 1930–1931, 1934–1939). The Sporting News Player Contract Cards, ScanID: 1099020611 Edward Bernard Borts, https://digital.la84.org/digital/collection/p17103coll3/id/100043/rec/5.

29. Charles David Stotz (1915–2005; 5–9 185), born in Jefferson, KY, spent two months with the Johnstown Johnnies (MATL) in 1936. In 1937, he played for the Dover Orioles. The Sporting News Player Contract Cards, ScanID: 1043002905 Charles Stotz, https://digital.la84.org/digital/collection/p17103coll3/id/140670/rec/1; World War II Draft Cards.

Paul William Swoboda (1916–1977; L/L 6–0 160), born in Baltimore, MD, had a 10-year minor league career from 1937 to 1948. He served in the U.S. Navy from 1944 to 1945. The Sporting News Player Contract Cards, ScanID: 1099025097 Paul Swoboda, https://digital.la84.org/digital/collection/p17103coll3/id/123123/rec/3.

30. Edwin Francis Vandegrift (1917–1944; R/R 5–11 165), born in Philadelphia, PA, spent four years in the Baltimore Orioles' farm system, including two seasons (1937–1938) with the Dover Orioles. He died of tuberculosis. The Sporting News Player Contract Cards, ScanID: 1045006181 Edwin Vanderfrift, https://digital.la84.org/digital/collection/p17103coll3/id/108865/rec/257.

31. Lyle Elliott tried out for the Dover Orioles in 1937. The Sporting News Player Contract Cards, ScanID: 1013003933 Lyle Elliott, https://digital.la84.org/digital/collection/p17103coll3/id/51429/rec/2.

Howard "Hal" Stock (1917–1979; R/? 5–10 165), born in Philadelphia, PA, played for the Dover Orioles in 1937 and the Centreville Colts in 1938. From 1942 to 1945, he served in the U.S. Coast Guard. The Sporting News Player Contract Cards, ScanID: 1043002119 Howard Stock, https://digital.la84.org/digital/collection/p17103coll3/id/147274/rec/65.

32. John Carl Wittig (1914–1999; R/R 6–0 180), born in Baltimore, MD, had a 15-year career (1934–1951) including five years with two major league teams, the New York Giants (1938–1939, 1941, 1943) and Boston Red Sox (1949). The Sporting News Player Contract Cards, ScanID: 1099028067 Johnnie Wittig, https://digital.la84.org/digital/collection/p17103coll3/id/161447/rec/1.

33. Possibly James Lester Christopher (1913–1976; 5–11 170), born in Bethlehem, MD, was on the roster of the Federalsburg Athletics from April to July 1937. The Sporting News Player Contract Cards, ScanID: 1008004291 Les Christopher, https://digital.la84.org/digital/collection/p17103coll3/id/24824/rec/66; World War II Draft Cards.

34. *Salisbury Daily Times*, 29 May 1937, p. 9.

35. Howard Dale Hudson (1910–1973; S/R 6–0 165), born in Pittsville, MD, played one season with the Federalsburg Athletics in 1937. The Sporting News Player Contract Cards, ScanID: 1021004935 Dale Hudson, https://digital.la84.org/digital/collection/p17103coll3/id/84275/rec/99.

36. *Salisbury Daily Times*, 27 May 1937, p. 1.

37. Stephen Joseph Gatier (1917–1999; 5–8 196), born in Vineland, NJ, played for the Baltimore organization and was a Triple A baseball player. He served in the U.S. Army from 1943 to 1945. *Vineland Daily Journal*, 4 Feb. 1999, p. 4; World War II Draft Cards.

James Myer Titcomb (1915–1986; 6–2 190), born in Washington, D.C., had a four-year career from 1937 to 1940. He served in the U.S. Army from 1941 to 1945. The Sporting News Player Contract Cards, ScanID: 1044006631 James Meyer Titcomb, https://digital.la84.org/digital/collection/p17103coll3/id/110871/rec/2; World War II Draft Cards.

Notes—Chapter Two

38. See page 207 for Fred Thomas's biography.

39. Nicholas Butcher (1917–1994; R/R 6-2 175), a Duquesne, PA, native, had a nine-year career from 1937 to 1949. From 1942 to 1946, he served in the U.S. Army. The Sporting News Player Contract Cards, ScanID: 1025009838 Nick Butcher, https://digital.la84.org/digital/collection/p17103coll3/id/5148/rec/26.

40. See page 194 for Moe Pucci's biography.

41. Clyde Delmar Lessig (1916–2002; R/? 5-11 168), born in Pen Argyl, PA, started the 1937 season with the Easton Browns. He was released in July and signed with the Dover Orioles. In 1938, he tried out for the Rome Colonels (CAML). The Sporting News Player Contract Cards, ScanID: 1026002979 Clyde Lessig, https://digital.la84.org/digital/collection/p17103coll3/id/141221/rec/1.

Richard Joseph Poydock (1920–1941; 6-3 190), born in DeLancey, PA, played five seasons of minor league baseball from 1937 until his career abruptly ended in 1941 when he was killed. The Sporting News Player Contract Cards, ScanID: 1036001169 Richard Poydock, https://digital.la84.org/digital/collection/p17103coll3/id/84126/rec/1; World War II Draft Cards.

42. Adelbert Henry "Bert" Pultz (1912–2004; R/R 5-10 155), born in Fleischmanns, NY, had a minor league career that spanned from 1935 to 1945. The Sporting News Player Contract Cards, ScanID: 1099019481 Bert Pultz, https://digital.la84.org/digital/collection/p17103coll3/id/103341/rec/1.

Michael P. Stiles (b. 1913; R/? 5-10 165) played for the Easton Browns in 1937. The Sporting News Player Contract Cards, ScanID: 1043001815 Michael Stiles, https://digital.la84.org/digital/collection/p17103coll3/id/131537/rec/15.

Robert W. Etts (1915–1995; R/R 6-1 182), born in Fleischmanns, NY, played for the Slatington ball club of the East Pennsylvania League in 1936. He played for two teams, the Easton Browns and the Cambridge Cardinals, in the 1937 season. In 1938, he tried out with the Rome Colonels. Sometime after that, he was severely injured when he was hit in the head with a baseball. Baseball-Reference; The Sporting News Player Contract Cards, ScanID: 1013006609 Robert Etts, https://digital.la84.org/digital/collection/p17103coll3/id/53200/rec/1.

43. Ernest Charles "Duke" Landgraf (1879–1965), born in Zella-Mehlis, Germany, either owned or managed a minor league baseball club from 1901 to 1926. He helped organize the Class A Eastern League in 1929 and the Class B Interstate League in 1939. He was a scout for the Detroit Tigers from 1931 to 1939. *Wilmington Morning News*, 6 Feb. 1965, p. 23; The Sporting News Player Contract Cards, ScanID: 1099036588 Ernest Landgraf, https://digital.la84.org/digital/collection/p17103coll3/id/36363/rec/2.

44. Alonzo Lee Nichols (1871–1947), a native of Easton, MD, was prominent as a livestock dealer. He held several official positions, such as a director and vice president of the Farmers and Merchants Bank and a member of the board of directors of the Eastern Wholesale Grocery Company and the Easton Publishing Company. *Easton Star-Democrat*, 1 Aug. 1947, p. 1.

Ivon Tennyson Morton (1889–1970), a native of Easton, MD, founded the Morton Sign Service, which was one of the largest outdoor advertising firms on the Eastern Shore. Before that, he taught industrial arts in the Annapolis Public School System from 1912 to 1920. *Baltimore Sun*, 23 Nov. 1970, p. 11.

45. George William "Doc" Jacobs (1900–1968; R/R 6-1 190), born in Hudson, MA, graduated from Boston College High School and Villanova College and played professional football and minor league baseball. He played for the Bridgeport Bears from 1928 to 1929 and the Hagerstown Hubs in 1930. He was manager and owner of the Easton Browns from 1937 to 1938 and manager of the Moultrie Packers (GFL) in 1940. From 1929 to 1943, he was the basketball, baseball and freshman football coach at Villanova College. In 1947, he became the director of athletics at St. Michael's College. The Sporting News Player Contract Cards, ScanID: 1022003087 George

Notes—Chapter Two

Jacobs, https://digital.la84.org/digital/collection/p17103coll3/id/85429/rec/43.

46. *Salisbury Daily Times*, 3 June 1937, p. 11.

47. Norman Wurst (1916–1939; S/? 6–2 195), born in Philadelphia, PA, spent the 1937 and the 1938 seasons with the Centreville Colts. *Philadelphia Inquirer*, 17 Mar. 1939, p. 16; https://www.baseball-reference.com/register/player.fcgi?id=wurst-000nor.

Ted Joe Tomczyk (1918–1985; 5–10 140) spent the 1937 season with the Centreville Colts. The Sporting News Player Contract Cards, ScanID: 1045000355 Ted Tomczyk, https://digital.la84.org/digital/collection/p17103coll3/id/121033/rec/2.

Louis Austin "Pete" Weimer (1915–1971; 5–11 168), born in Battle Creek, MI, played with the Centreville Colts and the Easton Browns during the 1937 season. He spent the 1938 season with the Kingsport Cherokees (APPY). The Sporting News Player Contract Cards, ScanID: 1047002435 L. Austin Weimer, https://digital.la84.org/digital/collection/p17103coll3/id/171799/rec/16; World War II Draft Cards.

48. Alexander "Spunk" Pitko (1914–2011; R/R 5–11 190), born in Burlington, NJ, had a five-year career from 1936 to 1940. This included stints with the Philadelphia Phillies (seven games in 1938) and the Washington Senators (four games in 1939). The Sporting News Player Contract Cards, ScanID: 1035004885 Alex Pitko, https://digital.la84.org/digital/collection/p17103coll3/id/102572/rec/1.

49. Lloyd E. Gross (1917–1977; R/R 6–2 198), born in California, PA, spent four seasons in the minor leagues (1937–1938, 1940–1941). He served in the U.S. Army from 1944 to 1945. The Sporting News Player Contract Cards, ScanID: 1025016794 Cloyd Gross, https://digital.la84.org/digital/collection/p17103coll3/id/66119/rec/19.

50. John Joseph Boylan (1916–1985 6–1 175), born in Philadelphia, PA, played for the Centreville Colts in 1937. He served in the U.S. Navy from 1942 to 1945. The Sporting News Player Contract Cards, ScanID: 1005002264 John J. Boylan, https://digital.la84.org/digital/collection/p17103coll3/id/9122/rec/3; World War II Draft Cards.

51. Edward Isidore Feinberg (1917–1986; S/R 5–9 165), born in Philadelphia, PA, had a three-year career from 1937 to 1939 with a 16-game stint with the Philadelphia Phillies in 1938–1939. He served in the U.S. Army from 1943 to 1946. The Sporting News Player Contract Cards, ScanID: 1014002739 Edward Feinberg, https://digital.la84.org/digital/collection/p17103coll3/id/69546/rec/1; World War II Draft Cards.

Gordon Vincent Troy (1915–2011; R/R 5–10 165), born in Gordon, PA, tried out with the Reading Red Sox (NYPL) in 1934. From 1937 to 1941, he played with several Philadelphia Phillies minor league teams. He served in the U.S. Army from 1941 to 1945. He was also an amateur golfer. The Sporting News Player Contract Cards, ScanID: 1045002641 Gordon Troy, https://digital.la84.org/digital/collection/p17103coll3/id/122568/rec/782.

52. Theodore Joseph Mezours (1914–1981; 5–10 180), born in New Brunswick, NJ, played for the Centreville Colts in 1937. He was a World War II Army veteran. *The Home News*, 13 Feb. 1981, p. 37; World War II Draft Cards.

53. Walter David "Toddy" Carroll, Jr. (1913–2001; R/R 6–3 178), born in Townley, AL, had a three-year career in the Philadelphia Phillies farm system from 1937 to 1939. He graduated from the University of Florida in 1936. He spent his entire career in the military, rising to the rank of lieutenant colonel. The Sporting News Player Contract Cards, ScanID: 1007005044 Walter Carroll, https://digital.la84.org/digital/collection/p17103coll3/id/20819/rec/166.

54. John Howard Davis tried out for three Eastern Shore League teams (Easton, Cambridge and Centreville) in 1937. The Sporting News Player Contract Cards, ScanID: 1011002719 John Howard Davis, https://digital.la84.org/digital/collection/p17103coll3/id/50905/rec/1.

55. *Cumberland Sunday Times*, 6 June 1937, p. 16.

Notes—Chapter Two

56. Harry Kuntashian (1913–2002; ?/R 6–0 180), born in New York, NY, had a five-year career from 1937 to 1941. The Sporting News Player Contract Cards, ScanID: 1025002507 Harry Kuntashian, https://digital.la84.org/digital/collection/p17103coll3/id/118146/rec/1.

57. Edgar Mahlon Beidleman (1915–2008; L/? 5–11 172), born in Hokendauqua, PA, played for five teams between 1937 and 1941 (Easton Browns 1937, Allentown Dukes [ISLG] 1939, Evansville Braves [IIIL] 1940, Bradford Bees [PONY] 1940, York/Bridgeport Bees [ISLG] 1940–1941). The Sporting News Player Contract Cards, ScanID: 1003004873 Ed Beidleman, https://digital.la84.org/digital/collection/p17103coll3/id/16638/rec/1.

58. Edward Franklin Zimmerman (1916–2007; R/? 5–8 155), born in Fullerton, PA, had a four-year career from 1937 to 1940. *Allentown Morning Call*, 27 Feb. 2007, p. 16; https://www.baseball-reference.com/register/player.fcgi?id=zimmer000edw.

59. James Barton "Mickey" Vernon (1918–2008; L/L 6–1 172), born in Marcus Hook, PA, started his baseball career playing for the Easton Browns in 1937. From 1938 to 1940, he split his time between several minor league teams (Greenville Spinners, Springfield Nationals and New Jersey Giants) and the Washington Senators. Starting in 1941, he spent his career in the major leagues, ending in 1960. He played for the Washington Senators (14 years), Cleveland Indians (three years), Boston Red Sox (two years), Pittsburgh Pirates (one year) and Milwaukee Braves (one year). From 1943 to 1945, he served in the U.S. Navy. The Sporting News Player Contract Cards, ScanID: 1099105998 Mickey Vernon, https://digital.la84.org/digital/collection/p17103coll3/id/43546/rec/1193.

Charles Moreskonich Metro (1919–2011; R/R 5–11 1/2 190), born in Nanty-Glo, PA, spent six years (1937–1942) in the minor leagues. In 1943, he joined the Detroit Tigers and played for them until his release on August 1, 1944. The Philadelphia Athletics signed him two weeks later, and he stayed there until August 1945, when he returned to the minor leagues. From 1947 to 1961, he began a stint being a player-manager in the Yankees, Tigers and Orioles farm systems. In 1962, he was a member of the Chicago Cubs' "College of Coaches," becoming "head coach" in June. He was a scout for the Cubs from 1963 to 1965 and was manager of the Kansas City Royals from August 1969 to June 1970. He returned to scouting by working for Detroit from 1971 to 1975 and with the Los Angeles Dodgers from 1977 to 1981. He was a coach with the Oakland Athletics from 1981 to 1982. His last position was with the Los Angeles Dodgers as a scout. The Sporting News Player Contract Cards, ScanID: 1099102226 Charlie Metro, https://digital.la84.org/digital/collection/p17103coll3/id/80269/rec/7.

60. Kenneth William Eck (1914–1996; R/? 5–10 150), born in Allentown, PA, had a four-year career from 1937 to 1940. The Sporting News Player Contract Cards, ScanID: 1013002135 Kenneth Eck, https://digital.la84.org/digital/collection/p17103coll3/id/52624/rec/10.

61. William John Savitsky (1915–2003; 6–4 190), born in Frackville, PA, was a minor league pitcher from 1937 to 1947. He served in the U.S. Army from 1941 to 1945 with the rank of staff sergeant. The Sporting News Player Contract Cards, ScanID: 1039004839 William Savitsky, https://digital.la84.org/digital/collection/p17103coll3/id/117482/rec/2.

62. Stephen Andrew Sefick (1911–1976; R/R 5–10 180), born in Johnstown, PA, was a minor league catcher who played from 1936 to 1946. A property of the New York Yankees, he also played baseball for the Hagerstown Owls and Allentown Wings in the Interstate League. *Allentown Morning Call*, 3 Apr. 1976, p. 9; The Sporting News Player Contract Cards, ScanID: 1099022816 Sefick Stephen Andrew, https://digital.la84.org/digital/collection/p17103coll3/id/123178/rec/37.

63. Michael Joseph Koons (1915–1985; R/R 5–11 3/4 195), born in Catasauqua, PA, spent two seasons with the Cambridge Cardinals (1937–1938), two

Notes—Chapter Two

seasons with the Hazleton Mountaineers (1939–1940) and one season with the Lancaster Red Roses (1941) until he was released to serve in the U.S. Army from 1942 to 1945. He spent six more seasons with several other minor league teams, including serving as player-manager for Mahanoy City Brewers (1949) and Berwick Slaters (1950). The Sporting News Player Contract Cards, ScanID: 1025020772 Michael Koons, https://digital.la84.org/digital/collection/p17103coll3/id/127990/rec/3.

64. James Martin Ettner (1918–1996; R/? 5–9 160), born in Danville, PA, was a minor league outfielder who played for the Cambridge Cardinals and the Monessen Red Wings (PASA) in 1937 and the Kinston Eagles (CPL) and the Cambridge Cardinals in 1938. The Sporting News Player Contract Cards, ScanID: 1013006605 James Ettner, https://digital.la84.org/digital/collection/p17103coll3/id/53054/rec/1.

65. Silvio Michael Giovanelli (1915–2005; 5–5 155), born in Valhalla, NY, played for the Cambridge Cardinals in 1937 and the Salisbury Indians in 1939. The Sporting News Player Contract Cards, ScanID: 1016006728 Silvio Giovanelli, https://digital.la84.org/digital/collection/p17103coll3/id/64280/rec/2; World War II Draft Cards.

William Francis Gagain (1919–1989; 6–0 210), born in Waterbury, CT, started the 1937 season with the Cambridge Cardinals until he was released in July, then he was with the Monessen Red Wings (PASA) and the Huntington Boosters (MTNS). The Sporting News Player Contract Cards, ScanID: 1016000010 William Gagain, https://digital.la84.org/digital/collection/p17103coll3/id/73452/rec/3; World War II Draft Cards.

66. Edward Thomas Kovis (1915–1990; ?/R 6–0 198), born in Manchester, CT, played for the Cambridge Cardinals in 1937 until he was released in July. He joined the Martinsville Manufacturers (BIST) from May to July 1938. The Sporting News Player Contract Cards, ScanID: 1025000311 Edward Kovis, https://digital.la84.org/digital/collection/p17103coll3/id/126928/rec/1.

67. Bernard F. Healy (1917–2010; R/? 5–11 185), born in Holyoke, MA, played for the Cambridge Cardinals in the 1937 season. He served in the U.S. Army from 1941 to 1945. The Sporting News Player Contract Cards, ScanID: 1019005827 Bernie Healy, https://digital.la84.org/digital/collection/p17103coll3/id/64582/rec/2.

William Myska (b. 1918; R/? 5–8 155) played for the Cambridge Cardinals in the first two months of the 1937 season. The Sporting News Player Contract Cards, ScanID: 1032003375 Bill Myska, https://digital.la84.org/digital/collection/p17103coll3/id/171944/rec/1.

68. Charles Amos Coleman (1916–1981; R/? 6–1 180), born in Sudlersville, MD, played for the Dover Orioles in 1937. The Sporting News Player Contract Cards, ScanID: 1009001756 Charles A. Coleman, https://digital.la84.org/digital/collection/p17103coll3/id/48614/rec/37.

69. Howard Harris Killen (1913–1994; R/R 5–10 155), born in Felton, DE, spent the 1937 season with the Dover Orioles and played for the Federalsburg Athletics in 1938. The Sporting News Player Contract Cards, ScanID: 1025020380 Howard Killen, https://digital.la84.org/digital/collection/p17103coll3/id/112375/rec/6.

70. Frank Messick played for the Pocomoke City Red Sox in 1937. The Sporting News Player Contract Cards, ScanID: 1030003441 Frank Messick, https://digital.la84.org/digital/collection/p17103coll3/id/134629/rec/1.

71. Irvin Gladstone Hall (1918–2006; R/R 5–10 160), born in Alberton, MD, played 12 seasons of minor league baseball (1937–1942, 1946–1951). He played four seasons for the Philadelphia Athletics from 1943 to 1946. The Sporting News Player Contract Cards, ScanID: 1025017086 Irvin G. Hall, https://digital.la84.org/digital/collection/p17103coll3/id/70266/rec/182.

72. Henry Charles Schluter (1917–1995; R/R 5–10 1/2 155), born in Baltimore, MD, had a six-year minor league career from 1936 to 1940 and 1942. The Sporting News Player Contract Cards,

Notes—Chapter Two

ScanID: 1099022451 Henry Schluter, https://digital.la84.org/digital/collection/p17103coll3/id/112988/rec/1.

Nelson Dudley Jester (1912–1967; R/R 5–9 180), born in Chincoteague, VA, played for the Pocomoke City Red Sox from June 1937 to July 1938. The Sporting News Player Contract Cards, ScanID: 1022004979 Nelson Jester, https://digital.la84.org/digital/collection/p17103coll3/id/81547/rec/1.

73. Maurice James Dugan (1914–1996; L/? 5–10 175), born in Baltimore, MD, spent the 1937 season with the Pocomoke City Red Sox. He was traded to the Milford Giants in May 1938 and stayed there until his release in July. The Sporting News Player Contract Cards, ScanID: 1012005713 Maurice Dugan, https://digital.la84.org/digital/collection/p17103coll3/id/57682/rec/28.

David Denenberg (1914–1992; L/? 5–10 175), born in Philadelphia, PA, started the 1937 season with the Centreville Colts until he was released in July 1937 and joined the Pocomoke City Red Sox for the rest of the season. The Sporting News Player Contract Cards, ScanID: 1011004861 David Denenberg, https://digital.la84.org/digital/collection/p17103coll3/id/53687/rec/1.

74. *Queen Anne's County Record-Observer*, 15 Apr. 1937.

75. Thomas Jefferson Ogden (1917–2005; R/R 6–1 180), born in Wayne, GA, spent the 1937 and 1938 seasons with the Centreville Colts and the 1939 season with the Hazelton Mountaineers (ISLG). He served in the U.S. Navy during World War II. The Sporting News Player Contract Cards, ScanID: 1033004025 Thomas Ogden, https://digital.la84.org/digital/collection/p17103coll3/id/161594/rec/736.

76. Nicholas "Dick" Petock (1912–1980; 5–11 165), born and raised in Mahanoy City, PA, was a catcher for several semiprofessional teams in Schuylkill County in the 1930s and 1940s. He tried out for the Centreville Colts in July 1937. *Pottsville Republican*, 3 Jan. 1980, p. 3; World War II Draft Cards; The Sporting News Player Contract Cards, ScanID: 1035002105 Dick Petock, https://digital.la84.org/digital/collection/p17103coll3/id/93248/rec/1.

77. Charles Howard "Hank" Harris (1914–1954; R/R 6–0 160), born in Baltimore, MD, played for the Pocomoke City Red Sox in 1937 after being signed by the Baltimore Orioles in 1933 and not making the roster with the Johnstown Johnnies (MATL) in 1934. He played for several other minor league teams from 1938 to 1942, when he was inducted into the U.S. Army and served until 1944. From 1952 to 1954, he was an umpire in the Western Association. The Sporting News Player Contract Cards, ScanID: 1025017408 Charles Harris, https://digital.la84.org/digital/collection/p17103coll3/id/64000/rec/94.

78. Michael Alexander "Mickey" Urban (1918–1999; R/R 5–9 165), born in Larksville, PA, had a five-year career (1937–1940, 1943). He served in the U.S. Army from 1943 to 1946. The Sporting News Player Contract Cards, ScanID: 1099026186 Michael Urban, https://digital.la84.org/digital/collection/p17103coll3/id/110947/rec/37.

John Joseph Francis "Tex" Gilmartin (1910–1969; 5–11 185), born in Jessup, PA, spent the 1937 season with the Crisfield Crabbers. He served in the 49th Fighter Squadron from 1942 to 1945. The Sporting News Player Contract Cards, ScanID: 1016006199 John Gilmartin, https://digital.la84.org/digital/collection/p17103coll3/id/65794/rec/3; World War II Draft Cards.

Harry Sylvester "Hal" Marnie (1918–2002; 6–1 182), born in Philadelphia, PA, had a seven-year career from 1937 through 1946, with three seasons (1943–1945) missed due to United States Army service in World War II. He appeared in 96 games over parts of three seasons (1940–1942) for the Philadelphia Phillies. The Sporting News Player Contract Cards, ScanID: 1099014332 Hal Marnie, https://digital.la84.org/digital/collection/p17103coll3/id/168839/rec/2; World War II Draft Cards.

79. Stephen Sherwood Barnes (1915–2010; R/L 5–10 165), born in Philadelphia, PA, started his five-year minor league career with the Crisfield Crabbers

Notes—Chapter Three

in 1937. He served in the U.S. Navy from 1944 to 1946. The Sporting News Player Contract Cards, ScanID: 1003000498 Sherwood Barnes Sr., https://digital.la84.org/digital/collection/p17103coll3/id/20889/rec/112.

80. Joseph Reha (1910–1986; R/? 5–8 151), born in Throop, PA, had a four-year minor league career (1937, 1940–1942). The Sporting News Player Contract Cards, ScanID: 1037001449 Joe Reha, https://digital.la84.org/digital/collection/p17103coll3/id/80985/rec/5; World War II Draft Cards.

81. Joseph Garbutt Cahall (1915–1977 6-1 165), born in Philadelphia, PA, started the 1937 season with the Centreville Colts. In June, he was released to the Crisfield Crabbers and stayed until the end of the season. The Sporting News Player Contract Cards, ScanID: 1007000800 Joseph Cahall, https://digital.la84.org/digital/collection/p17103coll3/id/7493/rec/1; World War II Draft Cards.

82. Possibly Stanley Edward Solinski (1905–1994; 5–10 156), born in Jersey City, NJ, played for the Cambridge Cardinals and the Crisfield Crabbers during the 1937 season. The Sporting News Player Contract Cards, ScanID: 1042002427 Stanley Solinski, https://digital.la84.org/digital/collection/p17103coll3/id/130692/rec/1; World War II Draft Cards.

83. Oscar Burton "Spike" Webb (1916–1967; L/? 5–10 170), born in Clarendon, VA, was with the Crisfield Crabbers in 1937. He spent the next three years bouncing around several minor league teams (Opelousas Indians [EVL], Elizabethton Betsy Red Sox [APPY], Kingsport Cherokees [APPY]) until he was released by the Rome Colonels (CAML) in June 1940. The Sporting News Player Contract Cards, ScanID: 1047001341 Burt Webb, https://digital.la84.org/digital/collection/p17103coll3/id/166118/rec/87.

84. Baltimore native William Edward "Buzz" Mahrer (1917–1961; 6–0 175) played for the 1937 Crisfield Crabbers and tried out for the Federalsburg Athletics in 1938. The Sporting News Player Contract Cards, ScanID: 1027005815 William E. Mahrer, https://digital.la84.org/digital/collection/p17103coll3/id/156333/rec/1; World War II Draft Cards; *Baltimore Evening Sun*, 3 Mar. 1961, p. 4.

Chapter Three

1. Robert Stephen Fuchs (1912–2004), son of Emil E. Fuchs, president of the Boston Braves, was president of the Harrisburg Senators in 1934. During World War II, he served with the U.S. Army in India with the rank of lieutenant colonel. *The Boston Globe*, 15 June 1947, p. 94.

2. *Baltimore Sun*, 21 June 1937, p. 13.

3. *Hanover Evening Sun*, 21 June 1937, p. 8.

4. *Baltimore Evening Sun*, 11 July 1980, p. 34.

5. Kenesaw Mountain Landis (1866–1944) was the first commissioner of baseball from November 1920 until his death. Before his appointment, he served as a federal judge in Illinois from 1905 to 1922. *Elmira Star-Gazette*, 13 Nov. 1920, p. 8; *Pittsburgh Sun-Telegraph*, 26 Nov. 1944, p. 21.

6. *Salisbury Daily Times*, 22 June 1937, p. 1.

7. *Wicomico News*, 24 June 1937, p. 7.

8. Rodger H. Pippen (1888–1959) was the sports editor for the *Baltimore News-Post* and *Baltimore Sunday American* from 1906 to 1957.

9. *Wicomico News*, 24 June 1937, p. 7.

10. Leslie Mann (1892–1962) was manager of Harrisburg Senators in 1934. The Sporting News Player Contract Cards, ScanID: 1099014213 Les Mann, https://digital.la84.org/digital/collection/p17103coll3/id/156253/rec/56.

11. John Joseph "Crab" Evers (1881–1947) was a scout for the Boston Braves in 1934 and manager of the Albany Senators in 1935. The Sporting News Player Contract Cards, ScanID: 1025014439 Johnny Evers, https://digital.la84.org/digital/collection/p17103coll3/id/62367/rec/14.

12. *Harrisburg Telegraph*, 22 June 1937, p. 17.

228

Notes—Chapter Four

13. Pierre Bertman Farrell (1894–1966), born in Auburn, NY, was president of the New York-Pennsylvania Baseball League from 1930 to 1940, succeeding his father, John H. Farrell. *Poughkeepsie Journal*, 3 Dec. 1966, p. 9.

14. *Wicomico News*, 24 June 1937, p. 7.

15. Among the players on the suspended list were Philip Sherr, Vernon Shelton, Alexander Trippe, J. Woodrow Bates, Philip Beihl, Frank Baroni and Clifton Keyser. National Association of National Baseball Leagues, *Official Bulletin. No. 4* (Durham: National Association of National Baseball Leagues, 5 July 1937).

16. *Easton Star-Democrat*, 25 June 1937, p. 2.

17. *Baltimore Sun*, 27 June 1937, p. 20.

18. *Salisbury Daily Times*, 9 Aug. 1937, p. 1.

19. Ibid.

20. Ibid.

21. Ibid.

22. *Salisbury Daily Times*, 9 Oct. 1965, p. 6.

Chapter Four

1. Thomas Taylor was sent to the Dover Orioles from the Baltimore Orioles in June 1937 and stayed the rest of the season. *Wilmington Morning News*, 18 June 1937, p. 30.

2. *Salisbury Daily Times*, 22 June 1937, p. 7.

3. Bill Mowbray, *The ESL Encyclopedia Eastern Shore League of Professional Baseball Clubs* (Cambridge, MD: B. Mowbray, 1984), p. 47.

4. *Salisbury Daily Times*, 22 June 1937, p. 7.

5. Ibid.

6. Franklin James Radler (1917–1981; R/R 5–11 176), born in Lehighton, PA, had a 13-year minor league career from 1937 to 1952. During his last five years, he was player-manager for the Stroudsburg Poconos (NATL) (1948–1950), the DeLand Red Hats (FLOR) (1951) and the Union City Greyhounds (KITTY) (1952). The Sporting News Player Contract Cards, ScanID: 1099019609 Franklin James Radler, https://digital.la84.org/digital/collection/p17103coll3/id/85274/rec/1.

7. See page 166 for Mike Depko's biography.

8. Alfred Bernard McNally (1918–1991; L/L 5–11 168), born in Philadelphia, PA, played for the Federalsburg Athletics in 1937. He served in the U.S. Army during World War II. World War II Draft Cards; The Sporting News Player Contract Cards, ScanID: 1030000165 Al McNally, https://digital.la84.org/digital/collection/p17103coll3/id/142861/rec/1.

9. John Matthew Manczak (1916–1996; R/R 5–8 155), born in Trenton, NJ, had a five-year minor league career from 1937 to 1940 and 1948 to 1949. He served in the U.S. Navy from 1941 to 1947 and 1950 to 1952. The Sporting News Player Contract Cards, ScanID: 1099014172 John Manczak, https://digital.la84.org/digital/collection/p17103coll3/id/168881/rec/1.

10. Sterling Monroe "Turney" Ecker (1915–1994; R/R 5–9 165), born in Littlestown, PA, tried out for the Federalsburg Athletics in 1937 and 1938. He played for the Staunton Presidents (VIRL) in 1942 and the Baltimore Orioles (IL) from 1943 to 1944. In 1945, he served in the U.S. Army. *Baltimore Evening Sun*, 21 Feb. 1994, p. 4; The Sporting News Player Contract Cards, ScanID: 1013002197 Sterling Ecker, https://digital.la84.org/digital/collection/p17103coll3/id/55213/rec/7.

11. *Salisbury Daily Times*, 28 June 1937, p. 7.

12. Harold Miller (b. ca. 1917; R/? 6–0 190) spent the 1937 season with the Centreville Colts and split the 1938 season between the Montgomery Rebels (SEAL) and the Dover Orioles. He served in the U.S. Marines in World War II. The Sporting News Player Contract Cards, ScanID: 1030005773 Harold Miller, https://digital.la84.org/digital/collection/p17103coll3/id/154738/rec/4.

13. Isadore "Ike" Mysel (1911–1972; R/? 6–0 195), born in Philadelphia, PA, spent the first two months of the 1937 season with the Centreville Colts. He served in the U.S. Army from 1942 to

Notes—Chapter Four

1945. The Sporting News Player Contract Cards, ScanID: 1032003371 Ike Mysel, https://digital.la84.org/digital/collection/p17103coll3/id/159616/rec/1.

14. Charles Parker "Buck" Smyth (1914–1987; 5–11 170), born in Philadelphia, PA, spent two seasons with the Centreville Colts from 1937 to 1938. World War II Draft Cards.

15. Raymond Anthony Rist (1913–1958; L/? 6–0 180), born in Pottsville, PA, had a five-year minor league career from 1937 to 1941. The Sporting News Player Contract Cards, ScanID: 1037006073 Ray Rist, https://digital.la84.org/digital/collection/p17103coll3/id/103425/rec/26.

16. See page 169 for Albert Elliott's biography.

17. Stanley Stanfield spent the 1937 season with the Cambridge Cardinals. The Sporting News Player Contract Cards, ScanID: 1042005583 Stanley Stanfield, https://digital.la84.org/digital/collection/p17103coll3/id/144949/rec/12.

18. Kenneth David Raffensberger (1917–2002; R/L 6–2 185), born in York, PA, had a 21-year professional baseball career from 1937 to 1957, including 15 years in the major leagues. From 1939 through 1954, he played for the St. Louis Cardinals (1939), Chicago Cubs (1940–1941), Philadelphia Phillies (1943–1947) and Cincinnati Reds/Redlegs (1947–1954). The Sporting News Player Contract Cards, ScanID: 1099019627 Ken Raffensberger, https://digital.la84.org/digital/collection/p17103coll3/id/90308/rec/1.

19. William Thomas "Red" Hoffner (1911–2007; R/R 5–8 155), born in Philadelphia, PA, played eight seasons between 1935 and 1949. He served in the U.S. Marines from 1943 to 1946. *The Tampa Tribune*, 22 Mar. 2007, p. 25; The Sporting News Player Contract Cards, ScanID: 1025018401 William Hoffner, https://digital.la84.org/digital/collection/p17103coll3/id/90267/rec/11.

20. *Salisbury Daily Times*, 3 July 1937, p. 7.

21. See page 203 for Joseph Shafnacker's biography.

22. During July 1937, Baltimore native Casimir Walter Macklin (b. 1915; 5–9 190) signed a contract with Salisbury Indians, who in turn released him to the Ayden Aces for a tryout. He returned to Salisbury and was released. World War II Draft Cards, The Sporting News Player Contract Cards, ScanID: 1027004861 Casimir Macklin, https://digital.la84.org/digital/collection/p17103coll3/id/163678/rec/1.

Philip Sherr (1915–1971; 6–0 180), born in Baltimore, MD, played semi-professional baseball in the 1930s for the Mt. Washington Pleasure Club and the Cross Country Club. He tried out for the Salisbury Indians in June 1937, was placed on the suspended list, reinstated in July 1937 and released soon after. *Baltimore Sun*, 28 June 1971, p. 7; World War II Draft Cards; The Sporting News Player Contract Cards, ScanID: 1041000363 Phillip Sherr, https://digital.la84.org/digital/collection/p17103coll3/id/134885/rec/1.

23. *Salisbury Daily Times*, 8 July 1937, p. 7.

24. Edward Guy Weatherlow (1909–1990; 5–11 198), born in Easton, MD, spent the 1937 season with the Dover Orioles. The Sporting News Player Contract Cards, ScanID: 1047001229 Edward Weatherlow, https://digital.la84.org/digital/collection/p17103coll3/id/174525/rec/1; World War II Draft Cards.

25. See page 160 for James Bergen's biography.

26. Norbert Anthony Desrosier (1913–1971; ?/R 5–7 168), born in Manchester, NH, spent the 1937 season with the Cambridge Cardinals. The Sporting News Player Contract Cards, ScanID: 1011005737 Tom Desrosier, https://digital.la84.org/digital/collection/p17103coll3/id/57994/rec/1.

27. See page 191 for Juan Montero's biography.

28. Richard Joseph Hutchison (1917–2002; 5–9 175), born in Philadelphia, PA, played for the Dover Orioles in 1937. He served in the U.S. Army Air Force during World War II. World War II Draft Cards; The Sporting News Player

Notes—Chapter Four

Contract Cards, ScanID: 1022000473 R. Hutchinson, https://digital.la84.org/digital/collection/p17103coll3/id/100395/rec/3.

29. Emlyn Evan Jones (1917–2009; R/L 5–6 142), born in Saint Clair, PA, had a four-year minor league career from 1937 to 1939 and 1941. He served in the U.S. Army from 1942 to 1945. The Sporting News Player Contract Cards, ScanID: 1023001275 Emlyn Evan Jones, https://digital.la84.org/digital/collection/p17103coll3/id/125053/rec/1.

30. Arthur Rosen was on the Pocomoke City Red Sox's roster from July to September 1937. The Sporting News Player Contract Cards, ScanID: 1038004361 Arthur Rosen, https://digital.la84.org/digital/collection/p17103coll3/id/83367/rec/1.

31. Thomas Joseph Daddino (1914–2007; L/L 6–0 170), born in Beverly, NJ, played for the Pocomoke City Red Sox from 1937 to 1938 and the North Wilkesboro Flashers (BLRI) from 1948 to 1950. He served in the U.S. Army from 1941 to 1945. The Sporting News Player Contract Cards, ScanID: 1025012575 Tom Daddino, https://digital.la84.org/digital/collection/p17103coll3/id/49147/rec/1.

32. John J. Halychik (1917–1962; 5–8 160), born in Saint Clair, PA, played 11 games for the Pocomoke City Red Sox in 1937 before injuring his eye. The next season he tried out for the Leaksville-Draper-Spray Triplets (BIST) but did not make the team. The Sporting News Player Contract Cards, ScanID: 1018005487 John Halychik, https://digital.la84.org/digital/collection/p17103coll3/id/72803/rec/1; World War II Draft Cards.

33. *Salisbury Daily Times*, 15 July 1937, p. 7.

34. Thomas Jacob Dousha (1914–1944; R/? 5–11 175), born in Baltimore, MD, spent three seasons (1937–1939) with the Pocomoke City Red Sox. He entered the U.S. Army in 1943 and was killed in France in 1944. The Sporting News Player Contract Cards, ScanID: 1012004105 Thomas Dousha, https://digital.la84.org/digital/collection/p17103coll3/id/53745/rec/1.

Hanna Raymond Humphreys (1916–2005; 5–11 150), born in White Stone, VA, spent the 1937 season with the Pocomoke City Red Sox. He served in the U.S. Army from 1943 to 1945. The Sporting News Player Contract Cards, ScanID: 1021006099 H. Raymond Humphreys, https://digital.la84.org/digital/collection/p17103coll3/id/94036/rec/15.

35. *Salisbury Daily Times*, 15 July 1937, p. 7.

36. Joseph Virgil "Tony" Hudson (1914–1968; 5–7 1/2 160), born in Dagsboro, DE, started the 1937 season with the Pocomoke City Red Sox until he was released in July and signed with the Crisfield Crabbers. The Sporting News Player Contract Cards, ScanID: 1021005021 Joseph Hudson, https://digital.la84.org/digital/collection/p17103coll3/id/98768/rec/148; World War II Draft Cards.

37. Joseph Max Millar (1916–1984; L/? 6–0 155), born in Washington, D.C., joined the Easton Browns in July 1937. He served in the U.S. Army from 1941 to 1945. The Sporting News Player Contract Cards, ScanID: 1030005145 Joseph Millar, https://digital.la84.org/digital/collection/p17103coll3/id/154950/rec/8.

38. Nathaniel Benson Riggin (1915–1958; R/? 5–8 163), born in Crisfield, MD, played for several Eastern Shore League teams (Crisfield, Milford and Salisbury) from 1937 to 1939. The Sporting News Player Contract Cards, ScanID: 1037005309 Nathaniel Riggin, https://digital.la84.org/digital/collection/p17103coll3/id/91047/rec/2.

Roy Edward "Stretch" Myers (1917–2004; 6–2 1/2 168), born in Los Angeles, CA, spent the 1937 season with the Crisfield Crabbers and the 1938–1939 seasons with the Bisbee Bees (AZTX). He served in World War II. *Fort Collins Coloradoan*, 7 Oct. 2004, p. 10; The Sporting News Player Contract Cards, ScanID: 1030004127 Roy Meyers, https://digital.la84.org/digital/collection/p17103coll3/id/141270/rec/75; World War II Draft Cards.

39. Dallas Wayne Rife (1916–1987; 5–11 150), born in Green Village, PA, spent the 1937 season with the Crisfield Crabbers and the 1938 season with the

Notes—Chapter Four

Pocomoke City Red Sox. He served in the U.S. Navy from 1945 to 1946. The Sporting News Player Contract Cards, ScanID: 1037005223 Dall Rife, https://digital.la84.org/digital/collection/p17103coll3/id/99288/rec/4; World War II Draft Cards.

40. Robert Herman List (1916–2006; R/R 6–4 200), born in Baltimore, MD, had a four-year career in the minor leagues from 1937 to 1940. The Sporting News Player Contract Cards, ScanID: 1026005329 Robert List, https://digital.la84.org/digital/collection/p17103coll3/id/133337/rec/28.

41. William Thomas "Rip" Shillingford (1910–1994; R/? 5–8 185), born in Clifton Heights, PA, had a three-year minor league career playing in the Northeastern and Eastern Shore Leagues (1934, 1937–1938). *Philadelphia Daily News*, 17 Oct. 1994, pp. 24–25; The Sporting News Player Contract Cards, ScanID: 1041000677 William Shillingford, https://digital.la84.org/digital/collection/p17103coll3/id/145919/rec/4.

Charles Oswald Knapp (1911–1956; R/R 5–11 175), born in Philadelphia, PA, had a three-year minor league career from 1936 to 1938. He played for the Philadelphia Eagles. He served in the U.S. Navy as a PT boat commander for four years. The Sporting News Player Contract Cards, ScanID: 1024004383 Charles Knapp, https://digital.la84.org/digital/collection/p17103coll3/id/112396/rec/4.

Queen Anne's Record-Observer, 22 July 1937, p. 4.

42. *Salisbury Daily Times*, 26 July 1937, p. 7.

43. Joseph Paul Scarbinsky (1913–2003; 6–0 186), born in Saint Clair, PA, spent the 1937 season with the Pocomoke City Red Sox. The Sporting News Player Contract Cards, ScanID: 1039005223 Joseph Scarbinsky, https://digital.la84.org/digital/collection/p17103coll3/id/124015/rec/19; World War II Draft Cards.

44. William John Zarowsky (1912–1991; R/R 6–2 180), born in Eckley, PA, had a four-year minor league career from 1937 to 1940. *Standard-Speaker*, 2 May 1991, p. 2; https://www.baseball-reference.com/register/player.fcgi?id=zarows000wil.

45. See Frank Deutsch's biography on page 167.

46. Charles Stockley "Choc" Millman (1915–2013; L/R 5–8 165), born in Philadelphia, PA, spent the 1937 season between the Ayden Aces and Federalsburg Athletics. In 1938, he tried out for the Union Springs Redbirds. He served in the U.S. Army from 1941 to 1945. The Sporting News Player Contract Cards, ScanID: 1030006855 Charles Millman, https://digital.la84.org/digital/collection/p17103coll3/id/138772/rec/1; World War II Draft Cards.

47. Paul Pletcher Martin (1914–1978; 6–0 200), a graduate of Lancaster High School and Franklin and Marshall College, taught German and English at Hershey Industrial School from 1937 to 1943. He served as a sergeant with Army Intelligence at SHAEF Headquarters in London and Berlin during World War II. He then became a professor of German at Franklin and Marshall College from 1946 to 1978. A Lancaster, PA, native, he played basketball during his collegiate career and was on the championship teams from 1935 to 1937. He was a member of the three-time state champion Hamilton Watch softball team from 1935 to 1938. *Lancaster New Era*, 9 Nov. 1978, p. 3; World War II Draft Cards; *Reading Times*, 28 July 1937, p. 15.

48. Raymond Moritz "Zeke" Zschau (1917–2002; R/L 6–2 176), born in Marshall, IL, had a three-year minor league career from 1937 to 1939. He served in the U.S. Navy from 1943 to 1946. https://www.baseball-reference.com/register/player.fcgi?id=zschau000zek; *Mattoon Journal Gazette*, 17 May 2002, p. 10.

49. Possibly Michael John Milici (1910–1995; R/R 5–10 180), born in Rehoboth, MA, tried out for the Fieldale Towlers (BIST) in 1935. In 1937, he spent the season with the Federalsburg Athletics. The Sporting News Player Contract Cards, ScanID: 1030005087 Michael, Milici, https://digital.la84.org/digital/collection/p17103coll3/id/146874/rec/2.

Notes—Chapter Five

50. Harold Wayne Lomas (1917–1994; R/R 6–0 170), born in Lenni, PA, had a four-year minor league career from 1937 to 1940. He served in the U.S. Navy from 1944 to 1945. The Sporting News Player Contract Cards, ScanID: 1027000057 H. Wayne Lomas, https://digital.la84.org/digital/collection/p17103coll3/id/143306/rec/7.

51. David Tomlinson, a southpaw pitcher, was on the Cambridge Cardinals' roster from July to September 1937. The Sporting News Player Contract Cards, ScanID: 1045000423 David Tomlinson, https://digital.la84.org/digital/collection/p17103coll3/id/123381/rec/10.

52. Frank Joseph Gunkel (1917–2003; R/R 6–1 1/2 195), born in Philadelphia, PA, had a five-year minor league career (1937–1938, 1940–1941, 1946). He served as a sergeant with the 4108 Army Air Corps in Marianna, FL, from 1941 to 1945. While stationed, he played for the Marianna Flyers baseball team. The Sporting News Player Contract Cards, ScanID: 1025016882 Frank Gunkel, https://digital.la84.org/digital/collection/p17103coll3/id/78188/rec/3.

53. Austin John O'Donnell (1916–1963; ?/L 5–11 150), born in Providence, RI, played for the Cambridge Cardinals from July 1937 to July 1938. The Sporting News Player Contract Cards, ScanID: 1033003733 Austin O'Donnell, https://digital.la84.org/digital/collection/p17103coll3/id/172723/rec/1.

54. Edward A. "Jiggs" Donahue (1891–1961; 5–7 148), born in Cohoes, NY, graduated from Washington & Lee University, where he was called "Little Wizard." He managed several minor league teams from 1923 to 1928 and 1937, 1938 and 1940. In 1941, he was an umpire for the Florida East Coast League. He coached football at Western Reserve University, Clemson University and Washington & Lee University from 1914 to 1921. The Sporting News Player Contract Cards, ScanID: 1099035695 Edward A. (Jiggs) Donahue, https://digital.la84.org/digital/collection/p17103coll3/id/34343/rec/2; World War II Draft Cards.

Chapter Five

1. *Salisbury Daily Times*, 4 Aug. 1937, p. 9.

Widely regarded as one of the greatest second basemen of all time, Charles Leonard "The Mechanical Man" Gehringer (1903–1993) played 19 seasons (1924–1942) for the Detroit Tigers. The Sporting News Player Contract Cards, ScanID: 1016003823 Charlie Gehringer, https://digital.la84.org/digital/collection/p17103coll3/id/70850/rec/2.

2. James Richard McInerney (1915–2008; R/R 5–10 165), born in Coatesville, PA, spent the 1937 season with three Eastern Shore League teams (Easton, Dover and Centreville). He served in the U.S. Army from 1941 to 1945. The Sporting News Player Contract Cards, ScanID: 1029005179 James R. McInerney, https://digital.la84.org/digital/collection/p17103coll3/id/141106/rec/1.

3. Ellsworth Minton "Jake" Outwin (1912–1977; 5–11 225), born in Chicago, IL, played several games for the Dover Orioles in August 1937. He served in the U.S. Navy from 1942 to 1966. The Sporting News Player Contract Cards, ScanID: 1034000549 Ellsworth M Outwin, https://digital.la84.org/digital/collection/p17103coll3/id/177910/rec/1; World War II Draft Cards.

4. Albert Baumann joined the Pocomoke City Red Sox in July 1937 and stayed the rest of the season. The Sporting News Player Contract Cards, ScanID: 1003002820 Albert Baumann, https://digital.la84.org/digital/collection/p17103coll3/id/15037/rec/1.

5. Frank LeRoy played for the Pocomoke City Red Sox in 1937 and 1938. The Sporting News Player Contract Cards, ScanID: 1026002801 Frank LeRoy, https://digital.la84.org/digital/collection/p17103coll3/id/143012/rec/5.

6. Price, MD, native Casper Dawson Clough (1908–1970; 6–1 1/2 216) was on the roster of the Pocomoke City Red Sox in August 1937. World War II Draft Cards; The Sporting News Player Contract Cards, ScanID: 1009000077 Casper D. Clough, https://digital.la84.org/digital/collection/p17103coll3/id/45970/rec/2.

Notes—Chapter Five

7. Herman Benjamin "Zulu" Gray (1912–1970; 5–11 1/2 165), born in Dagsboro, DE, spent the 1937 season with the Pocomoke City Red Sox. He served in the U.S. Army in World War II. The Sporting News Player Contract Cards, ScanID: 1017005089 Herman Gray, https://digital.la84.org/digital/collection/p17103coll3/id/73485/rec/1; World War II Draft Cards.

8. *Salisbury Daily Times*, 7 Aug. 1937, p. 4.

9. *Ibid.*

10. Allen David "Snowball" Klepper (1915–1974; 5–8 155), born in Lebanon, PA, played with the Cambridge Cardinals in 1937 and the Anderson A's in 1938. *Lebanon Daily News*, 31 May 1974, p. 2; https://www.baseball-reference.com/register/player.fcgi?id=kleppe001all.

11. See page 202 for Jose Salazar's biography.

12. Joseph Paul DiMaggio (1914–1999) played his entire 13-year career with the New York Yankees from 1936 to 1951. Nicknamed Joltin' Joe and the Yankee Clipper, he was a three-time MVP Award winner and helped the Yankees win nine World Series championships. The Sporting News Player Contract Cards, ScanID: 1025013380 Joe DiMaggio, https://digital.la84.org/digital/collection/p17103coll3/id/54814/rec/3.

13. Swedish native Johan Leander Tillman (1893–1964; S/R 5–11 170), also known as John Lawrence "Ducky" Tillman, was raised in Bristol, CT. He had a long baseball career from 1914 to 1934, including appearances in two major league games with the St. Louis Browns in 1915. The Sporting News Player Contract Cards, ScanID: 1099025665 Johnny Tillman, https://digital.la84.org/digital/collection/p17103coll3/id/122002/rec/27; World War I Draft Registration Cards.

14. Richard William "Rube" Marquard (1886–1980) had an 18-year career from 1908 to 1925. In 1912, he won 19 consecutive decisions. The Sporting News Player Contract Cards, ScanID: 1099014345 Richard William Marquard, https://digital.la84.org/digital/collection/p17103coll3/id/159658/rec/5.

15. *Salisbury Daily Times*, 11 Aug. 1937, p. 7.

16. Ralph Decker played for the Crisfield Crabbers in 1937. The Sporting News Player Contract Cards, ScanID: 1011001147 Ralph Decker, https://digital.la84.org/digital/collection/p17103coll3/id/51711/rec/363.

17. The Newark Bears ended the 1937 season with a record of 109 wins and 43 losses, with a winning percentage of .717. The Salisbury Indians finished with a winning percentage of .833. Both finished 25 1/2 games ahead of the second-place team.

18. Walter Harvey Cantwell (1909–1977; 5–9 160), born in Chester, PA, was with the Easton Browns during the latter months of the 1937 season. *Delaware County Daily Times*, 4 May 1977, p. 8; World War II Draft Cards.

19. Leroy Paul Mikus (1917–1985 R/R 6–2 190), born in Passaic, NJ, had a three-year minor league career from 1937 to 1939. He served in the U.S. Navy from 1943 to 1945. The Sporting News Player Contract Cards, ScanID: 1030004877 LeRoy Mikus, https://digital.la84.org/digital/collection/p17103coll3/id/139941/rec/1.

20. Harold Joseph "Pie" Traynor (1898–1972) was considered the best third baseman. He played his entire career with the Pittsburgh Pirates from 1920 to 1937. The Sporting News Player Contract Cards, ScanID: 1099025881 Pie Traynor, https://digital.la84.org/digital/collection/p17103coll3/id/110454/rec/3.

21. Harpel Aubrey Moore (1904–1987), born in Elliott, MD, operated an insurance company. World War II Draft Cards.

22. *Queen Anne's Record-Observer*, 12 Aug. 1937, p. 8.

23. See page 178 for Ed Hullings's biography.

24. *Camden Courier-Post*, 17 Aug. 1937, p. 15.

25. *Salisbury Daily Times*, 16 Aug. 1937, p. 7.

26. *Ibid.*

27. William Heim came to the Dover Orioles in September 1937. The Sporting News Player Contract Cards, ScanID:

Notes—Chapter Five

1019006705 W. Heim, https://digital.la84.org/digital/collection/p17103coll3/id/67300/rec/8.

28. Possibly Alfred Walton Anderson (1914–1985; R/R 5-11 165), born in Gainesville, GA, had an eight-year baseball career, including three years in the majors with the Pittsburgh Pirates (1941–1942, 1946). The Sporting News Player Contract Cards, ScanID: 1025007222 Alf Anderson, https://digital.la84.org/digital/collection/p17103coll3/id/1155/rec/4; *Atlanta Constitution*, 26 June 1985, p. 14.

29. Edwin Leonard Taylor (1919–2003; R/R 5-11 170), born in Louisville, KY, reported to the Baltimore Orioles (IL) following his graduation from DuPont Manual Training School in 1937. He spent four seasons in Baltimore's farm system until he was inducted into the U.S. Army in 1941. From 1951 to 1956, he worked as an umpire. The Sporting News Player Contract Cards, ScanID: 1099036334 Edwin Taylor, https://digital.la84.org/digital/collection/p17103coll3/id/34075/rec/301.

30. Harry Frederick "Scrap" Theurer (1918–2004; ?/L 6-0 180), born in Burlington, NJ, spent the 1937 season with the Dover Orioles. In 1938, he played 10 games before being released in July 1938. He served in the U.S. Coast Guard during World War II. The Sporting News Player Contract Cards, ScanID: 1044003711 Harry Theurer, https://digital.la84.org/digital/collection/p17103coll3/id/118603/rec/1.

31. Lawrence Wesley Burdsall (1911–1975; L/L 5-8 150), born in Lansdowne, PA, played several games for the Dover Orioles in August 1937. The Sporting News Player Contract Cards, ScanID: 1006004148 Lawrence Burdsall, https://digital.la84.org/digital/collection/p17103coll3/id/15280/rec/1; World War II Draft Cards.

32. Garrett Layton Grier II (1912–2003; 5-10 1/2 160), born in Milford, DE, was on the roster of the Federalsburg Athletics during the last two months of the 1937 season. In 1938 and 1940, he was with the Milford Giants. He served in the U.S. Navy as lieutenant commander of aviation ordnance during World War II. *News Journal*, 23 Jan. 2003, p. 16; World War II Draft Cards; The Sporting News Player Contract Cards, ScanID: 1018000029 Garrett Grier Sr., https://digital.la84.org/digital/collection/p17103coll3/id/77153/rec/5.

33. Tristram Edgar "the Gray Eagle" Speaker (1888–1958) was considered one of the greatest offensive and defensive center fielders. He played for 20 years with four different Major League teams (Boston Americans/Red Sox, 1907–1915; Cleveland Indians, 1916–1926; Washington Senators, 1927; Philadelphia Athletics, 1928). *Camden Courier-Post*, 9 Dec. 1958, p. 25; The Sporting News Player Contract Cards, ScanID: 1099024136 Tristram Speaker, https://digital.la84.org/digital/collection/p17103coll3/id/152603/rec/14.

Salisbury Daily Times, 16 Aug. 1937, p. 7.

34. Philip Asbury Insley (1908–2002), born in Cambridge, MD, earned his medical degree from the University of Maryland, College Park. He practiced surgical and general medicine in Salisbury, MD, from 1936 to 1979. *Salisbury Daily Times*, 16 Feb. 2002, p. 6.

35. James Aloysius Scully (1914–1975; R/R 5-10 160), born in Wilmington, DE, played for the Federalsburg Athletics for the 1937 season. The Sporting News Player Contract Cards, ScanID: 1040002963 James Scully, https://digital.la84.org/digital/collection/p17103coll3/id/123248/rec/4; World War II Draft Cards.

36. Edward Francis Lane (1915–1942; R/R 5-10 165), born in Philadelphia, PA, played for the Federalsburg Athletics in 1937. World War II Draft Cards; The Sporting News Player Contract Cards, ScanID: 1025004549 Edward Lane, https://digital.la84.org/digital/collection/p17103coll3/id/112343/rec/3.

37. *Salisbury Daily Times*, 19 Aug. 1937, p. 11.

38. See page 174 for Joe Garliss' biography.

39. John Charles Rozier (1879–1955) was employed as a plumber for the Centreville town commissioners. World War II Draft Cards.

40. Howard Wilkinson Jackson (1877–1960), born in Stemmers Run, MD, was the mayor of Baltimore, MD, from 1923 to 1927 and again from 1931 to 1943. *Baltimore Evening Sun*, 1 Sept. 1960, pp. 22, 36.

41. James E. White, Jr., played in the Northeast Arkansas League before joining the Dover Orioles in August during the 1937 season. The Sporting News Player Contract Cards, ScanID: 1047005589 James E. Jr. White, https://digital.la84.org/digital/collection/p17103coll3/id/164695/rec/1242.

42. Alexander Trakimas (1917–1979; 5–8 168), born in Philadelphia, PA; spent the 1937 season with the Dover Orioles and the 1939 season with the Trenton Senators. The Sporting News Player Contract Cards, ScanID: 1045001591 Alexander Trakimas, https://digital.la84.org/digital/collection/p17103coll3/id/121731/rec/5; World War II Draft Cards.

43. Edward Joseph Tantillo (1919–2002; 5–9 165), born in Rochester, NY, spent the 1937 season with the Dover Orioles and the 1938 season with the Pocomoke City Red Sox. He pitched a perfect game against the Centreville Colts on September 6, 1937. The Sporting News Player Contract Cards, ScanID: 1099025181 Edward Tantillo, https://digital.la84.org/digital/collection/p17103coll3/id/127080/rec/1; World War II Draft Cards.

Chapter Six

1. See page 183 for John Kruk's biography.

2. Henry "Hank" Greenberg (1911–1986; R/R 6–3 1/2 210), a New York City native, spent the majority of his major league baseball career with the Detroit Tigers (1930, 1933–1941, 1946), where he won four home run and four RBI titles as well as twice received the American League's Most Valuable Player Award. In 1947, which would be his last season, he was sold to the Pittsburgh Pirates. The Sporting News Player Contract Cards, ScanID: 1025016618 Hank Greenberg, https://digital.la84.org/digital/collection/p17103coll3/id/79684/rec/2; William Simons, "Hammerin' Hank," *Journal of Sport History* 27, no. 3 (2000): 533; https://digital.la84.org/digital/collection/p17103coll10/id/1495/rec/1.

3. *Salisbury Daily Times*, 2 Sept. 1937, p. 9.

4. *Salisbury Daily Times*, 21 Aug. 1937, p. 1.

5. *Salisbury Daily Times*, 2 Sept. 1937, p. 9.

6. *Salisbury Daily Times*, 2 Sept. 1937, p. 7.

7. Lincoln Modesto "Red" Lenzi (1913–1998; R/R 5–7 160), born in Hodgkins, IL, had a five-year minor league career from 1935 to 1938 and 1946. The Sporting News Player Contract Cards, ScanID: 1026002387 L.M. Lenzi, https://digital.la84.org/digital/collection/p17103coll3/id/131987/rec/2.

8. *Salisbury Daily Times*, 3 Sept. 1937, p. 7.

9. *Salisbury Daily Times*, 3 Sept. 1937, p. 6.

10. *Ibid*.

11. William Joseph Boyce (1916–1975; 6–1 1/2 179), born in Philadelphia, PA, had a six-year career in the minor leagues. The Sporting News Player Contract Cards, ScanID: 1005001922 William Boyce, https://digital.la84.org/digital/collection/p17103coll3/id/19998/rec/1; World War II Draft Cards.

12. *Salisbury Daily Times*, 23 July 1953, p. 14.

13. Carl Owen Hubbell (1903–1988), nicknamed "Meal Ticket" and "King Carl," spent his entire career with the New York Giants from 1928 to 1943. During 1936 and 1937, he set the record for consecutive wins by a pitcher with 24. *Baltimore Evening Sun*, 22 Nov. 1988, p. 41; The Sporting News Player Contract Cards, ScanID: 1099029803 Carl Hubbell, https://digital.la84.org/digital/collection/p17103coll3/id/30520/rec/6.

14. John Thomas Feeley (1917–1954; 5–11 180), born in New Philadelphia, PA, joined the Easton Browns in August 1937. In 1938, he played for the Fremont Reds (OSL). He served in the U.S. Army

Notes—Chapter Seven

Air Corps from 1941 to 1945. The Sporting News Player Contract Cards, ScanID: 1014002619 John Feeley, https://digital.la84.org/digital/collection/p17103coll3/id/76931/rec/6; World War II Draft Cards.

15. *Salisbury Daily Times*, 7 Sept. 1937, p. 8.

Chapter Seven

1. John G. Rodgers (b. 1912; R/R 5–9 190) of Providence, RI, played three seasons with the Cambridge Cardinals from 1937 to 1939. The Sporting News Player Contract Cards, ScanID: 1038002823 John G. Rogers, https://digital.la84.org/digital/collection/p17103coll3/id/105052/rec/530; https://www.baseball-reference.com/register/player.fcgi?id=rodger001joh.

2. Clyde William Humphrey (1912–1980; R/L 5–10 1/2 166), born in St. Clairsville, Ohio, had an eight-year professional baseball career between 1933 and 1945. He served in the U.S. Army in 1944. The Sporting News Player Contract Cards, ScanID: 1025018949 Clyde Humphrey, https://digital.la84.org/digital/collection/p17103coll3/id/95379/rec/29.

3. New York City native Henry Felix "Dutch" Franz (b. 1917; R/? 5–10 170) from 1937 to 1940 played for three teams (Cambridge Cardinals, Lynchburg Grays [VIRL] and Erwin Mountaineers [APPY]). The Sporting News Player Contract Cards, ScanID: 1015004009 Henry Franz, https://digital.la84.org/digital/collection/p17103coll3/id/75638/rec/2; World War II Draft Cards.

4. William Andrew "Andy" Johnson (1916–2003; L/L 5–11 160), born in Milstead, GA, had a four-year professional career from 1936 to 1939. The Sporting News Player Contract Cards, ScanID: 1023000529 William Andrew Johnson, https://digital.la84.org/digital/collection/p17103coll3/id/127325/rec/75.

5. *Salisbury Daily Times*, 11 Sept. 1937, p. 7.

6. Joseph Leo O'Rourke (1904–1990; L/R 5–7 145), son of Patsy O'Rourke (scout, vice president and director of the Phillies), born in Philadelphia, PA, was involved in professional baseball from 1923 to 1965. He was the manager of the Centreville Colts from 1937 to 1938. *Tampa Bay Times*, 2 July 1990, p. 19; The Sporting News Player Contract Cards, ScanID: 1099105362 Joe O'Rourke Jr., https://digital.la84.org/digital/collection/p17103coll3/id/43560/rec/2.

Douglas Christopher Voth (1915–1970; S/R 6–1 180), of New York, NY, had a four-year minor league career from 1937 to 1940. He served in the U.S. Army during World War II. The Sporting News Player Contract Cards, ScanID: 1046002737 Douglas Voth, https://digital.la84.org/digital/collection/p17103coll3/id/106407/rec/1.

7. *Salisbury Daily Times*, 15 Sept. 1937, p. 1.

8. Edward Olin Willis (1883–1952), born in Dover, DE, was an insurance man for 31 years and a leader in volunteer fire department activities. *Baltimore Sun*, 18 Sept. 1952, p. 6.

9. Known as the Wild Horse of the Osage for his daring, aggressive baserunning abilities, Johnny Leonard Roosevelt "Pepper" Martin (1904–1965) spent his 13-year career with the St. Louis Cardinals between 1928 and 1944. *St. Louis Post-Dispatch*, 5 Mar. 1965, p. 28; The Sporting News Player Contract Cards, ScanID: 1099014458 Pepper Martin, https://digital.la84.org/digital/collection/p17103coll3/id/160903/rec/2.

Chapter Eight

1. Spencer Arthur Abbott (1877–1951), born in Chicago, IL, became manager of the Trenton Senators on June 24, 1937, replacing Bud Shaney. Known as "the dean of minor league managers," he had a 50-plus-year career in professional baseball as a pitcher, manager and scout from 1899 to 1950. *The Evening Sun*, 24 June 1937, p. 32; The Sporting News Player Contract Cards, ScanID: 1025007362 Spencer Abbott, https://digital.la84.org/digital/collection/p17103coll3/id/2353/rec/19.

2. *Salisbury Daily Times*, 2 Sept. 1937, p. 7.

Notes—Chapter Eight

3. Matthew William Holmes (1910–1986; R/R 5–11 1/2 176), born in Syracuse, NY, had a four-year minor league career from 1936 to 1939. The Sporting News Player Contract Cards, ScanID: 1021000580 Matty Holmes, https://digital.la84.org/digital/collection/p17103coll3/id/91872/rec/82.

4. *Salisbury Daily Times*, 8 Sept. 1937, p. 7.

5. Rodger Hamill Pippen (1888–1959), a native of Baltimore, MD, had a 52-year career as a sports editor of the *Baltimore News-Post* and *Sunday American*. *Baltimore Evening Sun*, 8 June 1959, p. 10.

6. Wallace Moses (1910–1990; L/L 5–11 175), born in Uvalda, GA, spent 21 seasons in professional baseball (1931–1951) including 17 years in the major leagues from 1935 to 1951 (Philadelphia Athletics, Chicago White Sox and Boston Red Sox). Later he served as a coach for several teams (Philadelphia Athletics, 1952–1954; Philadelphia Phillies, 1955–1958; Cincinnati Reds, 1959–1960; New York Yankees, 1961–1962, 1966; and Detroit Tigers, 1967–1970). The Sporting News Player Contract Cards, ScanID: 1052009783 Wally Moses, https://digital.la84.org/digital/collection/p17103coll3/id/179570/rec/43.

Robert Lee "Indian Bob" Johnson (1906–1982; R/R 5–11 1/2 185), born in Pryor, OK, had a 22-year career (1929–1949, 1951) including 13 seasons for three major league teams (Philadelphia Athletics, 1933–1942; Washington Senators, 1943; Boston Red Sox, 1944–1945). The Sporting News Player Contract Cards, ScanID: 1025019613 Bob Johnson, https://digital.la84.org/digital/collection/p17103coll3/id/108589/rec/4.

Charles Eugene Hasson (1915–2003; L/L 6–3 207), born in Connellsville, PA, had a 13-year career (1935–1942, 1946–1950) including two seasons with the Philadelphia Athletics (1937–1938). He served in the U.S. Army from 1942 to 1946. The Sporting News Player Contract Cards, ScanID: 1025017589 Gene Hasson, https://digital.la84.org/digital/collection/p17103coll3/id/73594/rec/2.

Russell Dixon Peters (1914–2003; R/R 5–11 170), born in Roanoke, VA, had a 16-year career (1935–1944, 1946–1951) including 10 seasons in the major leagues (Philadelphia Athletics, 1936–1938; Cleveland Indians, 1940–1944, 1946; St. Louis Browns, 1947). The Sporting News Player Contract Cards, ScanID: 1099018465 Rusty Peters, https://digital.la84.org/digital/collection/p17103coll3/id/81112/rec/226.

Lynn Nelson (1907–1955; L/R 5–10½ 175), born in Sheldon, ND, had an 18-year career (1926–1943) including seven seasons in the major leagues (Chicago Cubs, 1930, 1933–34; Philadelphia Athletics, 1937–1939; Detroit Tigers, 1940). *The Kansas City Times*, 16 Feb. 1955, p. 14; Gary Gillette and Peter Palmer, eds., *The ESPN Baseball Encyclopedia* (New York: Sterling, 2007), p. 1283; The Sporting News Player Contract Cards, ScanID: 1099016981, Birchard Lynn P. Nelson, https://digital.la84.org/digital/collection/p17103coll3/id/172177/rec/3.

7. William Frederick Conroy (1899–1970; R/R 5–8 1/2 170), born in Chicago, IL, had a 16-year career from 1935 to 1944 and from 1946 to 1948 including six seasons in the major leagues (Philadelphia Athletics, 1935–1937; Boston Red Sox, 1942–1944). The Sporting News Player Contract Cards, ScanID: 1025011339 Bill Conroy, https://digital.la84.org/digital/collection/p17103coll3/id/46577/rec/40.

Wayne Harper Ambler (1915–1998; R/R 5–8 1/2 165), born in Abington, PA, entered the major leagues after graduating from Duke University. He spent three seasons with the Philadelphia Athletics from 1937 to 1939. After that, he spent two years in the minor leagues from 1940 to 1941. From 1943 to 1946, he served in the U.S. Navy. The Sporting News Player Contract Cards, ScanID: 1025007172 Wayne Ambler, https://digital.la84.org/digital/collection/p17103coll3/id/1273/rec/3.

8. George Anthony "Woody" Woodend (1917–1980; R/R 6–0 203), born in Hartford, CT, had a six-year career (1937–1940, 1944–45) including two seasons in the major leagues (Philadelphia Athletics, 1937; Boston Braves, 1944). The Sporting News Player Contract Cards,

Notes—Chapter Nine

ScanID: 1099028198 George Woodend, https://digital.la84.org/digital/collection/p17103coll3/id/174487/rec/1.

William Philip Kalfass (1916–1968; R/L 6–3 1/2 190), born in New York, NY, had a six-year career (1934, 1937–1940, 1946) including one season with Philadelphia Athletics (1937). The Sporting News Player Contract Cards, ScanID: 1025019966 Bill Kalfass, https://digital.la84.org/digital/collection/p17103coll3/id/110323/rec/2.

9. Warren Llewellyn Huston (1913–1999; R/R 6–0 170), born in Newton, MA, had a six-year career (1937–1938, 1942-1945) including two seasons in the major leagues (Philadelphia Athletics 1937; Boston Braves, 1944). The Sporting News Player Contract Cards, ScanID: 1025019021 Warren Huston, https://digital.la84.org/digital/collection/p17103coll3/id/89033/rec/21.

10. *Salisbury Daily Times*, 22 Sept. 1937, p. 7.

11. See page 193 for Richard Porter's biography.

12. Michael B. Janesko (1900–1978) spent 20 years playing for the House of David touring baseball team from 1928 to 1948. *St. Louis Post-Dispatch*, 3 Mar. 1978, p. 20.

13. *The Daily Mail*, 21 Sept. 1937, p. 4.

Chapter Nine

1. Lloyd Vernon Kennedy (1907–1993; S/R 6–0 175), born in Kansas City, MO, had a 12-year career from 1934 to 1945 with six teams (Chicago White Sox, Cleveland Indians, St. Louis Browns, Philadelphia Phillies, Detroit Tigers, Washington Senators and Cincinnati Reds). The Sporting News Player Contract Cards, ScanID: 1025020264 L. Vernon Kennedy, https://digital.la84.org/digital/collection/p17103coll3/id/126895/rec/110.

2. Arnold Revola "Red" Anderson (1912–1972; R/R 6–3 210), born in Lawton, IA, was playing for the Sioux Falls Canaries (NSL) in 1937 when he was sent to the Washington Senators. He served in the U.S. Navy aboard the USS *Gardner* from 1942 to 1945. The Sporting News Player Contract Cards, ScanID: 1025007226 Arnold Anderson, https://digital.la84.org/digital/collection/p17103coll3/id/1391/rec/56.

Richard Anthony Lanahan (1911–1975; L/L 6–0 186), born in Washington, D.C., had a 10-year career between 1935 and 1946 including four seasons with the Washington Senators and the Pittsburgh Pirates (1935, 1937, 1940–1941). The Sporting News Player Contract Cards, ScanID: 1025021195 Dick Lanahan, https://digital.la84.org/digital/collection/p17103coll3/id/113802/rec/3.

Newton Smith "Bucky" Jacobs (1913–1990; R/R 5–11 155), born in Altavista, VA, had a nine-year career from 1937 to 1945 including three seasons with the Washington Senators (1937, 1939–1940). https://www.baseball-reference.com/players/j/jacobbu01.shtml; *The ESPN Baseball Encyclopedia*, p. 1283.

3. James Charles Wasdell (1914–1983; L/L 5–11 185), born in Cleveland, OH, had an 11-year career from 1937 to 1947. The Sporting News Player Contract Cards, ScanID: 1099026967 James Wasdell, https://digital.la84.org/digital/collection/p17103coll3/id/165249/rec/3.

4. William Murray Werber (1908–2009; R/R 5–11 172), born in Berwyn Heights, MD, had an 11-year major league career between 1930 and 1942 with five teams (Boston Red Sox, Cincinnati Reds, New York Yankees, Philadelphia Athletics and New York Giants). The Sporting News Player Contract Cards, ScanID: 1099027283 Wm. M. Werber, https://digital.la84.org/digital/collection/p17103coll3/id/171806/rec/3.

5. *The Evening Star*, 20 Sept. 1937, p. 15.

6. *Ibid.*

7. *Ibid.*

Player Biographical Sketches

1. *Wilmington Morning News*, 11 Oct. 1975, p. 24; *Evening Journal*, 25 Aug. 1975, p. 33 *Wilmington Morning News*, 9 Sept. 1935, p. 12; *Wilmington Morning News*, 11 July 1936, p. 13; *Wilmington

Notes—Player Biographical Sketches

Morning News, 9 May 1936, p. 13; *Wilmington Morning News*, 8 May 1937, p. 15; *Wilmington Morning News*, 16 July 1936, p. 13; *Wilmington Morning News*, 14 July 1936, p. 16; *Wilmington Morning News*, 23 June 1937, p. 15; *Journal-Every Evening*, 26 Apr. 1938, p. 21; *Wilmington Morning News*, 29 Apr. 1939, p. 26; *Wilmington Morning News*, 13 Sep. 1939, p. 16; *Journal-Every Evening*, 3 May 1940, p. 27; *Journal-Every Evening*, 1 May 1934, p. 24; *Wilmington Morning News*, 24 May 1934, p. 11; *Journal-Every Evening*, 1 May 1935, p. 17; *Wilmington Morning News*, 28 May 1932, p. 12; *Wilmington Morning News*, 12 May 1945, p. 14; World War II Draft Cards; The Sporting News Player Contract Cards, ScanID: 1001003581 Walter Andrews, https://digital.la84.org/digital/collection/p17103coll3/id/1299/rec/102.

2. *Sheboygan Press*, 20 Mar. 1935, p. 12; *Sheboygan Press*, 27 Apr. 1934, p. 15; *Sheboygan Press*, 18 Apr. 1935, p. 22; *Waco News-Tribune*, 24 July 1936, p. 9; *Greenville News*, 28 Aug. 1939, p. 7; *Sheboygan Press*, 19 July 1980, p. 6; *Sheboygan Press*, 15 Apr. 1937, p. 27; baseball-reference.com; World War II Draft Cards; The Sporting News Player Contract Cards, ScanID: 1003002042 J Bassler, https://digital.la84.org/digital/collection/p17103coll3/id/6463/rec/1.

3. *Salisbury Daily Times*, 20 July 1937, p. 7; World War II Draft Cards; The Sporting News Player Contract Cards, ScanID: 1004000574 James Bergen, https://digital.la84.org/digital/collection/p17103coll3/id/4202/rec/6.

4. *Hanover Evening Sun*, 13 Sept. 1978, p. 12; *Hanover Evening Sun*, 19 Aug. 1935, p. 3; *Hanover Evening Sun*, 18 Apr. 1936, p. 8; *Times Recorder*, 7 Aug. 1937, p. 8; *Hanover Evening Sun*, 21 May 1941, p. 8; *Frederick News*, 10 May 1938, p. 7; World War II Draft Cards.

5. *The Plain Speaker*, 13 Nov. 1936, p. 29; *Johnson City Press*, 14 Sept. 1995, p. 2; *Elizabethan Star*, 12 June 1936, p. 5; *Johnson City Chronicle*, 13 Mar. 1940, p. 7; *Greenwood Commonwealth*, 7 May 1940, p. 5; *Spokesman-Review*, 19 Apr. 1939, p. 31; World War II Draft Cards; The Sporting News Player Contract Cards, ScanID: 1025010403 Thaddeus Cash, https://digital.la84.org/digital/collection/p17103coll3/id/7599/rec/1.

6. Barry Sparks, "Comebacks and Fisticuffs: The Many Lives of the Eastern Shore League 1922–1949," *Maryland Historical Magazine* 87, no. 2 1992, 162; *Salisbury Daily Times*, 30 Aug. 1937, p. 6; *Charlotte Observer*, 8 Jan. 1938, p. 11; *Greenville News*, 27 Mar. 1938, p. 15; *Greenville News*, 6 Aug. 1939, p. 15; *Journal-Every Evening*, 27 Jan. 1941, p. 17; *Berkshire Eagle*, 30 Aug. 1941, p. 14; *St. Louis Post-Dispatch*, 7 Sep. 1943, p. 17; *Pittsburgh Sun-Telegraph*, 8 May 1944, p. 15; *Richmond Times-Dispatch*, 24 June 1945, p. 24; *Salt Lake Tribune*, 9 Dec. 1945, p. 25; *Fort Worth Star-Telegram*, 4 July 1946, p. 9; *Richmond Times-Dispatch*, 23 Dec. 1948, p. 21; *Salisbury Daily Times*, 26 Sept. 1962, p. 25; *Milwaukee Journal*, 6 May 1946, p. 5; *Berkshire County Eagle*, 24 Dec. 1947, p. 18; *Berkshire Evening Eagle*, 16 July 1946, p. 12; *Diario Las Americas*, 25 Jan. 1974, p. 15; The Sporting News Player Contract Cards, ScanID: 1025011250 George Comellas, https://digital.la84.org/digital/collection/p17103coll3/id/46446/rec/1.

7. *Danville Bee*, 14 Apr. 1937, p. 2; *Wilkes-Barre Record*, 23 June 1937, p. 18; *Wilkes-Barre Record*, 5 Aug. 1937, p. 18; *Standard-Sentinel*, 23 June 1937, p. 14; *Ottawa Journal*, 26 June 1937, p. 26; *Wilkes-Barre Evening News*, 20 Aug. 1937, p. 15; *Greenville News*, 13 Apr. 1938, p. 8; *Wilkes-Barre Record*, 13 May 1938, p. 26; *The Plain Speaker*, 27 Sept. 1951, p. 5; *Wilkes-Barre Times Leader*, 25 Sept. 1951, p. 8; *Wilkes-Barre Times Leader*, 24 Sept. 1951, p. 22; World War II Draft Cards; The Sporting News Player Contract Cards, ScanID: 1025013180 Michael Depko, https://digital.la84.org/digital/collection/p17103coll3/id/57366/rec/1.

8. *Allentown Morning Call*, 2 June 1938, p. 6; *Salisbury Daily Times*, 4 Mar. 1938, p. 9; *Allentown Morning Call*, 5 July 1938, p. 14; *Allentown Morning Call*, 10 Apr. 1939, p. 16; *Allentown Morning Call*, 12 May 1939, p. 34; *Allentown Morning Call*, 9 Mar. 1940, p. 13; *Allentown Morning Call*, 11 May 1940, p. 7;

Notes—Player Biographical Sketches

Morning News, 22 May 1941, p. 24; *Allentown Morning Call*, 26 May 1942, p. 18; *Allentown Morning Call*, 1 Mar. 1995, p. 18; *Salisbury Daily Times*, 22 July 1938, p. 6; *Allentown Morning Call*, 17 May 1938, p. 7; *Allentown Morning Call*, 25 July 1937, p. 15; *Salisbury Daily Times*, 27 Aug. 1937, p. 7; World War II Draft Cards; The Sporting News Player Contract Cards, ScanID: 1011005875 Frank Deutsch, https://digital.la84.org/digital/collection/p17103coll3/id/56235/rec/3.

9. *Salisbury Daily Times*, 1 July 1937, p. 5; *York Sunday News*, 12 Dec. 1993, p. 21; *York Daily Record*, 2 July 1937, p. 10; *York Gazette and Daily*, 8 July 1937, p. 10; *York Dispatch*, 21 Sept. 1995, p. 16; *Arizona Republic*, 27 Mar. 1947, p. 12; *Arizona Republic*, 3 May 1948, p. 37; *Dayton Journal*, 14 June 1948, p. 17; *Arizona Republic*, 27 May 1949, p. 43; *Arizona Republic*, 21 Feb. 1953, p. 4; World War II Draft Cards; The Sporting News Player Contract Cards, ScanID: 1099104242 Buck Elliott Jr., https://digital.la84.org/digital/collection/p17103coll3/id/43610/rec/1.

10. *Tampa Bay Times*, 28 Dec. 1962, p. 12; *Salisbury Daily Times*, 28 Dec. 1962, p. 8; *Salisbury Daily Times*, 10 Oct. 1953, p. 10; *Journal-Every Evening*, 17 July 1923, p. 16; *Springfield News-Leader*, 28 Mar. 1924, p. 5; *St. Louis Globe-Democrat*, 31 Aug. 1924, p. 10; *Oakland Tribune*, 30 Sept. 1925, p. 17; *Allentown Morning Call*, 16 June 1931, p. 43; *St. Louis Post-Dispatch*, 29 Jan. 1932, p. 31; *Baltimore Sun*, 9 Feb. 1933, p. 12; *Montreal Gazette*, 20 Mar. 1935, p. 16; *St. Louis Star and Times*, 29 Jan. 1935, p. 20; *Tampa Tribune*, 22 Apr. 1956, p. 33; *Salisbury Daily Times*, 7 Aug. 1956, p. 9; *McAllen Monitor*, 16 Feb. 1960, p. 8; The Sporting News Player Contract Cards, ScanID: 1025015035 Jake Flowers, https://digital.la84.org/digital/collection/p17103coll3/id/66939/rec/9.

11. *Baltimore Sun*, 23 May 1989, p. 4; *Montgomery Advertiser*, 23 July 1946, p. 6; *Baltimore Evening Sun*, 7 Feb. 1946, p. 24; *Daily Press*, 13 Mar. 1940, p. 6; *Daily Press*, 20 Apr. 1940, p. 7; *Orlando Sentinel*, 9 July 1940, p. 6; *Daily Press*, 26 May 1940, p. 20; *Minneapolis Star*, 25 June 1940, p. 24; *Orlando Sentinel*, 8 July 1940, p. 6; *Chattanooga Daily Times*, 3 May 1941, p. 9; *Chattanooga Daily Times*, 19 May 1941; *Asheville Citizen-Times*, 28 Apr. 1939, p. 15; "Joe Garliss." Pro Football Archives. https://www.profootballarchives.com/playerg/garl01000.html; World War II Draft Cards; The Sporting News Player Contract Cards, ScanID: 1025015682 Joseph Allen Garliss, https://digital.la84.org/digital/collection/p17103coll3/id/65885/rec/2.

12. Roberto Gonzalez Echavarria, *The Pride of Havana: A History of Cuban Baseball* (Oxford: Oxford University Press, 2001), 76; *Baltimore Evening News*, 16 July 1936, p. 16; *Baltimore Evening Sun*, 25 Mar. 1936, p. 26; *Rutland Daily Herald*, 3 June 1936, p. 13; *The Evening Star*, 20 Sept. 1937, p. 15; *Salisbury Daily Times*, 2 June 1938, p. 1; *Charlotte News*, 12 Apr. 1938, p. 12; *Philadelphia Inquirer*, 20 Sept. 1937, p. 21; *Akron Beacon Journal*, 6 Mar. 1960, p. 45; *Salisbury Daily Times*, 31 Jan. 1958, p. 12; *Salisbury Daily Times*, 7 July 1953; *New York Daily News*, 23 July 1953, p. 21C; *Decatur Daily Review*, 5 June 1956, p. 14; *Salisbury Daily Times*, 26 Sept. 1962, p. 25; *Montgomery Advertiser*, 24 Apr. 1960, p. 21; *San Francisco Examiner*, 27 Dec. 1959, p. 8; The Sporting News Player Contract Cards, ScanID: 1025016842 Mike Guerra Romero, https://digital.la84.org/digital/collection/p17103coll3/id/77977/rec/15.

13. *Camden Courier-Post*, 17 Aug. 1937, p. 15; World War II Draft Cards; The Sporting News Player Contract Cards, ScanID: 1021005855 Edward Hullings, https://digital.la84.org/digital/collection/p17103coll3/id/104121/rec/1.

14. *York Dispatch*, 12 Jan. 1934, p. 14; *Harrisburg Sunday Courier*, 29 Apr. 1934, p. 5; *Philadelphia Inquirer*, 25 June 1934, p. 14; *Indiana Gazette*, 23 Feb. 1935, p. 2; *Pottsville Republican*, 22 Mar. 1935, p. 22; *Reading Times*, 24 May 1935, p. 29; *Scranton Times-Tribune*, 20 Apr. 1936, p. 20; *Wilkes-Barre Record*, 11 Aug. 1936, p. 14; *Wilkes-Barre Record*, 11 May 1936, p. 16; *Wilkes-Barre Record*, 15 Jan. 1937, p. 22; *Vineland Evening Times*, 17 Apr. 1937, p. 8; *Denton Journal*, 4 June 1938,

Notes—Player Biographical Sketches

p. 8; *The Plain Speaker*, 2 Sept. 1938, p. 21; *Wilmington Morning News*, 11 Oct. 1938, p. 15; *New York Daily News*, 15 July 1939, p. 55; *Knoxville Journal*, 2 Dec. 1939, p. 5; *Vineland Evening Times*, 18 Sept. 1940, p. 8; *Elmira Star-Gazette*, 18 Mar. 1941, p. 12; *Vineland Evening Times*, 19 Apr. 1941, p. 8; *The Daily Advertiser*, 15 Aug. 1933, p. 8; *The Daily Advertiser*, 4 Apr. 1941, p. 3; *Anniston Rams*, 6 June 1941, p. 10; *Anniston Star*, 5 May 1942, p. 6; *Birmingham News*, 20 May 1942, p. 18; *Anniston Star*, 1 Mar. 1943, p. 8; *Salisbury Daily Times*, 2 June 1938, p. 1; *Salisbury Daily Times*, 29 Dec. 1937, p. 1; *Camden Courier-Post*, 21 Apr. 1937, p. 18; *Salisbury Daily Times*, 30 Aug. 1937, p. 6; *Salisbury Daily Times*, 9 Sep. 1957, p. 8; World War II Draft Cards; The Sporting News Player Contract Cards, ScanID: 1025020728 Joe Kohlman, https://digital.la84.org/digital/collection/p17103coll3/id/129231/rec/1.

15. *Baltimore Sun*, 15 June 1937, p. 16; *Baltimore Sun*, 30 May 1938, p. 9; World War II Draft Cards; The Sporting News Player Contract Cards, ScanID: 1025000321 Frank Kowal, https://digital.la84.org/digital/collection/p17103coll3/id/130244/rec/1.

16. *Salisbury Daily Times*, 1 Sep. 1937, p. 8; *Greenville News*, 8 Apr. 1938, p. 18; John Kruk. Interview with Buddy Kruk. Personal interview. Kearny, NJ, 1990); World War II Draft Cards; The Sporting News Player Contract Cards, ScanID: 1025001467 John Krook, https://digital.la84.org/digital/collection/p17103coll3/id/114776/rec/865.

17. *Scranton Tribune*, 31 Aug. 1936, p. 14; *Greenville News*, 28 Aug. 1939, p. 7; *Greenville News*, 30 Apr. 1940, p. 7, *San Bernardino County Sun*, 24 July 1941, p. 18; *Pittsburgh Press*, 5 Sep. 1941, p. 40; *Wilkes-Barre Record*, 4 May 1942, p. 12; *Cincinnati Enquirer*, 27 Sept. 1942, p. 26; *The Daily Republican*, 17 Jan. 1946, p. 2; *Elmira Star-Gazette*, 11 Apr. 1946, p. 37; *Charlotte News*, 1 Feb. 1947, p. 24; *Charlotte News*, 5 Mar. 1948, p. 21; World War II Draft Cards; https://www.baseball-reference.com.

18. *Charlotte Observer*, 3 Sept. 1933, p. 23; *Hackensack Record*, 6 Aug. 1932, p. 12; *Greenville News*, 17 Aug. 1939, p. 8; *Greenville News*, 3 June 1940, p. 7; *Greenville News*, 21 June 1940, p. 21; *Chicago Tribune*, 3 Sept. 1933, p. 15; *Burlington Daily News*, 8 Sept. 1936, p. 8; *Troy Record*, 25 Feb. 1947, p. 15; World War II Draft Cards; The Sporting News Player Contract Cards, ScanID: 1027003505 William Michael Luzansky, https://digital.la84.org/digital/collection/p17103coll3/id/158509/rec/1.

19. *Scranton Tribune*, 16 June 1934, p. 15; *Scranton Tribune*, 23 Apr. 1935, p. 14; *Scranton Tribune*, 8 May 1935, p. 14; *Scranton Tribune*, 23 May 1935, p. 16; *Scranton Times-Tribune*, 1 May 1935, p. 24; *Scranton Republican*, 28 Mar. 1936, p. 14; *Scranton Tribune*, 14 May 1936, p. 15; *Scranton Tribune*, 9 June 1936, p. 14; *Scrantonian*, 21 Feb. 1937, p. 23; *Salisbury Daily Times*, 9 Aug. 1937, p. 6; *Salisbury Daily Times*, 30 Aug. 1937, p. 6; *Philadelphia Inquirer*, 20 Sep. 1937, p. 21; *Scranton Times-Tribune*, 28 Oct. 1937, p. 36; *Scranton Times-Tribune*, 14 Aug. 1937, p. 13; *Charlotte Observer*, 10 Apr. 1938, p. 33; *Charlotte Observer*, 4 Jan. 1939, p. 14; *Scrantonian*, 28 Jan. 1940, p. 25; *Elmira Star-Gazette*, 16 Aug. 1945, p. 24; *Charlotte News*, 15 May 1946, p. 17; *The Index-Journal*, 17 Apr. 1947, p. 3; *Charlotte Observer*, 5 July 1947, p. 7; "Archibald 'Moonlight' Graham, Jerry Lynn and Scranton Baseball," January 15, 2007, https://finner68.wordpress.com/2007/01/15/archibald-%e2%80%9cmoonlight%e2%80%9d-graham-and-scranton-baseball/; World War II Draft Cards; The Sporting News Player Contract Cards, ScanID: 1027003925 Jerry Lynn, https://digital.la84.org/digital/collection/p17103coll3/id/167277/rec/2.

20. *Salisbury Daily Times*, 17 Sept. 1938, p. 4; *Baltimore Evening Sun*, 10 May 1938, p. 23; *Ottawa Journal*, 26 June 1937, p. 26; *Find a Grave*; World War II Draft Cards; The Sporting News Player Contract Cards, ScanID: 1030005235 Tony Miller, https://digital.la84.org/digital/collection/p17103coll3/id/147004/rec/4.

21. Dr. Layton Revel and Luis Munoz, "Forgotten Heroes: Manuel 'Cocaina' Garcia," *Center for Negro*

Notes—Player Biographical Sketches

League Baseball Research, http://www.cnlbr.org/Portals/0/Hero/Manuel-Cocaina-Garcia.pdf.; https://www.baseball-reference.com/bullpen/Juan_Montero_(minors01); *The Plain Speaker*, 15 July 1937, p. 4; *Salisbury Daily Times*, 15 July 1937, p. 8; *Shamokin News-Dispatch*, 8 July 1937, p. 6; *Pampa Daily News*, 5 May 1952, p. 4; The Sporting News Player Contract Cards, ScanID: 1099016143 Juan Montero, https://digital.la84.org/digital/collection/p17103coll3/id/131074/rec/12.

22. Allen Historical Society, Dick Porter collection 2019.110, Edward H. Nabb Research Center for Delmarva History and Culture, Salisbury University, Salisbury, MD; James R. Trader papers 2012.292, Edward H. Nabb Research Center for Delmarva History and Culture, Salisbury University, Salisbury, MD; The Sporting News Player Contract Cards, ScanID: 1099019212 Dick Porter, https://digital.la84.org/digital/collection/p17103coll3/id/92197/rec/115.

23. *The Home News*, 31 Aug. 1980, p. 74; *Reading Times*, 7 Sept. 1937, p. 13; *Salisbury Daily Record*, 5 Aug. 1939, p. 7; *The Central New Jersey Home News*, 21 Aug. 1949, p. 19; World War II Draft Cards.

24. *Salisbury Daily Times*, 13 Sep. 1938, p. 6; *Charlotte Observer*, 7 Feb. 1939, p. 15; *Orlando Sentinel*, 3 Jan. 1940, p. 6; *Orlando Evening Star*, 22 May 1939, p. 6; *Charlotte Observer*, 1 June 1939, p. 23; *Charlotte Observer*, 31 Dec. 1939, pp. 33–34; *Charlotte News*, 6 May 1940, p. 12; *Greenville News*, 16 June 1940, p. 17; *Greenville News*, 23 Mar. 1941, p. 11; *Anniston Star*, 30 Mar. 1941, p. 16; *Clarion-Ledger*, 25 May 1941, p. 16; *Chattanooga Daily Times*, 6 Aug. 1940, p. 11; *Allentown Morning Call*, 12 Apr. 1943, p. 16; *Lancaster New Era*, 10 Apr. 1943, p. 3; *Montgomery Advertiser*, 9 June 1946, p. 10; *Lancaster Intelligencer Journal*, 19 Apr. 1947, p. 10; *Miami News*, 18 Mar. 1949, p. 6; *Miami Herald*, 27 Apr. 1949, p. 46; *Pocono Record*, 29 May 1950, p. 9; *Pocono Record*, 19 June 1950, p. 8; *Tallahassee Democrat*, 18 Mar. 1951, p. 10; *Tallahassee Democrat*, 14 Feb. 1952, p. 9; *Nashville Banner*, 2 Apr. 1953, p. 38; *Pensacola News Journal*, 9 May 1953, p. 2; *Dothan Eagle*, 10 May 1953, p. 23; World War II Draft Cards; The Sporting News Player Contract Cards, ScanID: 1099019544 Charles Marion Quimby, https://digital.la84.org/digital/collection/p17103coll3/id/100928/rec/6.

25. *Salisbury Daily Times*, 2 Aug. 1938, p. 9; *Daily Record*, 5 Aug. 1939, p. 7; *The Daily Home News*, 1 Sept. 1942, p. 8; *The Daily Home News*, 5 June 1943, p. 12; *The Daily Home News*, 17 July 1945, p. 8; *Plainfield Courier-News*, 10 Oct. 1947, p. 23; *Home News Tribune*, 16 Mar. 2008, p. 25; *The Daily Home News*, 22 May 1936, p. 39; *The Daily Home News*, 14 June 1936, p. 16; *The Daily Home News*, 2 June 1957, p. 31; World War II Draft Cards; The Sporting News Player Contract Cards, ScanID: 1037002931 Leon Revolinsky, https://digital.la84.org/digital/collection/p17103coll3/id/97176/rec/1.

26. *Reading Times*, 5 May 1937, p. 17; *Sunbury Daily*, 12 Apr. 1937, p. 8; *Wilkes-Barre Times Leader*, 4 May 1937, p. 1; *Harrisburg Evening News*, 20 May 1937, p. 22; *South Amboy Citizen*, 4 June 1937, p. 6; *Salisbury Daily Times*, 21 July 1937, p. 1; *Salisbury Daily Times*, 9 Aug. 1937, p. 8; *The Daily Home News*, 19 Aug. 1937, p. 1; *Asbury Park Press*, 7 Apr. 1991, p. 15; *Salisbury Daily Times*, 2 June 1938, p. 1; World War II Draft Cards; The Sporting News Player Contract Cards, ScanID: 1037003457 Joe Reznichak, https://digital.la84.org/digital/collection/p17103coll3/id/84787/rec/1.

27. *Salisbury Daily Times*, 21 May 1938, p. 7; *Salisbury Daily Times*, 1 Sept. 1937, p. 8; *Salisbury Daily Times*, 9 Aug. 1837, p. 8; *Hartford Courant*, 12 Apr. 1938, p. 13; *Salisbury Daily Times*, 17 May 1938, p. 1; *Salisbury Daily Times*, 14 June 1938, p. 8; The Sporting News Player Contract Cards, ScanID: 1039002153 Joe Salazar, https://digital.la84.org/digital/collection/p17103coll3/id/126827/rec/51.

28. *The Daily Home News*, 10 June 1935, p. 8; *The Daily Home News*, 4 May 1936, p. 12; *The Daily Home News*, 3 July 1937, p. 8; *The Daily Home News*, 24 May 1937, p. 14; *The Daily Home News*, 5 May 1938, p. 25; *The Daily Home News*, 14

Notes—Player Biographical Sketches

May 1938, p. 12; *The Home News*, 7 July 1977, p. 22; World War II Draft Cards; *Find a Grave*.

29. The Sporting News Player Contract Cards, ScanID: 1040006759 Vernon Shelton, https://digital.la84.org/digital/collection/p17103coll3/id/153978/rec/86; *Richmond News Leader*, 2 Aug. 1936, p. 19; *Richmond News Leader*, 9 Aug 1937, p. 14; *Richmond News Leader*, 12 Aug. 1938, p. 29; *Find a Grave*.

30. *Ottawa Journal*, 25 May 1938, p. 18; *Ottawa Citizen*, 30 June 1938, p. 11; *Lancaster Eagle-Gazette*, 5 May 1936, p. 9; World War II Draft Cards; The Sporting News Player Contract Cards, ScanID: 1043000205 Art Steinfadt, https://digital.la84.org/digital/collection/p17103coll3/id/144853/rec/1.

31. *Reading Times*, 28 May 1937, p. 32; *Reading Times*, 29 May 1937; *Salisbury Daily Times*, 21 May 1938, p. 7; *Staunton News-Leader*, 10 Jan. 1937, p. 6; *The Daily Mail*, 27 May 1937, p. 13; *Greenbelt Cooperator*, 25 Sept. 1942, p. 3; *Frederick News*, 13 May 1947, p. 8; *Washington Post*, 18 Mar. 2007, p. C7; World War II Draft Cards; The Sporting News Player Contract Cards, ScanID: 1044004107 Fred Thomas, https://digital.la84.org/digital/collection/p17103coll3/id/129088/rec/33.

32. *The Daily Home News*, 7 Mar. 1946, p. 14; *Minneapolis Star*, 5 May 1948, p. 37; *Charlotte Observer*, 25 May 1948, p. 26; *The Courier-Journal*, 14 July 1948, p. 19; *Minneapolis Star*, 24 Feb. 1949, p. 48; *Charlotte Observer*, 19 June 1951, p. 14; *Star Tribune*, 19 Jan. 1989, p. 32; *Scranton Times-Tribune*, 28 Oct. 1937, p. 36; *Philadelphia Inquirer*, 20 Sep. 1937, p. 21; *Plainfield Courier-News*, 3 Nov. 1937, p. 15; *Plainfield Courier-News* 2 Sept. 1937, p. 20; World War II Draft Cards; The Sporting News Player Contract Cards, ScanID: 1099030100 Frank Trechock, https://digital.la84.org/digital/collection/p17103coll3/id/26784/rec/1.

Bibliography

Newspapers

Akron Beacon Journal
Allentown Morning Call
Anniston Rams
Anniston Star
Arizona Republic
Asbury Park Press
Asheville Citizen-Times
Atlanta Constitution
Baltimore Evening Sun
Baltimore Sun
Barre Daily Times
Berkshire County Eagle
Berkshire Eagle
Berkshire Evening Eagle
Birmingham News
Boston Globe
Burlington Daily News
Camden Courier-Post
Charlotte News
Charlotte Observer
Chattanooga Daily Times
Chicago Tribune
Cincinnati Enquirer
Clarion-Ledger
Courier-Journal (Louisville, KY)
Crisfield Times
Cumberland Evening Times
Cumberland Morning Times
Daily Advertiser (Lafayette, LA)
Daily Home News (New Brunswick, NJ)
Daily Mail (Hagerstown, MD)
Daily Press (Newport News, VA)
Daily Republican (Monongahela, PA)
Danville Bee
Dayton Journal
Decatur Daily Review
Delaware County Daily Times
Denton Journal
Diario Las Americas
Dothan Eagle
Easton Star-Democrat
Eau Claire Leader
Elizabethan Star
Elmira Star-Gazette
Evening Journal (Wilmington, DE)
Evening News (Wilkes-Barre, PA)
Evening Star (Washington, D.C.)
Fort Collins Coloradoan
Fort Worth Star-Telegram
Frederick News
Greenbelt Cooperator
Greenville News
Greenwood Commonwealth
Hackensack Record
Hagerstown Morning Herald
Hanover Evening Sun
Harrisburg Evening News
Harrisburg Sunday Courier
Harrisburg Telegraph
Hartford Courant
Home News (New Brunswick, NJ)
Home News Tribune (New Brunswick, NJ)
Index-Journal (Greenwood, SC)
Indiana Gazette
Johnson City Chronicle
Johnson City Press
Journal–Every Evening (Wilmington, DE)
Kansas City Times
Knoxville Journal
Lancaster Eagle-Gazette
Lancaster Intelligencer Journal
Lancaster New Era
Lebanon Daily News
Maryland Historical Magazine
Mattoon Journal Gazette
McAllen Monitor
Miami Herald
Miami News

Bibliography

Milwaukee Journal
Minneapolis Star
Montgomery Advertiser
Montreal Gazette
Morning Times (Scranton, PA)
Nashville Banner
New York Daily News
New York Times
News and Observer (Raleigh, NC)
Oakland Tribune
Orlando Sentinel
Ottawa Citizen
Ottawa Journal
Pampa Daily News
Pensacola News Journal
Philadelphia Daily News
Philadelphia Inquirer
Pittsburgh Press
Pittsburgh Sun-Telegraph
Plain Speaker (Hazleton, PA)
Plainfield Courier-News
Pocono Record
Pottsville Republican
Poughkeepsie Journal
Reading Times
Richmond News Leader
Richmond Times-Dispatch
Rutland Daily Herald
St. Louis Globe-Democrat
St. Louis Post-Dispatch
St. Louis Star and Times
Salisbury Daily Times
Salt Lake Tribune
San Bernardino County
San Francisco Examiner
Scranton Republican
Scranton Times
Scranton Times-Tribune
Scrantonian (Scranton, PA)
Shamokin News-Dispatch
Sheboygan Press
South Amboy Citizen
Spokesman-Review (Spokane, WA)
Springfield Leader and Press
Springfield News-Leader
Standard-Sentinel (Hazleton, PA)
Standard-Speaker (Hazleton, PA)
Star Tribune (Minneapolis, MN)
Staunton News-Leader
Sunbury Daily
Tallahassee Democrat
Tampa Bay Times
Tampa Tribune
Times Recorder
Troy Record
Vineland Evening Times
Waco News-Tribune
Washington Post
Wicomico News
Wilkes-Barre Evening News
Wilkes-Barre Record
Wilkes-Barre Times Leader
Wilmington Morning News
Worcester Democrat and the Ledger-Enterprise
York Daily Record
York Dispatch
York Gazette and Daily
York Sunday News

Books

Aaron, Mark Z., ed. *Who's on First: Replacement Players in World War II.* Phoenix: Society for American Baseball Research, 2015.

Dickson, Paul. *The Dickson Baseball Dictionary.* Third Edition. New York: W.W. Norton, 2009.

Echevarria, Roberto Gonzalez. *The Pride of Havana: A History of Cuban Baseball.* New York: Oxford University Press, 2001.

Gillette, Gary, and Pete Palmer, eds. *The ESPN Baseball Encyclopedia.* New York: Sterling, 2007.

Kraus, Rebecca S. *Minor League Baseball: Community Building Through Hometown Sports.* New York: Haworth, 2003.

Lambert, Mike. *Eastern Shore League.* Charleston, SC: Arcadia, 2010.

Mowbray, Bill. *The Eastern Shore Baseball League.* Centreville, MD: Tidewater, 1989.

Mowbray, Bill. *The ESL Encyclopedia: Eastern Shore League of Professional Baseball Clubs and Other Delmarva Baseball Testimonials.* Cambridge, MD: B. Mowbray, 1984.

Bibliography

Periodicals

National Association of National Baseball Leagues. *Official Bulletin. No. 4.* Durham: National Association of National Baseball Leagues, 1937.

Websites

Ancestry.com. *U.S., World War I Draft Registration Cards, 1917–1918* [database online]. Provo, UT, USA: Ancestry.com Operations, Inc., 2005.
Ancestry.com. *U.S., World War II Draft Cards Young Men, 1940–1947* [database online]. Lehi, UT, USA: Ancestry.com Operations, Inc., 2011.
"Archibald 'Moonlight' Graham, Jerry Lynn and Scranton Baseball." January 15, 2007. https://finner68.wordpress.com/2007/01/15/archibald-%e2%80%9cmoonlight%e2%80%9d-graham-and-scranton-baseball/.
Baseball-Reference.com.
Canadian Attic. http://canadianattic.blogspot.com/2019/08/august-28-2019.html.
Find a Grave. http://www.findagrave.com.
"Frank James, Jr." *YMCA of Frederick County's Alvin G. Quinn Sports Hall of Fame.* https://frederick-hof.org/inductee/lewis-frank-james-jr/.
"Joe Garliss." *Pro Football Archives.* https://www.profootballarchives.com/playerg/garl01000.html.
Kestenbaum, Lawrence. *PoliticalGraveyard.com: The Internet's Most Comprehensive Source of U.S. Political Biography.* https://politicalgraveyard.com.
Revel, Dr. Layton, and Luis Munoz. "Forgotten Heroes: Manuel "Cocaina" Garcia. *Center for Negro League Baseball Research.* http://www.cnlbr.org/Portals/0/Hero/Manuel-Cocaina-Garcia.pdf.
Simons, William. "Hammerin' Hank." *Journal of Sport History* 27, no. 3 (2000): 533–536. https://digital.la84.org/digital/collection/p17103coll10/id/1495/rec/1.
The Sporting News Baseball Player Contract Cards Collection. The LA84 Foundation. https://digital.la84.org/digital/collection/p17103coll3.

Archival Resources

Allen Historical Society, Dick Porter collection 2019.110, Edward H. Nabb Research Center for Delmarva History and Culture, Salisbury University, Salisbury, Maryland.
James R. Trader papers 2012.292, Edward H. Nabb Research Center for Delmarva History and Culture, Salisbury University, Salisbury, Maryland.

Interviews

Kruk, John. Interview with Buddy Kruk. Personal interview. Kearny, NJ, 1990.

Index

Numbers in ***bold italics*** indicate pages with illustrations

Abbott, Spencer A. 150, 237*n*1
Albany Senators 13–14, 162, 176, 185, 187, 215*n*18, 228*n*11
Ambler, Wayne H. 151, 238*n*7
Anderson (Crisfield Crabbers) 23
Anderson, Alfred W. 107, 235*n*28
Anderson, Arnold R. "Red" 154, 239*n*2
Andrews, Walter *see* Andrzejewski, Wladylaw A.
Andrzejewski, Wladylaw A. 16, 20, 68, 157–*158*
Archer, Joseph 28, 69–70, 94, 96, 107, 120, 221*n*27

Baker, John F. "Home Run" 7- 8, 214*n*8
Baltimore Orioles 7, 12, 8, 66, 82, 91
Barnes, Stephen S. 48, 77–78, 109–110, 123, 129, 227*n*79
Baroni, Frank 229*n*15
Bassler, John 15, 19, 21, 23, 28–30, 37–39, 41–42, 46, 58, 60–64, 67, 69–71, ***73***, 78–79, 84, 88–89, 93, 98, ***101***, 108, 111–112, 116–***117***, 120–124, 129, 132, ***134***, 136, 145–146, 148, 151–152, 158–***159***, 160
Bates, John W. 15–16, 217*n*23, 229*n*15
Baumann, Albert 96–97, 233*n*4
Beidleman, Edgar M. ***32***, 38, 40, 61–62, 71, 74–75, 82, 104, 106, 225*n*57
Beihl, Philip 229*n*15
Bergen, James 69–78, 81, 109, 160–161
Bloodsworth, Olen H. 7, 214*n*8
Boston Braves 54, 122
Boston Red Sox 12, 152, 156
Boyce, Arthur W. ***135***
Boyce, Harry J. 25, 62–63, 85, 117, 221*n*24
Boyce, William J. 130–131, 236*n*11
Boyer, James M. 12, 58, 114, 137, 215*n*16

Boylan, John J. 36, 46, 224*n*50
Brady, Robert S. 16, 20, 30–41, 43, 47, 51–58, 63, 85, ***161***–162, ***206***–207
Bramham, William G. 5–***6***, 52, 54–55, 57, 186, 213*n*2
Brittingham, Hezekiah 24, 220*n*15
Britton, Samuel G. 16, 218*n*28
Brooklyn Dodgers 12, 14
Brown, Larry A. 20–21, 219*n*2
Burdsall, Lawrence W. 108, 111, 235*n*31
Butcher, Leslie W. 15, 217*n*25
Butcher, Nicholas 29, 31, 223*n*39
Butler, Harry C. 7, 214*n*8

Cahall, Joseph G. 49, 228*n*81
Cambria, Joseph C. 8, 12–***13***, 14–***15***, 16, ***18***, 20, 23, 38, 52–55, 74., 85, 99–100, 105, 120, 126, 128, 135–136, 150, 157, 164–***165***, 176, 183, 191, 202, 215*n*18, 216*n*20
Cambridge Canners 14, 171, 216*n*21
Cambridge Cardinals 12, 16, 19–23, 34, 40–42, 54, 58–61, 64–68, 72, 85, 89–92, 99–100, 105, 109, 114, 118, 121, 136–141, 153, 156, 169, 219*n*30, 219*n*2–3, 219*n*6–7, 220*n*8–10, 224*n*54, 225*n*63, 226*n*64–67, 228*n*82, 230*n*17, 230*n*26, 233*n*51, 233*n*53, 234*n*10, 237*n*1, 237*n* 3
Cantwell, Walter H. 103–104, 234*n*18
Carr, Joseph F. 6–8, 213*n*7
Carrington, Henry W. 12, 20, 85, 137, 215*n*16
Carroll, Walter D., Jr. 37–38, 46, 80, 86, 114, 142–146, 224*n*53
Cash, Thaddeus G. 16, ***18***, 20–23, 25, 27, 29, 68, 84, 162–***163***
Centreville Colts 2, 12, 21, 34–***35***,

249

Index

36–38, 40, 43, 45–46, 60, 65–66, 68, 79–81, 85–89, 92, 107, 109, 112–115, 121–123, 132, 135–137, 141–148, 222n31, 224n47, 224n52, 224n54, 227n73, 227n75–76, 228n81, 229n12–14, 233n2, 236n43, 237n6
Christopher, James L. 30, 222n33
Clark, Albert 12, 34, 43, 137, 215n16
Clarke, Robert M. 11, 24, 75, 136
Clas, Ralph E. 7, 213n8
Clough, Casper D. 97, 233n6
Coleman, Charles A. 42, 226n68
Comellas, Jorge 2, 19–21, 23–25, 27–28, 31–32, 34, 37–38, 40, 44–45, 48, 51, 60–61, 63–66, 68, 72–73, 76–77, 81, 85–86, 89–90, 92, 94, 96–97, 100–*101*, 102–103, 105–106, 110, 113–115, 120–123, 125, 130–132, *134*, 136, 138–143, 145, 148–149, 151–153, 155, 163–*165*, 176
Conlan, James *135*
Conroy, William F. 151, 238n7
Crane, Thomas 12, 20, 215n16
Crawford (Crisfield Crabber) 49
Crisfield Crabbers 11–12, 16, 21, 23–24, 31, 34, 48–49, 52, 60, 75, 77–79, 81, 92–93, 96, 100, 102–103, 109–110, 123, 125, 129–131, 136, 149, 153, 190, 205, 213n6, 220n11–12, 220n15, 227n78–79, 228n81–84, 230n36, 230n38–39, 234n16
Cullen, Harold S. 24, 220n15

Daddino, Thomas J. 46, 75, 107, 124, 132, 231n31
Davis, John H. 38, 224n54
Decker, Ralph 102–103, 110, 234n16
Denenberg, David 44, 46–47, 122, 227n73
Depko, Michael F. 62, 97, 149, 166–167
Desrosier, Norbert A. 72, 230n26
Deutsch, Frank A. 82–*83*, 84, 87, 89–91, 94–*95*, 96–100, 103–109, 111–114, 116, 118, 120–124, 126, 129–132, *134*, 139–141, 144–145, 147–148, 151–152, 167–*168*, 169
Diehl, George *32*
DiMaggio, Joseph P. 101, 188, 234n12
Disharoon, Elijah C. 14, 128, 216n20
Dize, Wallace E. 24, 220n17
Donahue, Edward A. "Jiggs" 91, 119, 233n54
Dousha, Thomas J. 76–77, 81, 97–98, 121–122, 124, 132, 231n34

Dover Orioles 12, 21, 23, 27–29, 34, 42–43, 53–54, 58, 60, 63–64, 68–70, 72–74, 89, 91, 94–96, 102, 107–108, 115–116, 118–120, 135–136, 160, 191, 199, 219n6, 220–221n21, 221n26–27, 222–28–31, 223n41, 226n68–69, 229n1, 229n12, 230n24, 230n28, 233n2–3, 234n27, 235n30–31, 236n41–43
Dugan, Maurice J. 44, 46–47, 76–77, 97–98, 122, 227n73

Easton Browns 12, 21, 31–*32*, *33*–34, 38–40, 53–54, 60–62, 65, 68, 70–71, 74–75, 82–83, 92, 103–106, 111, 119, 125, 129–130, 132–134, 136–137, 141–142, 153, 156, 207, 223n41, 224n54, 224n57, 224n59, 230n37, 233n2, 234n18, 236n14
Eck, Kenneth W. *32*, 40, 61, 71, 83, 104, 130, 133, 225n60,
Ecker, Sterling M. "Tucker" 63, 229n10
Ekaitis, George L. 12, 29, 215n16
Elliott, Albert W., Jr. 66–67, 80–81, 169–*170*, 171
Elliott, Albert W., Sr. 66, 169
Elliott, Lyle 28, 222n31
Ettner, James M. 41, 226n64
Etts, Robert W. 33, 223n42
Evers, John J. 54, 228n11

Farrell, Pierre B. 54, 229n13
Federalsburg Athletics 12, 16, 21, 25–*26*, 29–31, 24, 53, 60–63, 68, 84–86, 92, 102, 105, 108, 111–112, 116–*117*, 121, 136–137, 153, 218n30, 220n21–24, 222n33, 222n35, 226n69, 228n84, 229n8, 229n10, 232n46, 232n49, 235n32, 235n35–36
Feeley, John T. 133, 236n14
Feinberg, Edward I. 35, 37–38, 46, 79–80, 86, 88, 114, 121, 142–143, 145–146, 224n51
Fields, Maurice L. 14, 43, 124–125, 128, *134*, 216n21
Finta, Stephen J., Jr. 27, 42–43, 96, 119, 221n26
Flowers, D'Arby R. 14, 16–22, 28–29, *39*, 51–54, 59–61, 64, 78, 82, 85, 91, 94, 98, 100–*101*, 103–104, 109–110, 117–118, 121–122, 124, 126–128, 133–*134*, *135*–136, 138, 140, 145–146, 150–151, 171–*172*, 173, 191, 201
Foskey, Ernest T. 14, 128, 131, 216n20

250

Index

Franz, Henry F. 139, 237*n*3,
Fuchs, Robert S. 52, 228*n*1

Gagain, William F. 41, 59–60, 64, 226*n*65
Garliss, Joseph A. *101*, 112–114, 116–120, 123–124, 126, 130, 132–*134*, 138–139, 141–143, 145–146, 148, 151–152, 174–*175*, 176
Gatier, Stephen J. 31, 222*n*37
Gehringer, Charles L. 94, 101, 188, 233*n*1
Gilbert, James R. 12, 215*n*16
Gilmartin, John J. F. 48, 77–78, 93, 227*n*78
Giovanelli, Silvio M. 41–42, 59, 64, 67, 226*n*65
Glen Burnie ball club 153
Gordy, Samuel E. 14
Gordy, William S. 127
Gray, Herman B. 77, 97–98, 121–122, 132, 234*n*7
Greenberg, Henry 126, 236*n*2
Grier, Garrett L. 108, 117, 235*n*32
Griffith, Clark C. 13, 31, 55–*56*, 57, 126–127, 129, 135, 154
Gross, Lloyd E. 35–38, 80, 142–144, 147, 224*n*49
Guerra, Fermin R. 2, 15, 20–25, 27–31, 33, 35–*39*, 40–43, 47–49, 51–52, 58, 60–62, 64–67, 69, 71–76, 78–84, 87, 89–93, 95–96, 98–*101*, 102–105, 107–113, 116, 118–122, 124–126, 128–131, *134*, 138–141, 143–144, 148–149, 154–155, 176–*177*, 178
Gunby, Lewis W. 20
Gunkel, Frank J. 90, 100, 139, 233*n*52
Gurth, Russell W. 15, 217*n*25

Hagerstown Old Export ball club 153
Hall, Irvin G. 44, 46–47, 122, 124, 132, 226*n*71
Halychik, John J. 75, 77, 81, 231*n*32
Haneles, Lewis *135*
Harris, Bucky 155, 178
Harris, Charles H. 46, 75, 98, 123–124, 227*n*77
Harrisburg Senators 51–53, 55
Hasson, Charles E. 151, 238*n*6
Hayden, Edward J. 21, 219*n*6
Healy, Bernard F. 42, 64, 67, 100, 139, 141, 226*n*67
Heim, William 107, 120, 234*n*27
Hoffner, William T. 67–68, 105, 139–140, 230*n*19
Holmes, Matthew W. 150, 238*n*3
Horsey, Hanson 7, 214*n*7

House of David 144, 152–153, 193, 203, 239n12
Hubbell, Carl O. 1, 133, *180*, 236*n*13
Hudson, Howard D. 30, 62, 92, 223*n*35
Hudson, Joseph V. 77–79, 93, 231*n*36
Hullings, Edwin J. 106–109, 111, 178–*179*
Humphrey, Clyde W. 139, 237*n*2
Humphreys, Hanna R. 76, 231*n*34
Huston, Warren L. 151, 239*n*9
Hutchison, Richard J. 73, 230*n*28

Insley, Philip A. 110, 131, 235*n*34
Iwanicki, Robert J. 22, 41, 67–68, 90–91, 121, 138–141, 220*n*10

Jackson, Frank E. 20–22, 41–42, 59, 68, 90–91, 138–140, 219*n*4
Jackson, Howard W. 118, 236*n*40
Jacobs, George W. *32*, 34, 104, 223*n*45
Jacobs, Newton S. 154, 239*n*2
James, Lewis F. 16, 218*n*28
Janesko, Michael B. 153, 239*n*12
Jarrett, Paul B. 16, 218*n*27
Jester, Nelson D. 46–47, 75–77, 97–98, 122, 124, 227*n*72
Johnson, Robert L. 151, 155, 238*n*6
Johnson, William A. 90–91, 100, 140, 237*n*4
Johnson, Wilmer 116
Jones, Emlyn E. 75–77, 97, 121–122, 124, 231*n*29
Jones, Ernest S. 20, 219*n*1
Jutkiewicz, Charles *135*

Kalfass, William P. 151, 239*n*8
Keen, Howard V. 16, 40, *44*, 121, 126, 129, 219*n*30
Kennedy, Lloyd V. 154, 239*n*1, 229*n*15
Keyser, Clifton B. 15, 68, 217*n*24
Kibler, John T. 2, 8–*9*, 10–12, 51–57, 66, 96, 144–145, 147, 214*n*13
Killen, Howard H. 43, 69–70, 94, 107, 115, 226*n*69
Klepper, Allen D. 99, 234*n*10
Knapp, Charles O. 80, 86, 88, 115, 142, 144, 146–147, 232*n*41
Knotts, William K. 7, 214*n*8
Kohlman, Joseph J. 2, 21–22, 24, 27, 31, 35–38, 40–42, 45–46, 49, 51, 60–62, 64, 66–67, 69, *73*, 75–76, 79–80, 82–83, 86–87, 91–92, 95–96, 98, 100–*101*, 103–106, 110, 112, 115, 118–123, 125, 129–*134*, 136, 140–141, 143–144, 147–148, 150, 155, 179–*180*, 181–182

251

Miracle on the Eastern Shore

Koons, Michael J. 40–41, 72, 89–90, 99, 138, 225*n*63
Kovis, Edward T. 41–42, 58, 226*n*66
Kowal, Francis J. 25, 30, 37–39, 64, 68, 136, 149, 182
Kravitz, Samuel 16, 218*n*27–28
Kruk, John 126, 141, 148, 150, *183*–184
Kubski, Albert *32*
Kuntashian, Harry *32*, 34, 38–40, 61–62, 70–71, 104, 129–130, 225*n*56

Lanahan, Richard A. 154, 239*n*2
Landgraf, Ernest C. *32*, 34, 223*n*43
Landis, Kenesaw M. 53–56, 228*n*5
Lane, Edward F. 112, 235*n*36
LaPointe, George *135*
Larned, Claude M. 15–16, 217*n*24
Lee, Francis E. *32*
LeGates, George H. 25, 30, 84, 86, 116–118, 121, 221*n*22
Leip, Edgar E. 16, 20, 22–23, 28–33, 35–39, 41–49, 58, 61–77, 79–*83*, 85–92, 94–*95*, 96–*101*, 103–109, 111–116, 120–122, 124, 126, *128*–*134*, 138–141, 143–145, 147–148, 151–153, 155, 184–*185*, 186
Lenzi, Lincoln M. 104, 130, 133, 236*n*7
LeRoy, Frank 97, 104, 233*n*5
Lessig, Clyde D. 32, 38–39, 71, 223*n*41
Levan, Anthony 23–24, 220*n*12
List, Robert H. 79, 88, 122, 145–146, 232*n*40
Lomas, Harold W. 86–87, 112–113, 233*n*50
Lucas, Frederick W. 16, 21–22, 137, 139, 219*n*30
Luzansky, William M. 16, 20–23, 25, 28, 31–34, 36–*39*, 40–43, 47–49, 58, 60–91, 93–*101*, 102–111, 113–114, 116, 118–126, 129–*134*, 138–153, 186–*187*, 188
Lyman, William S. 15, 217*n*23
Lynn, Jerome E. 2, 25, 27–33, 35–43, 45–49, 51, 61–76, 78–*83*, 84–94, 96–*101*, 102–104, 107–108, 110–114, 116, 118–125, 129–*134*, 138, 140–142, 144–152, 154–155, 188–*189*, 190

Macklin, Casimir W. 68, 230*n*22
Mahrer, William E. 49, 93, 228*n*84
Maier, Robert *135*
Mann, Leslie 54, 228*n*10
Manczak, John M. 63, 84, 108, 112, 116–117, 229*n*9

Marchlewicz, Charles A. 20–22, 41–42, 59, 67, 105, 156, 219*n*4
Marnie, Harry S. 48, 69, 70, 73, 78–79, 102, 107, 119–120, 123, 131, 227*n*78,
Marquard, Richard W. 102, 106, 112, *165*, 234*n*14
Marshall, Chip *see* Marchlewicz, Charles
Martin, Johnny L. R. 146, 237*n*9
Martin, Paul P. 85, 232*n*47
Maryland blue laws 30–31, 38
Mast, Charles H. 20, 219*n*3
McInerney, James R. 95–96, 107, 233*n*2
McNally, Alfred B. 62, 229*n*8
Messick, Frank 44–45, 47, 76, 226*n*70
Mezours, Theodore J. 37–38, 46, 224*n*52
Metro, Charles M. 39–40, 225*n*59
Mikus, Leroy P. *32*, 104–106, 130, 133, 234*n*19
Milici, Michael J. 86, 117, 232*n*49
Millar, Joseph M. 77–78, 93, 110, 231*n*37
Miller, Anthony J. 16, 149, 190–191
Miller, Charles L. 25, 221*n*23
Miller, Harold 46, 65–66, 79–80, 88–89, 114, 146, 229*n*12
Miller, Walter B. 5, 231*n*1
Millman, Charles S. 62, 84, 232*n*46
Milton, John 14, 127, *134*, 216*n*20
Montero, Juan F. 72–*73*, 74, 77–78, 80, 87, 92, 97, 99, *101*, 103–104, 109, 111, 115–116, 121–122, 126, 128, *134*, 136, 139, 141, 146, 148, 150, 153, 191–*192*, 193
Moore, Harpel A. 105, 234*n*21
Moran, Kendall A. 25, 116, 221*n*21
Morris, Charles S. 25, 62, 221*n*23
Morton, Ivon T. 34, 223*n*44
Moses, Wallace 151, 238*n*6
Mosher, Michael S. 27–28, 221*n*25
Murphy, Melvin 14, 55, 110–111, 127, *134*–*135*, 150, 216*n*20
Murtaugh, Daniel E. 21–22, 41, 59–60, 67–68, 100, 138–140, 156, 219*n*7
Myers, Roy E. 77–79, 93, 123, 131, 156, 231*n*38
Mysel, Isadore 46, 65–66, 229*n*13
Myska, William 42, 64, 226*n*67

Nelson, Lynn B. 151, 238*n*6
New York Giants 7, 12, 102, 133, 136, 156
Newark Bears 103, 152, 194, 234*n*17
Nichols, Alonzo L. 34, 223*n*44
no-hitter 109, 114–115, 129–130, 135, 147, *180*, *198*–199

Nine—Index

O'Buzz, Anthony J. 23, 31, 220*n*11
O'Connor, James J. H. 12, 58–60, 90, 114, 215*n*16
O'Donnell, Austin J. 90, 233*n*53
Ogden, John 7–8
Ogden, Thomas J. 45, 65–66, 87–89, 108, 113–114, 142, 145–146, 227*n*75
O'Rourke, Joseph L. *35*, 66, 142, 145, 237*n*6
O'Rourke, Patsy 8, *35*
Outwin, Ellsworth M. 95–96, 233*n*3

Pasquella, Daniel H. 6–7, 11, 16–17, 23–24, 75, 213*n*6
Perez, Regino A. 16, 218*n*27
Peters, Russell D. 151–152, 238*n*6
Petock, Nicholas 46, 227*n*76
Philadelphia Athletics 8, 12, 151–152, 155
Philadelphia Phillies 7–8, *35–36*, 156
Pierson, Herbert F. 15, 217*n*25
Pippen, Rodger H. 53, 122, 150, 238*n*5
Pitko, Alexander *36*–38, 45–46, 66, 80, 86, 89, 107, 114, 121, 142–144, 146, 224*n*48,
Pocomoke City Red Sox 11–12, 21, 23, 34, 40, *44*, 46–47, 53, 60, 75–77, 81, 92, 95–99, 121–124, 126–127, 128, 129, 132, 136, 153, 173, 214*n*8, 216*n*21, 219*n*30, 226*n*70, 227*n*72–73, 227*n*77, 231*n*30–32, 231*n*34, 231*n*36, 231–233*n*39, 232*n*43, 233*n*4–7, 236*n*43
Porter, Richard T. 152, *193*–194
Poydock, Richard J. 32, 223*n*41
Pucci, Mario R. 31–33, 136, 194–*195*
Pultz, Adelbert H. 32, 40, 61, 71, 74, 104, 106, 130, 133, 223*n*42

Quimby, Charles M. 15, 20, 23, 25, 27–29, 31, 33, 35–43, 45–49, 52, 59–67, 69–72, 74–82, 84–88, 91–92, 94, 96, 98, 100, *101*, 102, 104–105, 107–112, 114, 116, 118–120, 122, 124, 126, 129–*134*, *135*, 138–139, 141, 143, 145–148, 151–152, 195–*196*, 197

Radler, Franklin J. *32*, 60–61, 74, 229*n*6
Raffensberger, Kenneth D. 64, 67, 91, 121, 138–140, 156, 230*n*18
Ralph, James A. 15, 217*n*23
Ratterree, William W. 25, 31, 84, 108, 220*n*21
Reha, Joseph 49, 77–79, 103, 130, 228*n*80
Revolinsky, Leon J. 15, 28–29, 34, 37, *39*, 42–43, 47, 58–61, 63–64, 67–70, 73–75, 77–78, 80, 86, 88, 96–98, *101*, 103, 107–110, 115–120, 122, 125, *127*, 129, 133–*134*, *135*–136, 139–141, 143, 148, 153, *198*–199
Rew, James H. 5, 213*n*1
Reznichak, Joseph T., Jr. 27, 29, 31, 33–38, 41–43, 45, 47–49, 60–63, 65–67, 69–84, 87–97, 99–101, 103, 106, 109, 113, 120–121, 127, 174–*175*, 179, 188, *200*–201
Rife, Dallas W. 78–79, 93, 100, 231*n*39
Riggin, Nathaniel B. 77–79, 93, 131, 231*n*38
Rist, Raymond A. 46, 66, 80, 86–88, 114, 142–144, 146, 230*n*15
Rodgers, John G. 138, 237*n*1
Roetz, Edward B. 28, 42, 70, 73, 222*n*28
Ronchetti, Samuel, Jr. 21, 220*n*8
Rosen, Arthur 75–76, 231*n*30
Ross, Edward W. 7, 214*n*8
Rozier, John C. 115, 235*n*39

Sabo, Alex 209
St. Louis Browns 12, 32
St. Louis Cardinals 12, 14, 156
Salazar, Jose F. 100–*101*, 126, 128, *134*, 150–152, 176, *202*–203
Salisbury Indians Boosters' Committee 127
Salisbury State Teachers College 17
Salisbury White Clouds 20, 14
Savitsky, William J. 40, 44–45, 225*n*61
Scarbinsky, Joseph P. 81, 96–97, 129, 232*n*43
Schluter, Henry C. *44*, 46, 77, 96–98, 121, 124, 226*n*72
Schoen, Maynard O. 25, 29, 221*n*21
Schoolfield, Allen P. 7, 214*n*8
Scully, James A. 111, 235*n*35
Sefick, Stephen A. 40, 46, 225*n*62
Semple, Thomas 21–22, 48, 220*n*9
Shafnacker, Joseph R. 68, 70, 136, 203–*204*
Shaughnessy playoff system 10, 214*n*14
Shelton, Vernon W. 24, 136, 204–*205*, 206, 229*n*15
Sherr, Philip 68, 229*n*15, 230*n*22
Shillingford, William T. 80, 88–89, 114–115, 146, 232*n*41
Shires, Felix L. 14, 216*n*22
Short, George E. 16, 63, 84, 86, 102, 105, 139–140, 218*n*30
Smithson, Robert *135*

Miracle on the Eastern Shore

Smyth, Charles P. 66, 79–80, 87, 230*n*14
Solinski, Stanley E. 49, 228*n*82
Soltis, Carmen S. 16, 218*n*27
South Philadelphia Hebrews 46, 97, 149, 166, 182, 190
Speaker, Tristram E. 1, 110, 234*n*33
Spring, Frank S. 14–15, 217*n*23
Stanfield, Stanley 66–67, 230*n*17
Stant, Robert E. 25, 63, 111, 117, 221*n*22
Steinfadt, Arthur A. 16, 21, 25, 27–29, 52, 68, **206**–207
Sterling, Columbus W. 24, 220*n*18
Sterling, Elwood 24, 220*n*16
Sterling, Raydie J. 100
Stiles, Michael P. **32**–33, 38, 40, 61–62, 71, 82–83, 104, 106, 130, 223*n*42
Stock, Howard 28, 119, 222*n*31
Stotz, Charles D. 28, 42–43, 222*n*29
Swoboda, Paul W. 28, 43, 107, 119–120, 222*n*29

Tantillo, Edward J. 120, 135, 236*n*43
Tawes, James C. W. 7, 11, 78, 214*n*8
Tawes, John M. 7, 214*n*8
Taylor, Edwin L. 107, 119–120, 235*n*29
Taylor, Rex A. 30–31, 38
Taylor, Thomas 58, 72, 94, 118–119, 229*n*1
Thawley, Mager B. 5, 213*n*1
Theurer, Harry F. 107–108, 119–120, 235*n*30
Thomas, Frederick B. 31, 37, **39**, 41–43, 48–49, 58–61, 63–72, 76–80, 85–86, 88–89, 94, 98–99, **101**–102, 104–106, 109, 114–119, 121, 123, 132, **134**, 142–143, 146–153, 207–**208**, 209
Thomas, Preston E. 24, 220*n*17
Tillman, Johan L. 102, 234*n*13
Titcomb, James M. 31, 222*n*37
Toach, John J. 12, 43, 98, 121, 215*n*16
Toland, James P. 25, 30, 68, 72, 149, 221*n*21
Tomczyk, Ted J. 35, 224*n*47
Tomlinson, David 90, 233*n*51
Trakimas, Alexander 119–120, 236*n*42
Traynor, Harold J. 105, 234*n*20
Trechock, Frank A. 2, 16, 19–23, 25, 27, 29–31, 33, 35–**39**, 40–41, 43–49, 58, 60–76, 78–**83**, 84–87, 89–90, 92–**95**, 96–97, 99–**101**, 102–114, 116, 118–121, 123–125, 129–**134**, 138–142, 144–150, 152–155, 209–**210**, 211
Trenton Senators 7–8, **13**, 15–16, 31, 51, 62, 74, 77, 80–81, 79, 99, 106, 109, 150

Trippe, Alexander 15, 218n25, 229*n*15
Troy, Gordon V. 37, 46, 65–66, 80, 123, 143–144, 146, 224*n*51
Truitt, Alfred T. 7, 20, 84, 127, 150, 201, 213*n*8
Truitt, Charles J. 12, 213*n*8, 215*n*17

Urban, Michael A. 48–49, 93, 102, 131, 227*n*78,

Vandegrift, Edwin F. 28, 42–43, 69–70, 73, 94, 222*n*30
Vernon, James B. "Mickey" **32**, 39–40, 61, 71, 74, 104–106, 130, 156, 225*n*59
Voth, Douglas C. 142–143, 145, 147, 237*n*6

Waldron, Thomas A. 25, 220*n*21
Walters, Harrison M. 7, 214*n*8
Ward, Ryland B. 24, 220*n*14
Wasdell, James C. 154, 239*n*3
Washington Elite Giants 153
Washington Senators 7, 12–**13**, 31, **36**, 55–**56**, 82, 121, 126, 135, 154–156
Weatherlow, Edward G. 70, 73, 94, 230*n*24
Webb, Oscar B. 49, 77–79, 100, 123, 125, 228*n*83
Webber, Fred **32**
Weimer, Louis A. "Pete" **32**, 35, 38, 61–62, 71, 74, 83, 104, 224*n*47
Werber, William M. 155, 239*n*4
Wexler (Pocomoke City Red Sox) 44, 46–47
Whalen, John J. "Poke" 7, 10, 14–15, **18**, 127, 157, 216*n*21
White, James E., Jr. 119–120, 236*n*41
Willis, Edward O. 145, 237*n*8
Wittig, John C. 27–28, 63–64, 69, 72, 95–96, 115, 156, 222*n*32
Woodend, George A. 151, 238*n*8
Wurst, Norman 35, 37–38, 66, 80, 88–89, 114, 142–143, 224*n*47

York White Roses *see* Trenton Senators

Zarowsky, William J. 31–**32**, 82–83, 105–106, 132–133, 232*n*44
Zimmerman, Edward F. **32**, 38, 40, 71, 82–83, 104, 106, 130, 133, 225*n*58
Zschau, Raymond M. 85–86, 111–112, 116–117, 232*n*48